Cost Accounting Revision Guide

Other books in this series
Quantitative Methods Revision Guide   Paul Goodwin
Economics Revision Guide   Rob Dixon and Keith West

Cost Accounting
Revision Guide

Colin Drury

Heinemann Professional Publishing

Heinemann Professional Publishing Ltd
Halley Court, Jordan Hill, Oxford OX2 8EJ

OXFORD   LONDON   MELBOURNE   AUCKLAND

First published 1988

© Colin Drury 1988

British Library Cataloguing in Publication Data
Drury, Colin
  Cost accounting revision guide.
  1. Cost accounting
  I. Title
  657'.42   HF5686.C8

ISBN 0 434 90415 5

Typeset by Keyset Composition, Colchester, Essex
Printed in Great Britain by Richard Clay Ltd, Chichester

Contents

Preface ix

Part One   How to Use This Book 1

Part Two   Revision Notes
1 Introduction to cost and management accounting   3
2 Accounting for materials and labour   11
3 Accounting for overheads   19
4 Accounting entries for job costing and contract costing   34
5 Process costing   46
6 Joint product and by-product costing   59
7 Absorption and variable costing systems   65
8 Cost-volume-profit analysis   72
9 Accounting information for decision-making   81
10 Capital investment appraisal   90
11 Budgeting and budgetary control   98
12 Standard costing   111

Part Three   Past Examination Questions and Worked Answers   125

Index   205

Table of contents

Contents	Syllabuses
	CIMA (1) CIMA (2) CACA AAT ICAEW ICAS ICAI SCCA (3) SCCA (10) IPS ICSA

Part 1 How to Use This Book

Part 2 Revision Notes

Chapter 1 *Introduction to cost and management accounting*

	CIMA(1)	CIMA(2)	CACA	AAT	ICAEW	ICAS	ICAI	SCCA(3)	SCCA(10)	IPS	ICSA
1.1 Differences between financial and management accounting	*	*	*	*	*	*	*	*	*	*	*
1.2 Objectives of cost and management accounting	*	*	*	*	*	*	*	*	*	*	*
1.3 Classification of costs	*	*	*	*	*	*	*	*	*	*	*
1.4 Classification of costs for stock valuation and profit measurement	*	*	*	*	*	*	*	*	*	*	*
1.5 Classification of costs for decision-making	*	*	*	*	*	*	*	*	*	*	*
1.6 Classification of costs for control	*	*	*	*	*	*	*	*	*	*	*

Chapter 2 *Accounting for materials and labour*

2.1 Control of material stocks	*	*	*	*	*	*	*	*	*	*	*
2.2 Perpetual inventory system	*	*	*	*	*	*	*	*	*	*	*
2.3 Stores pricing	*	*	*	*	*	*	*	*	*	*	*
2.4 Labour cost accounting	*	*	*	*	*	*	*	*	*	*	*
2.5 Incentive schemes	*	*	*	*	*	*	*	*	*	*	*

Chapter 3 *Accounting for overheads*

3.1 Definition of overheads	*	*	*	*	*	*	*	*	*	*	*
3.2 Reasons for apportioning overheads	*	*	*	*	*	*	*	*	*	*	*
3.3 Apportioning overheads – an overview of the procedure	*	*	*	*	*	*	*	*	*	*	*
3.4 Blanket overhead and departmental overhead rates	*	*	*	*	*	*	*	*	*	*	*
3.5 Procedure for calculating departmental overhead rates	*	*	*	*	*	*	*	*	*	*	*
3.6 Pre-determined overhead rates	*	*	*	*	*	*	*	*	*	*	*
3.7 Under- and over-recovery of overheads	*	*	*	*	*	*	*	*	*	*	*
3.8 Overhead absorption rates	*	*	*	*	*	*	*	*	*	*	*
3.9 Inter-service department transfers		*	*	*	*	*	*	*	*	*	*

Chapter 4 *Accounting entries for job costing and contract costing*

4.1 Integrated and interlocking accounts	*	*	*	*	*	*	*	*	*		
4.2 Control accounts	*	*	*	*	*	*	*	*	*		
4.3 Accounting entries for an integrated accounting system	*	*	*	*	*	*	*	*	*		
4.4 Interlocking accounts	*	*	*	*	*	*	*	*	*		
4.5 Contract costing		*	*	*	*	*	*	*	*	*	*

Chapter 5 *Process costing*

5.1 Job costing and process costing	*	*	*	*	*	*	*	*	*	*	*
5.2 Accounting procedure for a process costing system		*	*	*	*	*	*	*	*	*	*
5.3 Normal and abnormal losses		*	*	*	*	*	*	*	*	*	*
5.4 Revenue received from process losses		*	*	*	*	*	*	*	*	*	*

Table of contents

Contents	CIMA (1)	CIMA (2)	CACA	AAT	Syllabuses ICAEW	ICAS	ICAI	SCCA (3)	SCCA (10)	IPS	ICSA
5.5 Abnormal losses and gains		*	*	*	*	*	*	*	*		*
5.6 Closing WIP and equivalent production		*	*	*	*	*	*	*	*		*
5.7 Equivalent production and normal and abnormal losses at the end of the process		*	*	*	*	*	*	*	*		*
5.8 Equivalent production and losses part way through a process		*	*	*	*	*	*	*	*		*
5.9 Opening WIP: FIFO method		*	*	*	*	*	*	*	*		*
5.10 Opening WIP: Weighted average method		*	*	*	*	*	*	*	*		*

Chapter 6 *Joint product and by-product costing*
6.1 Joint products and by-products		*	*	*	*	*	*		*		*
6.2 Apportionment of joint costs		*	*	*	*	*	*		*		*
6.3 Joint product costs and decision-making		*	*	*	*	*	*		*		*
6.4 Accounting for by-products		*	*	*	*	*	*		*		*

Chapter 7 *Absorption and variable costing systems*
7.1 Absorption and variable costing	*	*	*	*	*	*	*	*	*	*	*
7.2 Internal and external reporting	*	*	*	*	*	*	*	*	*	*	*
7.3 Differences in profit calculations	*	*	*	*	*	*	*	*	*	*	*
7.4 Arguments supporting variable costing	*	*	*	*	*	*	*	*	*	*	*
7.5 Arguments supporting absorption costing	*	*	*	*	*	*	*	*	*	*	*

Chapter 8 *Cost-volume-profit analysis*
8.1 Cost-volume-profit analysis	*	*	*	*	*	*	*	*	*	*	*
8.2 A comparison of the accountants' model and economic theory		*	*	*	*	*	*	*	*	*	*
8.3 CVP analysis assumptions		*	*	*	*	*	*	*	*	*	*
8.4 A numerical approach to CVP analysis		*	*	*	*	*	*	*	*	*	*
8.5 CVP analysis: a graphical approach		*	*	*	*	*	*	*	*	*	*

Chapter 9 *Accounting information for decision-making*
9.1 Relevant costs and revenues		*	*	*	*	*	*		*	*	*
9.2 Discontinuing a segment		*	*	*	*	*	*		*	*	*
9.3 Special selling price decisions		*	*	*	*	*	*		*	*	*
9.4 Make or buy decisions		*	*	*	*	*	*		*	*	*
9.5 Limiting factors		*	*	*	*	*	*		*	*	*

Chapter 10 *Capital investment appraisal*
10.1 Distinguishing feature of capital investment decisions				*							
10.2 Opportunity cost of an investment				*							
10.3 Compounding and discounting				*							
10.4 Net present value				*							
10.5 Internal rate of return				*							
10.6 Payback method				*							
10.7 Accounting rate of return				*							

viii Cost Accounting Revision Guide

Table of contents

Contents	CIMA (1)	CIMA (2)	CACA	AAT	ICAEW	ICAS	ICAI	SCCA (3)	SCCA (10)	IPS	ICSA

Chapter 11 *Budgeting and budgetary control*
11.1 Definition of a budget * * * * * * * * * * *
11.2 Objectives of budgetary planning and control systems * * * * * * * * * * *
11.3 Organization required for preparation of budgets * * * * * * * * * * *
11.4 Stages in the budget process * * * * * * * * * * *
11.5 Preparation of functional budgets * * * * * * * * * * *
11.6 Cash budgets * * * * * * * * * * *
11.7 Responsibility accounting * * * * * * * * * * *
11.8 Flexible budgets * * * * * * * * * * *

Chapter 12 *Standard costing*
12.1 Standard costs and budgeted costs * * * * * * * * * * *
12.2 Setting standard costs * * * * * * * * * * *
12.3 Standard hours produced * * * * * * * * * * *
12.4 Types of cost standards * * * * * * * * * * *
12.5 Variance analysis * * * * * * * * * * *
12.6 Material variances (1) * * * * * * * * * *
12.7 Labour variances (1) * * * * * * * * * *
12.8 Fixed overhead variances (1) * * * * * * * * * *
12.9 Variable overhead variances (1) * * * * * * * * *
12.10 Sales margin variances * * * * *
12.11 Reconciliation of budgeted and actual profit * * * * * *
12.12 Control ratios * * * * *
12.13 Accounting entries * * * * *

Part 3 Past Examination Questions and Worked Answers

Note: (1) Total cost variances only.

Preface

The aim of this book is to provide a comprehensive revision programme for students who are preparing for the costing examinations of the various professional accountancy bodies. It should also prove useful to candidates preparing for the other accounting examinations such as GCE advanced level, degrees in business and accountancy studies and BTEC national and higher national diplomas.

The purpose of this book is not to provide an examination 'crammer' or a mass of model answers to be learned parrot fashion. The emphasis is on a clear and concise explanation of the basic facts, concepts and points of perspective essential to an overall understanding of the subject. Past examination questions and answers are used extensively throughout, but they are used for guidance on the different approaches to a particular topic and as a means of illustrating how to approach and structure answers. Emphasis is given to all types of questions set in the cost accounting examinations of the major professional accountancy bodies.

My appreciation goes to the Chartered Institute of Management Accountants (CIMA), the Chartered Association of Certified Accountants (CACA), the Institute of Chartered Accountants in England and Wales (ICAEW), the Association of Accounting Technicians (AAT) and the Institute of Chartered Secretaries and Administrators (ICSA) for permission to reproduce examination questions. The questions in Parts 2 and 3 of this book have been labelled with the above abbreviations to indicate the examination to which they refer. The accompanying answers are my own and are in no way the approved solutions of the above professional bodies.

Finally, and most importantly, I would like to thank my wife Bronwen, who has converted my original manuscript into one final typewritten form, and our children Martin, Robert and Caroline for their patience and understanding.

Part One
How to Use this Book

The notes in Part 2 (pages 5–124) will give you the key information on each topic. Part 2 consists of twelve chapters and the objective of this part is to cover the content of your examination syllabus in a clear and concise manner and to emphasize the basic facts, concepts and points of perspective essential to an overall understanding of each topic. Worked answers from past examinations are used to reinforce your understanding of each topic.

You should pay special attention to the informal notes which are set next to the main text. These highlight specific problems and common pitfalls. Remember that your examination syllabus may not include all the topics which are covered in Part 2. The chart on pages vi–viii shows how the topics relate to the syllabuses of the various examining bodies.

Part 3 (pages 125–203) consists of questions and worked answers to past examination questions. Note that questions labelled 1.1, 1.2, etc. refer to questions which relate to Chapter 1 in Part 2. Similarly, questions labelled 2.1, 2.2, etc. refer to questions which relate to Chapter 2. It is advisable that you attempt these questions without referring to the notes in Part 2. You should then check your answer with the author's worked solution and pay particular attention to the informal notes. If you are not satisfied with your level of understanding you should refer back to the appropriate chapter.

You should read Chapter 1 in Part 2 and then attempt the appropriate questions relating to Chapter 1 in Part 3. When you are satisfied with your understanding of Chapter 1 and your ability to answer the questions you should read Chapter 2 and then answer the questions relating to Chapter 2 in Section 3. Continue this process for Chapters 3 to 12. An alternative approach is to read the whole of Part 2 first and then move on to Part 3. When you have completed this book you might find it useful to return to Part 3 and attempt the questions under examination conditions.

Analysis of examination syllabuses

The table on pages vi–viii shows how the contents of this book relate to the specific syllabuses of the examining bodies. Most syllabuses are phrased in general terms and the table represents the author's interpretation of each syllabus. Syllabuses also change over time and *you should therefore check for yourself the contents of the most recent syllabus*. It is a good idea to look at recent examination papers as this will give you an indication of how the current examiners have interpreted the syllabus.

The following abbreviations are used to describe the various examination syllabuses shown on pages vi–viii.

CIMA (1)   Chartered Institute of Cost and Management Accountants – Stage 1 Accounting Examination (Cost Accounting Practice).

CIMA (2)   Chartered Institute of Cost and Management Accountants – Stage 2 Cost Accounting Examination.

CACA   Chartered Association of Certified Accountants – Level 1 Costing Examination (Paper 1.2).

AAT   Association of Accounting Technicians – Cost Accounting and Budgeting Examination (Paper 10).

ICAEW   Institute of Chartered Accountants in England and Wales – Accounting Techniques P1 Examination.

ICAS   Institute of Chartered Accountants of Scotland – Management Accounting Part II Examination.

ICAI   Institute of Chartered Accountants in Ireland – Paper 4 Management Accounting Examination.

SCCA (3)   Society of Company and Commercial Accountants – Paper 3 Cost Accounting Examination.

SCCA (10)   Society of Company and Commercial Accountants – Paper 10 Management Accounting Examination.

ICSA   Institute of Chartered Secretaries and Administrators – Part 2 Introduction to Accounting and Part 3 Management Accounting Examinations.

IPS   Institute of Purchasing Supply – Business Accounting Examination.

Part Two
Revision Notes

1
Introduction to cost and management accounting

1.1 Differences between financial and cost and management accounting

Users of accounting information   Cost and management accounting is concerned with the provision of information *to managers* to help them in decision-making, planning and control, whereas financial accounting is concerned with the provision of information *to external users* outside the business.

Segments   Financial accounting reports refer to the whole of the organization, whereas cost and management accounting focuses on small parts of the organization, for example individual products or activities.

Emphasis on the future   Financial accounting reports what has happened in the past, whereas management accounting is concerned with future information as well as past information.

Legal requirements   There is a legal requirement for public limited companies to produce annual financial accounts. Cost and management accounting is entirely optional and information should only be produced if the benefits from using the information exceed the cost of collecting it.

Frequency of reporting   Financial accounts are published annually but management requires information quickly if they are to act on it. Therefore management accounting reports may be prepared at daily, weekly or monthly intervals.

Note that less detailed published financial accounts are normally prepared on a semi-annual basis.

Approximations   Financial accounting information must be accurate, otherwise external users would have little confidence in the content of the published accounts. Management requires information rapidly, and more approximate information which is speedily prepared is normally sufficient for management purposes.

1.2 Objectives of cost and management accounting

Cost and management accounting is concerned with:

(a)   Accumulating costs for *stock valuation* to meet the requirements of external reporting

(b) Provision of financial information that will assist managers in their *decision-making* and planning activities
(c) Provision of financial information to help managers *control* the activities for which they are responsible.

1.3 Classification of costs

A cost and management accounting system should be capable of supplying different financial information for different purposes. It is therefore important that costs are classified in various ways according to their nature and the information needs of management.

1.4 Classification of costs for stock valuation and profit measurement

If there are no opening stocks and production is 100 units and 80 units are sold, the matching concept requires that costs for 80 units are matched against sales of 80 units. The closing stock of 20 units must be valued and deducted from the production costs.

The *matching* concept requires that costs are matched with revenue for the purpose of calculating profits. Therefore closing stocks must be deducted from the production costs. In an organization which undertakes a wide range of different jobs, it will be necessary, for stock valuation purposes, to charge the costs to each individual job. The work in progress (WIP) and finished goods stock valuations are ascertained from the total of the individual job costs; the total of the costs attached to the incomplete jobs represents the WIP valuation, and the total of the completed jobs in the finished goods store represents the finished goods stock valuation.

Not all costs are attached to products and included in the stock valuation. Costs which are not included in the product costs, and as a result are treated as an expense in the period in which they are incurred, are classified as *period costs*. Those costs which are allocated to the product and included in the stock valuation are classified as *product costs*. Product costs are therefore matched against sales and classified as an expense in the period when the goods are sold. SSAP9 requires that, for stock valuation, only manufacturing costs should be classified as product costs and non-manufacturing costs should be classified as period costs.

Classification by direct and indirect costs

An example of direct cost is the wood which is used in making a chair. An example of an indirect cost is factory rent and rates.

Direct costs are those costs which can be specifically traced to or identified with a particular product. The total of the direct costs is sometimes called *prime cost*. Indirect costs are those costs which cannot be identified with a particular product and which are incurred for the benefit of all products. Indirect expenses are also called *overheads*.

The objective for which the cost is required is called a cost objective. A cost objective might be a product, a sales territory, a department or anything for which one wants to measure the resources used. If a cost can be specifically allocated to a cost objective then it is a direct cost of the cost objective.

The distinction between direct and indirect costs depends on the purposes for which the information is required. We have assumed in the previous paragraph that the objective is to allocate costs to products. For *decision-making* the focus might be on the profitability of sales territories. Therefore costs are also allocated to sales territories. Sales staff salaries and the rental of sales offices will be classified as direct expenses of the sales territories, whereas the apportionment of general advertising which is applicable to *all* territories will be regarded as an indirect expense. For *control* purposes costs will be allocated to departments. The salary of a departmental supervisor will be a direct expense of the department, whereas the rent of the factory which is apportioned to departments will be an indirect expense.

1.5 Classification of costs for decision-making

Classification by relevant and irrelevant costs

Relevant costs are those future costs which will be changed by a decision, whereas irrelevant costs are those costs which will not be affected by a decision. Consider a situation where a company is considering the alternatives of either purchasing a component from an outside supplier or producing the component itself. The outside supplier has quoted a cost of £1000 for supplying the component. The estimated costs of producing the component are:

	£
Direct materials	200
Direct labour	300
Variable overhead	400
Fixed overhead	500
	1400

At first glance it appears that it is cheaper to purchase the component. However, it is assumed that the fixed overhead represents a share of factory overhead which would still continue if the component was not produced. In other words the fixed overhead expenditure will not be affected by the decision. It is assumed that the cost of direct labour, direct materials and variable overheads will be zero if the component is not produced. In other words these costs will be changed by the decision and are relevant to the decision. The relevant cost of producing the component is £900. The components should not therefore be purchased from the outside supplier.

Sunk costs

These are costs that have been created by a decision in the past and which cannot be changed by any decision that will be made in the future. Sunk costs are irrelevant for decision-making. For example the purchase price of materials which are already in stock represents a sunk cost. If the materials are used regularly then the decision to use materials on a particular job will necessitate their replacement. Future costs will increase by the cost of replacing the materials. Therefore the relevant cost of the materials is the replacement cost.

Opportunity costs

An opportunity cost is a cost which measures the opportunity which is lost or sacrificed when the choice of one course of action requires that an alternative course of action be given up. Consider the situation where materials are in stock but are not used regularly. The materials can either be sold or used on a particular contract. Hence the decision to allocate the materials to the contract will result in a loss of sale proceeds. The lost sale proceeds represent the opportunity cost of using the materials.

The relevant cost for an alternative course of action will include additional labour and overhead costs plus the opportunity cost of the materials. Opportunity costs are therefore part of the relevant cost of choosing an alternative course of action.

Classification by cost behaviour

This enables costs to be estimated at different output levels. Such information is important for decision-making – for example, expansion and contraction decisions.

Variable costs vary in direct proportion with the level of activity, so that doubling the level of activity will double the total variable cost. Hence, *total* variable costs are linear and *unit* variable cost is constant (see Figure 1.1). Examples of variable manufacturing costs include direct materials and power. These costs fluctuate with operating activity.

Linearity does not normally apply throughout the whole output range. For a discussion of non-linearity see Chapter 8.

Fixed costs such as depreciation and rent remain constant over a wide range of activity for a specified period. Note that *total* fixed costs are constant at all levels of activity whereas *unit* fixed costs decrease proportionally with the level of activity (see Figure 1.1).

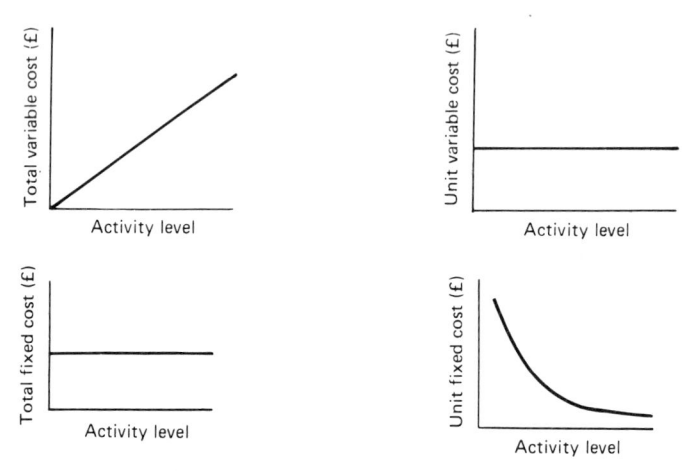

Figure 1.1 Variable costs and fixed costs

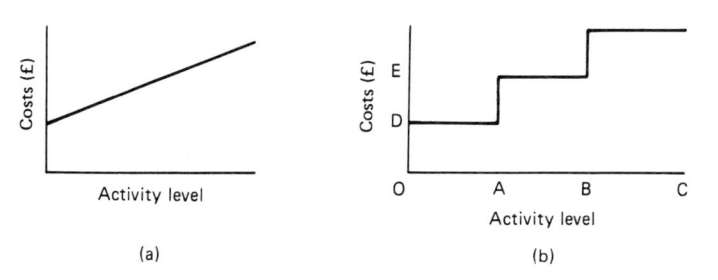

Figure 1.2 (a) Semi-variable and (b) semi-fixed costs

Semi-variable costs include both a fixed and a variable component (see Figure 1.2a). An example of a semi-variable cost is the maintenance of machinery which consists of planned fixed maintenance that is undertaken whatever the level of activity, and a variable element that is directly related to the level of activity.

Semi-fixed or step costs are fixed for a given level of activity but eventually increase by a constant amount at some critical point. Examples of semi-fixed costs include supervisory salaries and the hire of machinery. You can see from Figure 1.2b that costs of OD are incurred for output levels between O and A, OE between output levels A and B, and so on.

For a further discussion of semi-fixed costs see Chapter 8.

1.6 Classification of costs for control

For control purposes costs should be allocated to the individual who is responsible for incurring them. This system of cost accumulation is known as *responsibility accounting* and is based on the recognition of individual areas of responsibility. These areas of responsibility are known as *responsibility centres*.

Controllable and non-controllable costs

Costs which are allocated to responsibility centres should be classified according to whether they are controllable or non-controllable by the manager of the responsibility centre. A controllable cost is defined as a cost which is reasonably subject to regulation by the manager of the responsibility centre. If this condition does not hold then the cost should be regarded as non-controllable. Labour and materials are normally controllable costs whereas apportioned costs such as factory rent and depreciation are non-controllable.

Typical examination questions
The following are some recent examination questions on cost classification:

1 'Costs may be classified in a variety of ways according to their nature and the information needs of management.' Explain and discuss this statement illustrating with examples of the classifications required for different purposes. (ICSA Part 4 Management Accounting) (22 marks)
2 Explain and show by drawing two separate diagrams what is meant by:
   (a) A semi-variable cost
   (b) A stepped fixed cost
   and give one example of each.   (CIMA Cost Accounting 1)
3 Cost must be classified to facilitate its arrangement in as flexible a manner as possible. Explain the meaning of the 'classification of cost' and give some practical examples of the ways in which cost is classified.
(AAT) (7 marks)

4 Cost classifications used in costing include:
   (a) Period costs
   (b) Product costs
   (c) Variable costs
   (d) Opportunity costs
   Explain each of these classifications, with examples of the types of costs that may be included. (CACA) (17 marks)

2
Accounting for materials and labour

2.1 Control of material stocks

It is important that an effective system of controlling material stocks is implemented. The benefits which accrue from a sound materials control system are:

(a) Investment in stocks is minimized.
(b) Sufficient materials are available at the right quality and in a satisfactory condition. The materials should be purchased at the most competitive price available.
(c) Stock is protected from deterioration, damage, pilferage and waste.
(d) Information is readily available for financial reporting.
(e) The need for a costly periodic stocktaking is eliminated.

An effective materials stock control system should ensure that procedures are established for:

(a) Setting optimal stock levels
(b) Purchasing of materials
(c) Receipt of materials
(d) Issue of materials
(e) Stocktaking to ensure that actual stocks agree with the clerical records.

Setting optimum stock levels

Stock control models should be used to set minimum stock levels, reorder points and economic order quantities. It is important that accurate clerical or computer records are maintained for each stores item. When items of materials have reached their reorder point the storekeeper makes out a purchase requisition requesting the purchasing department to obtain the reorder quantity from the appropriate supplier.

Stock control models such as the economic order quantity model should be used to set optimal stock levels. Stock control models are normally included in a quantitative methods course.

Purchase of materials

When the purchasing department receives a copy of the purchase requisition the purchasing officer will select the appropriate supplier based on the department's expert knowledge, and then complete a purchasing order requesting the supplier to supply the materials listed on the order.

Receipt of materials

When the goods are received by the stores department they are inspected and checked with the supplier's delivery note and a copy of the purchase order. The goods received are listed on a goods received note (GRN) and recorded on the appropriate bin card. A copy of the GRN is passed to the accounts department so that it can be checked with the invoice. The prices on the invoice are entered against the items listed on the GRN. The items of the GRN are then entered as a receipt in the appropriate stores ledger account.

A separate stores ledger account is maintained for each item of stock. The stores ledger account records quantities and values, whereas a bin card records only quantities. For many companies bin cards and stores ledger records are maintained on a computer.

Issue of materials

Materials should only be issued from stores against a duly authorized stores requisition. A stores requisition contains details of the materials issued and the job or overhead account number to which the materials should be charged. The storekeeper enters the details from the stores requisitions in the issue column of the appropriate bin card and forwards the requisition to the costing department. The costing department prices the materials listed on the stores requisition. This information is obtained from the receipts column of the appropriate stores ledger account. The costing department will now record the following transactions:

Note that a separate bin card is maintained for each item of stock.

(a) Reduce raw material stocks by recording the values issued in the stores ledger accounts
(b) Charge the amount of material issued to the appropriate job or overhead account.

Stocktaking

Periodic checks must be made for each item of material in stock to ensure that actual stocks agree with the clerical records. The stock should be physically counted at regular intervals. To do this effectively there must be either a complete periodic stockcount or some form of continuous stocktaking. With a *complete periodic stockcount* all the stores items are counted at one point in time, whereas *continuous stocktaking* involves a sample of stores items being counted regularly, on, say, a daily basis. Continuous stocktaking is preferable because it is likely that the complete stockcount will cause production to be disrupted.

Actual stock may differ from the clerical records for the following reasons:

(a) Arithmetical errors when calculating the balance on the bin card
(b) Entries on the wrong bin card
(c) Items placed in the wrong physical location
(d) Theft of stock.

When a discrepancy arises the individual stores ledger account and the bin card must be reduced so that they both agree with the actual stock. Any stock lost must be valued and charged to an overhead account for stock losses.

Frequent checks should be made to ensure that stocks have not deteriorated and are not obsolete. The storekeeper should ensure as far as possible that items in store are protected from damage and deterioration. Slow-moving stocks should be identified by checking the frequency of issues. Any obsolete stocks or stocks no longer required should be disposed of and the losses charged to the stock losses account. Management should be provided with periodic reports giving details of the amounts and reasons for stock losses.

2.2 Perpetual inventory system

This system simply means that records are available which always show the current balance of stock for each individual item of material. This information will be recorded on bin cards or a computer.

Typical examination questions
You should now be able to answer the following questions:

1 Describe the essential requirements of an effective material stock control system. (CACA Level 1 Costing)
2 Outline the accountant's contribution to the process of material cost control in a manufacturing organization where material is a significant element of total cost. (CACA Level 1 Costing)
3 Describe the main elements of an efficient stores control system and list the principal advantages to management of implementing such a system. (ICAS Part 1 Management Accounting)

2.3 Stores pricing

It is likely that the stores record for a particular item of material will show that materials were acquired at different purchase prices. Some assumption must therefore be made about the flow of costs out of the stores ledger account. Consider the situation illustrated in Example 2.1.

Example 2.1

During a six-month accounting period the following materials were purchased:

1 January	1000 units at £1 per unit
1 June	1000 units at £2 per unit

On 30 June 1000 units were sold at £2.40 per unit. For simplicity we shall assume that no labour or overhead costs are incurred and there are no opening stocks. There are several possible methods of interpreting which cost should be used to calculate the cost of the issue and the value of the closing stock. First, we can assume that the first item received was the first

item to be issued – that is, first in, first out (FIFO). Second, we can assume that the last item to be received into stock was the first item to be issued – that is, last in, first out (LIFO). Third, we can assume that the items are issued at the average cost per unit of materials in stock. The effect of using each of the three methods is as follows:

	Sales £	Cost of sales £	Raw materials closing stock £	Profit £
FIFO	2400	1000 (1000 × £1)	2000 (1000 × £2)	1400
LIFO	2400	2000 (1000 × £2)	1000 (1000 × £1)	400
Average cost	2400	1500 (1000 × £1.50)	1500 (1000 × £1.50)	900

You should note that pricing of stores issues is required for profit measurement and stock valuation for financial accounting, and in the provision of decision-making information for management accounting. We shall initially consider the suitability of FIFO, LIFO and the average cost methods for financial accounting.

Financial accounting

FIFO appears to be the most logical method because it makes the same assumptions as the physical flow of materials; that is, the first material received is normally the first material issued. During periods of inflation, the earliest materials which have the lowest prices will be issued first. You can see that this assumption leads to a lower cost of sales calculation and a higher profit than would be obtained using either LIFO or average cost. Note that the closing stock is valued at the latest and therefore higher prices.

LIFO ignores the physical flow of materials. The latest and higher costs are used up first. This will normally result in a higher cost of sales charge and lower profits compared with FIFO and average cost. Closing stock will be valued at the oldest costs and this results in the lowest stock valuation.

With the average cost system the issue price is recalculated after each issue. The issue price is calculated by dividing the total cost of material in stock by the total quantity of material in stock after each new purchase. The cost of sales and closing stock value will tend to fall approximately midway between the values recorded for the FIFO and LIFO methods.

The average cost method tends to be easier to operate and smooths out fluctuations in issue prices. LIFO is not acceptable for taxation purposes. Also SSAP 9 implies that LIFO is not acceptable for external reporting. Therefore FIFO or the average cost method should be used for financial accounting.

Note that records maintained at standard prices may be acceptable for financial accounting.

Decision-making

For decision-making purposes, management requires information on the future costs of the raw materials. If materials are already in stock and are regularly used then the decision to issue materials to a particular job will necessitate their replacement. Therefore the relevant cost of issuing the materials is the replacement cost. Assume that the replacement cost of the materials in Example 2.1 is £2.60 at 30 June. You can see that the materials have been sold for £2400 (1000 units at £2.40). The cash proceeds from the sale are insufficient to replace the materials.

If FIFO, LIFO or average cost is used then the cost allocated to the order will be £1000 for FIFO, £2000 for LIFO and £1500 for the average cost method. Each method incorrectly suggests that the company is making satisfactory profits by selling the materials at £2.40 per unit. A company should, however, seek to ensure that future cash inflows are sufficient to replace the materials. Stores issues should therefore be priced at replacement cost for decision-making purposes. Pricing issues at replacement cost also provides a better indication of whether profits are being earned in real terms. There are practical difficulties in operating a replacement cost pricing system. It is extremely time consuming to keep prices up to date in an organization which carries several thousand different items in stock. A possible solution is to use a stores pricing method which provides a reasonably close approximation to replacement cost. You can see that LIFO provides the closest approximation, but this method is unacceptable for external reporting. It would be possible to use LIFO for decision-making and FIFO or average cost for external reporting, but operating two separate stores pricing systems is expensive.

Note that pricing issues at replacement cost is not acceptable for financial accounting.

If stock turnover is fast and material prices are changing slowly then FIFO, LIFO and average cost methods will provide a close approximation to replacement cost.

Many firms issue materials at a standard price. This is a target pre-determined price of what future purchases of material should cost when buying efficiently. Checks can therefore be made on the efficiency of the purchasing department by comparing actual prices paid with the target standard prices. The standard price is used for all issues over a period and it is therefore easier to operate than other methods. The disadvantage is that setting standard prices is very time consuming. Standard prices are acceptable for external reporting in certain circumstances and, because the emphasis is on future costs, they should lead to a closer approximation of replacement cost than FIFO or average cost.

For a more detailed description of standard prices you should refer to Chapter 12.

Typical examination question
You should now be able to answer the following question:

Describe and discuss the relative merits of the various methods that may be used for pricing the issue of raw materials to production.
(CACA Level 1 Costing)

2.4 Labour cost accounting

Documents such as job cards, time sheets and idle time cards are used to record the amount of time that productive workers spend on various activities. The foreman enters the starting and finishing time for each job on a job card or time sheet. Both documents contain the job number or overhead account number. The hourly rate of pay is applied to the job card or time sheet and the labour cost can then be calculated. If a productive worker is unoccupied for short periods then an idle time card should be used to record the waiting time.

Overtime and shift premiums

These should normally be included as part of the manufacturing overheads. For example, consider a situation where an employee is paid time and a half for weekly hours in excess of 40 hours. Assume that an operative works 46 hours (including 6 hours' overtime on job A) and that the normal wage rate is £5 per hour. The employee's weekly wage is:

	£
Normal time rate wage: 46 hours at £5	230
Overtime premium (0.5 × 6 hours × £5)	15
	245

It is unfair to charge the overtime premium of £15 to job A merely because it was scheduled to be produced during the overtime period. Overtime and night shift work usually results from a generally high level of production. It is preferable to charge the premiums to the departmental overhead account for overtime and shift work so that the costs are apportioned to *all* jobs worked on during the period. On the other hand if the overtime or shift premiums are a direct result of a customer's urgent request for the completion of the order then the premiums should be charged directly to the job. For control purposes it is important that overtime and shift premium costs are analysed by departments and are reported to management at frequent intervals.

Employment costs

These include the employer's share of National Insurance contribution and pension costs. For each employee an average hourly rate for employment costs should be ascertained and this should be added to the employee's hourly wage rate. The revised rate represents the employee's charging-out rate.

Idle time

Idle time should be charged to a separate overhead account for each department and reported to management at frequent intervals.

Typical examination question
You should now be able to answer the following question:

The management of a company manufacturing electrical components is considering the introduction of a historic batch costing system into the factory. You are required to:

(a) Outline the information and procedures required to obtain the actual direct material cost of each batch of components manufactured;

(7 marks)

(b) Identify the elements which could make up a direct operative's gross wage and for each element explain, with supporting reasons, whether it should be regarded as part of the prime cost of the components manufactured. (10 marks)
(CACA Level 1 Costing)

2.5 Incentive schemes

Both the firm and the employees should benefit from the introduction of an incentive scheme. Employees should receive an increase in wages arising from the increased production. The firm should benefit from a reduction in the fixed overhead per unit and an increase in sales volume. Other advantages of incentive schemes include:

(a) The opportunity to earn higher wages may encourage more efficient workers to join the company.
(b) Morale may be improved if extra effort is rewarded.

Disadvantages include:

(a) Incentive schemes can be complex and difficult to administer.
(b) Establishing performance levels leads to frequent and continuing disputes.
(c) The quality of the output may decline.

Typical examination question
A company is undecided on what kind of incentive scheme to introduce. From the following information you are required to calculate for each employee his earnings, using

(a) Guaranteed hourly rates only (basic pay),
(b) Piecework, but with earnings guaranteed at 75 per cent of basic pay where the employee fails to earn this amount, and
(c) Premium bonus in which the employee receives two-thirds of time saved in addition to hourly pay.

	Employees			
	A	B	C	D
Actual hours worked	38	36	40	34
Hourly rate of pay	£3	£2	£2.50	£3.60
Output (units) X	42	120	—	120
Y	72	76	—	270
Z	92	—	50	—

Standard time allowed (per unit): X, 6 minutes; Y, 9 minutes; Z, 15 minutes. Each minute earned is valued at £0.05 for piecework calculation.
(16 marks)
(AAT)

Answer

Employee	(i) Hourly rate	(ii) Piecework	
A	$38 \times £3 = £114$	$(42 \times £0.30) + (72 \times £0.45) + (92 \times £0.75)$	$= £114$
B	$36 \times £2 = £72$	$(120 \times £0.30) + (76 \times £0.45)$	$= £70.20$
C	$40 \times £2.50 = £100$	$(50 \times £0.75)$	$= £37.50$
D	$34 \times £3.60 = £122.40$	$(120 \times £0.30) + (270 \times £0.45)$	$= £157.50$

Note that with the piecework system the employees are paid an agreed rate per unit produced. The piece rates are £0.30 per unit of X (6 minutes × £0.05), £0.45 for Y (9 × £0.05) and £0.75 for Z (15 × £0.05). Only employee C earns less than 75 per cent of basic pay. Therefore C will receive a gross wage of £75. The piecerate wages should be charged directly to the products, and the difference between the guaranteed minimum wage of £75 and the piecework wage of £37.50 for employee C should be charged to an appropriate overhead account.

With a bonus scheme a set time is allowed for each job and a bonus is paid based on the proportion of time saved. The calculations for each employee are:

	Time allowed hours	Time saved hours	Bonus £	Total wages £
A	$42(6/60) + 72(9/60) + 92(15/60) = 38$	0	0	114
B	$120(6/60) + 76(9/60) = 23.4$	0	0	72
C	$50(15/60) = 12.5$	0	0	100
D	$120(6/60) + 270(9/60) = 52.5$	18.5	$(2/3)(18.5)(£3.60) = £44.40$	$£122.40 + £44.40 = £166.80$

Employees A, B and C do not earn a bonus because the time taken is in excess of time allowed.

3
Accounting for overheads

3.1 Definition of overheads

Overheads consist of indirect labour, indirect materials and indirect expenses.

3.2 Reasons for apportioning overheads to products

All *manufacturing* overheads are incurred in the production of a firm's output, and so each unit of the product produced receives some benefit from the costs. Consequently each unit of output should be charged with some of the overhead costs. It is also a requirement of the Statement of Standard Accounting Practice (SSAP) 9 that all manufacturing overheads must be applied to jobs when calculating profit and determining the stock entry in the balance sheets. Remember that for stock valuation purposes *non-manufacturing* overheads are not charged to the product.

3.3 Apportioning overheads: an overview of the procedure

The objective is to allocate the total *manufacturing* overheads incurred during a period to the cost units produced during the period. This process normally requires the calculation of hourly overhead absorption rates such as direct labour or machine hour overhead rates. For example if total overheads for the period are £100 000 and 25 000 direct labour hours are worked, then overheads will be recovered at a rate of £4 per direct labour hour. Each cost unit will therefore be charged with overhead at a rate of £4 per direct labour hour.

3.4 Blanket overhead rates and departmental overhead rates

A blanket overhead rate refers to a situation where a single overhead rate is established for the factory as a whole and this rate is charged to all jobs irrespective of the departments in which they were produced. In most circumstances blanket overhead rates should not be used. You can see why by considering Example 3.1.

Example 3.1

A firm has three production departments, X, Y and Z. Total factory overheads and direct labour hours (DLHs) for the period are:

Cost Accounting Revision Guide

Department	Overheads	DLHs
X	100 000	5 000
Y	60 000	15 000
Z	40 000	20 000
	200 000	40 000

Blanket overhead rate

$$= \frac{\text{total factory overheads}}{\text{total direct labour hours}} = \frac{£200\,000}{40\,000} = £5 \text{ per DLH}$$

Departmental overhead rates:

X	£20 per DLH	(£100 000/5000)
Y	£4 per DLH	(£60 000/15 000)
Z	£2 per DLH	(£40 000/20 000)

Consider a situation where job A spends 100 hours in department Z but does not pass through departments X and Y. If a blanket overhead rate is used, job A will be charged £500 consisting of 100 direct labour hours at £5 per hour. If a departmental overhead rate is used, job A will be charged £200 consisting of 100 hours at £2 per hour. Typical examination questions will ask you to justify the method which should be used. The answer is that departmental rates should be used so that job A will be charged only with a fair share of the overheads of department Z. You should also indicate that if the blanket overhead rate is used, all the factory overhead rates will be averaged out and job A will be indirectly charged with a share of the overheads of department X. This is unacceptable because job A does not pass through department X and this department incurs the largest amount of overhead expenditure.

A blanket rate is often called a plantwide overhead rate. A blanket rate should only be used when all jobs spend approximately the same proportion of time in each department. You will see from Example 3.1 that the total hours for the three departments is 40 000. The proportion for each department is 12.5 per cent for X (5000/40 000), 37.5 per cent for Y and 50 per cent for Z. Consider a job requiring 25 hours in X, 75 hours in Y and 100 hours in Z. The proportionate amount of time which this job spends in the three departments is 12.5 per cent, 37.5 per cent and 50 per cent — the same as the total hours for the three departments. When departmental overhead rates are used, £1000 will be charged to the job (that is, (25 h × £20) + (75 h × £4) + (100 h × £2)). Now calculate the overhead charge using a blanket overhead rate; the overhead charged to the job is also £1000 (200 total hours at £5 per hour).

3.5 Procedure for calculating departmental overhead rates

The procedure involves the following stages:

1. Allocation of overheads to production and service departments
2. Apportionment of service department overheads to production departments
3. Calculation of appropriate departmental overhead rates
4. Charging overhead to jobs.

Typical examination question: calculating departmental overhead rates

A company manufactures and sells two products, X and Y, whose selling prices are £100 and £300 respectively, and each product passes through two manufacturing processes, A and B. In process A, product X takes two hours per unit and product Y takes four hours. In process B, product X takes one hour per unit, and product Y takes three hours. Labour in process A is paid £4 per hour, and in process B £5 per hour.

The two products are made out of materials P, Q and R, and the quantities of each material used in making one unit of each product are:

Material	Product X	Product Y
P	37 kg	93 kg
Q	10	240
R	20 m²	75 m²

Material prices are £1 per kg for P, £2.40 per dozen for Q and £0.20 per square metre for R.

Salesmen are paid a commission of 5 per cent of sales. The packing materials are £1 for X and £4 for Y. The costs of transporting the goods to the customer are £2 for X and £5 for Y. Other annual costs are:

	£	£
Indirect wages: process A	25 000	
process B	40 000	
stores	20 000	
canteen	10 000	
		95 000
Indirect materials: process A	51 510	
process B	58 505	
stores	1 310	
canteen	8 425	
		119 750
Rent and rates		450 000
Depreciation of plant and machinery		140 000
Power		50 000
Insurance: fire on buildings		3 750
workmen's compensation at 2 per cent of wages		12 000
Heating and lighting		4 500
Advertising		90 000

A royalty of £1 per unit is payable on product X. The annual quantities sold are 15 000 units of X and 10 000 units of Y.

Other relevant information is:

Cost centre	Floor area	Book value of plant and machinery	Horsepower of machinery	Direct labour	Number of employees	Number of stores issue notes
	m²	£	%	hours		
Process A	100 000	1 000 000	80	70 000	40	10 000
Process B	50 000	200 000	20	45 000	30	5 000
Stores	100 000	150 000			10	
Canteen	50 000	50 000			5	
	300 000	1 400 000	100	115 000	85	15 000

You are required to:

(a) Prepare a production overhead analysis and apportionment sheet, showing clearly the bases of apportionment used; (10 marks)
(b) Calculate appropriate rates of overhead recovery for processes A and B; (2 marks)
(c) Calculate the full (absorption) cost of making and selling one unit of each product; (6 marks)

(CIMA Stage 1 Accounting)

Answer

(a) *Production overhead analysis and apportionment sheet*

Overhead	Bases of apportionment	Annual cost	Production processes A	B	Service departments Stores	Canteen
		£	£	£	£	£
Indirect wages	Direct	95 000	25 000	40 000	20 000	10 000
Indirect materials	Direct	119 750	51 510	58 505	1 310	8 425
Rent and rates	Area	450 000	150 000	75 000	150 000	75 000
Depreciation, plant	Book value, plant	140 000	100 000	20 000	15 000	5 000
Power	HP of plant	50 000	40 000	10 000		
Fire insurance	Area	3 750	1 250	625	1 250	625
Workers' insurance	2% of wages	12 000	6 100	5 300	400	200
Heat and light	Area	4 500	1 500	750	1 500	750
Total 1		875 000	375 360	210 180	189 460	100 000
Canteen	No. of employees	–	50 000	37 500	12 500	(100 000)
Stores	No. of stores issues	–	134 640	67 320	(201 960)	
Total 2		875 000	560 000	315 000	–	–

In addition to overhead costs, a question might also include the direct materials and direct labour costs for each department. A common mistake is to include these items in the overhead analysis. Remember that you are calculating overhead rates. Direct expenses should not therefore be included in the analysis. Note that royalties are a direct expense.

Another common mistake is to regard an assembly department as a service department. In most examination questions, production departments consist of machine departments and assembly departments.

You can see that overhead expenditure is initially allocated to production and service departments as indicated by total 1. For this question, production departments are represented by processes A and B. The second stage in the procedure is to reapportion service department costs to production departments so that manufacturing costs are analysed to production departments only. This is indicated by total 2. The next stage (part (b) of the question) is to calculate an overhead rate for each production department; this rate is then charged to all jobs which pass through the various production departments.

From the overhead analysis sheet you can see that indirect wages and materials cannot be allocated to specific jobs, but they can normally be allocated specifically to appropriate departments. These items are therefore charged directly to a department on an actual basis. You will normally be given this allocation in the question. For the remaining items an appropriate basis of apportioning overheads to departments should be established. Commonly used apportionment bases are:

Cost	Basis of apportionment
Rent, rates, insurance of buildings and lighting and heating	Area
Employee-related expenditure such as works management, works canteen, time and wages office	Number of employees
Depreciation and insurance of plant and machinery	Value of items of plant and machinery
Reapportionment of stores servicing department	Material usage such as value of materials or number of stores requisitions issued
Reapportionment of maintenance service department	Direct labour hours or value of wages incurred by maintenance department in various departments

Several alternative methods of apportioning costs may be appropriate for certain expenses. The objective is to choose a method which is related to the benefits which each department receives from the expenditure. You should not be unduly concerned if, for a single expense, you select an inappropriate apportionment method. Your objective is to indicate that you know how to apportion overheads, reallocate service departments to production departments and calculate appropriate absorption rates.

You will have noted from the question that workmen's compensation insurance premium is based on a charge of 2 per cent of wages. Consequently an insurance charge of 2 per cent of the total wages should be allocated to each department. The calculations are:

	Process A £	Process B £	Stores £	Canteen £
Direct wages	280 000 (W1)	225 000 (W2)	–	–
Indirect wages	25 000	40 000	20 000	10 000
Total wages	305 000	265 000	20 000	10 000
Allocation at 2 per cent of total wages	6 100	5 300	400	200

		£
(W1)	Product X (15 000 units × 2 h × £4)	120 000
	Product Y (10 000 units × 4 h × £4)	160 000
		280 000

		£
(W2)	Product X (15 000 units × 1 h × £5)	75 000
	Product Y (10 000 units × 3 h × £5)	150 000
		225 000

(b) *Overhead recovery rates*

	Process A	Process B
Direct labour hours	70 000	45 000
Production overhead	£560 000	£315 000
overhead rate per direct labour hour	£8	£7

(c) *Product costs*

	Product X £	Product X £	Product Y £	Product Y £
Direct materials: P	37		93	
Q	2		48	
R	4		15	
	—	43	—	156
Direct wages: process A	8		16	
process B	5		15	
	—	13	—	31
Production overhead (W3): process A	16		32	
process B	7		21	
	—	23	—	53
Royalty		1		–
Absorption (manufacturing) cost		80		240
Commission		5		15
Packing materials		1		4
Transport		2		5
Advertising (W4)		2		6
Total cost		90		270

(W3) The overhead absorption rates are £8 per hour for process A and £7 per hour for process B. Product X spends 2 hours in process A and 1 hour in process B. The production overhead charge is thus £23 for product X.

(W4) Apportionments should be based on the benefits which the products receive from advertising. Therefore advertising is apportioned on the basis of total sales revenue. Total sales revenue is £4 500 000 consisting of 15 000 units of X at £100 and 10 000 units of Y at £300. Advertising is 2 per cent of sales (£90 000/£4 500 000). Therefore advertising is allocated to products at the rate of 2 per cent of the selling price.

3.6 Predetermined overhead rates

Overhead absorption rates should be calculated by dividing *estimated annual* overhead expenditure by *estimated annual* activity. Overhead rates based on *actual* costs and activity should not be used because:

(a) Job cost calculations have to be delayed until the end of the accounting period as the overhead rate calculations cannot be obtained before this date, but cost information is required quickly if it is to be useful for management.

(b) The calculation of *monthly* overhead rates might resolve the above timing problem, but the impact of fixed overheads will cause monthly overhead rates to fluctuate. Consider Example 3.2.

Example 3.2

The *fixed* overheads of a company are £120 000 per annum and monthly production varies from 2000 hours to 5000 hours. The monthly overhead rate for fixed overheads will therefore fluctuate as follows:

Monthly overhead	£10 000	£10 000
Monthly production	2000 hours	5000 hours
Monthly overhead rate	£5 per hour	£2 per hour

Fixed overhead expenditure remains constant each month but monthly production fluctuates. Consequently, the overhead rate varies from £2 to £5 per hour. It would be unreasonable for a job worked on in one month to be charged at £5 per hour for overhead and an identical job worked on in another month to be charged at only £2 per hour.

3.7 Under- and over-recovery of overheads

There will be an under- or over-recovery of overheads whenever actual activity or overhead expenditure is different from the calculations used to estimate the overhead rate. Consider Example 3.3.

Example 3.3

Estimated fixed overheads	£100 000
Estimated activity	100 000 hours
Estimated overhead rate	£1 per hour

Calculate the under/over-recovery of overheads for each of the following:

(a) Actual activity is 90 000 hours and actual expenditure is £100 000
(b) Actual activity is 100 000 hours and actual expenditure is £96 000.

Answer

	(a) £	(b) £
Actual overhead expenditure	100 000	96 000
Overhead recovered	90 000 (90 000 × £1)	100 000 (100 000 × £1)
Under/(over) recovery	10 000	(4 000)

The Statement of Standard Accounting Practice (SSAP) 9 on stocks and work in progress recommends that any under- or over-recovery of overheads should be written off against the profit and loss statement for the period in which they occur. Consequently any under-recovery is regarded as a period cost and is not included in the stock valuation.

3.8 Overhead absorption rates

Overheads should normally be allocated to cost units on the basis of the amount of time a cost unit spends in a department. For example, a direct labour hour rate should be used for a non-machine department, whereas in the case of a machine department a machine hour rate is preferable. The justification for time-based overhead rates is that the greater the amount of time a cost unit spends in a department, the greater the amount of overhead facilities it is utilizing. Therefore cost units which require a large proportion of a department's hours will be charged with a large proportion of the department's overheads.

Where both machine work and non-machine work is undertaken in a department it is preferable to establish two separate cost centre overhead rates – one related to machinery and the other related to jobs which involve direct labour hours only. Alternatively a machine hour rate may be appropriate if the majority of the department overheads are incurred as a consequence of running the machines.

Examination questions are sometimes set requiring you to calculate other absorption rates besides the machine hour rate and the direct labour hour rate. You should therefore be aware of these absorption rates. They are:

Direct wages percentage
Units of output
Direct materials percentage
Prime cost percentage.

Typical examination question: overhead absorption rates
A manufacturing company with machining and assembly departments seeks your advice about methods of absorbing production overhead.
From the information given below you are required to:

(a) List four methods of absorbing production overhead and show the rates for each department in respect of the four methods;
(b) Complete a comparative statement showing, for each of the four methods chosen in (a), the total production cost attributable to job 987;
(c) State for each department which rate you recommend should be used and why;
(d) Recalculate (or restate) the total production cost attributable to job 987 on the basis of your answer to (c).

A cost centre is a location to which costs can be attached. Cost centres can be regarded as separate sections within a department and overhead rates can be calculated for each cost centre if jobs spend different proportions of time in each cost centre. In most circumstances a departmental overhead rate will be satisfactory and the calculation of overhead rates for each cost centre within a department will be unnecessary.

	Machining department	Assembly department
Data for the year:		
Direct material	£100 000	£40 000
Direct labour	£250 000	£480 000
Production overhead	£300 000	£120 000
Direct labour hours	120 000	180 000
Machine hours	100 000	50 000
Output (units)	50	60

Data relating to job 987:

Direct material	£8 000	£2 000
Direct labour	£2 500	£4 500
Direct labour hours	1 000	1 500
Machine hours	800	300

(30 marks)
(CIMA Cost Accounting 1)

Answer

(a) We shall calculate six different overhead absorption rates so that you are familiar with all possible methods. The following formula is used for each calculation:

$$\text{absorption rate} = \frac{\text{departmental overheads}}{\text{amount (or units) of chosen method}}$$

Remember to multiply this formula by 100 if you are calculating direct wages, direct materials or prime cost *percentage* overhead rates.

Method	*Machining dept*	*Assembly dept*
Direct labour hours (DLH)	$\dfrac{£300\,000}{120\,000 \text{ DLHs}}$ = £2.50 per DLH	$\dfrac{£120\,000}{180\,000 \text{ DLHs}}$ = £0.667 per DLH
Machine hours	$\dfrac{£300\,000}{100\,000 \text{ M/C h}}$ = £3 per M/C hour	$\dfrac{£120\,000}{50\,000 \text{ M/C h}}$ = £2.40 per M/C hour
Direct wages percentage	$\dfrac{£300\,000}{£250\,000} \times 100$ = 120% of direct wages	$\dfrac{£120\,000}{£480\,000} \times 100$ = 25% of direct wages
Direct materials percentage	$\dfrac{£300\,000}{£100\,000} \times 100$ = 300% of direct materials	$\dfrac{£120\,000}{£40\,000} \times 100$ = 300% of direct materials
Prime cost percentage	$\dfrac{£300\,000}{£350\,000} \times 100$ = 86% of prime cost	$\dfrac{£120\,000}{£520\,000} \times 100$ = 23% of prime cost
Units of output	$\dfrac{£300\,000}{50 \text{ units}}$ = £6000 per unit	$\dfrac{£120\,000}{60 \text{ units}}$ = £2000 per unit

(b) The total production cost of job 987 is:

	£	£
Direct labour hours method:		
Machining (1000 × £2.50)	2 500	
Assembly (1500 × £0.667)	1 000	
Prime cost	17 000	
		20 500
Machine hours method:		
Machining (800 × £3.00)	2 400	
Assembly (300 × £2.40)	720	
Prime cost	17 000	
		20 120
Direct wages percentage method:		
Machining (120% × £2500)	3 000	
Assembly (25% × £4500)	1 125	
Prime cost	17 000	
		21 125
Direct materials percentage method:		
Machinery (£8000 × 300%)	24 000	
Assembly (£2000 × 300%)	6 000	
Prime cost	17 000	
		47 000
Prime cost percentage method:		
Machining (£10 500 × 86%)	9 030	
Assembly (£6500 × 23%)	1 495	
Prime cost	17 000	
		27 525
Units of output method:		
Machining	6 000	
Assembly	2 000	
Prime cost	17 000	
		25 000

(c) The overhead absorption rate should normally be related to the amount of time that jobs spend in each department. In the machine department a *machine hour rate* should be used because a considerable proportion of overheads will normally be incurred as a result of machine running time. The *direct labour hour rate* is recommended for the assembly department because machine activity will not be a dominant part of the department's activities.

Examination questions normally require you to explain why other overhead recovery rates are unsatisfactory. The *direct wages percentage method* will yield exactly the same results as the direct labour hour rate where uniform wage rates exist within a department. You should, therefore, emphasize that this method is only suitable where uniform wage rates apply. For example, two jobs which both require 100 direct labour hours should be allocated the same amount of overheads. However, if highly paid skilled labour is used on one job and low-paid unskilled labour is used on the other, then the job requiring highly skilled labour will be charged with the greater share of departmental overheads.

The *direct material* and *prime cost percentage methods* are not recommended because the overheads charged to jobs are unlikely to be related to the amount of time which jobs spend in each department. With the *units of output method* each cost unit is charged the same amount of overhead; for example, in the machine department each job is charged £6000 per unit. The units of output method is only suitable where all units produced within a department are identical. For example, if another job which is completed by the machining department requires 2400 machine hours then this job would be charged to £6000 for overheads even though it required considerably more machine hours than job 987. The units of output method is therefore inappropriate for a job costing system – but note that it can be recommended for a process costing system.

(d) On the basis of the above recommendation, the production cost of job 987 will be as follows:

		£
Prime cost		17 000
Production overhead: machining dept (800 × £3)	2400	
assembly dept (1500 × £0.667)	1000	3 400
Total production cost		20 400

3.9 Inter-service department transfers

Most examination questions which require you to prepare an overhead analysis sheet and compute overhead absorption rates assume that service departments provide services for production departments only (see Section 3.5). However, service departments normally provide services for other service departments as well as for production departments. For example, a personnel department provides services for other service departments and such interactions must be taken into account in the allocation process. Examination questions may require you to allocate service department overheads using one or more of the following methods:

(a) Repeated distribution method
(b) Simultaneous equation method

Typical examination question: inter-service department transfers

(a) In a factory with four production departments and two service departments, the operating costs for the month of October were as shown below. The cost of running the canteen is apportioned to each department on the basis of the estimated use of the canteen by the employees in each department. Similarly, the cost of the boiler house is apportioned on the basis of the estimated consumption of power used by each department.

Costs for October		£
Production department:	1	200 000
	2	500 000
	3	300 000
	4	400 000
Service department:		
Canteen		50 000
Boiler house		100 000
Total		£1 550 000

The service departments are apportioned as follows:

	Canteen %	Boiler house %
Production department: 1	10	20
2	30	10
3	20	30
4	30	20
Service department:		
Canteen	–	20
Boiler house	10	–
	100	100

You are required to prepare a cost statement showing the costs of operating the four production departments after the costs of the service departments have been reapportioned to each production department.

(b) Comment briefly on the problems associated with apportioning service department costs to production departments.

(15 marks)
(CIMA Cost Accounting I)

Answer

(a) The question does not specify which allocation method you should use, so you can select either method. Each method is explained below.

Repeated distribution method

Line	Production departments 1 £	2 £	3 £	4 £	Canteen £	Boiler house £
1 Allocation per overhead analysis	200 000	500 000	300 000	400 000	50 000	100 000
2 Allocation of boiler house	20 000 (20%)	10 000 (10%)	30 000 (30%)	20 000 (20%)	20 000 (20%)	(100 000)
3 Allocation of canteen	7 000 (10%)	21 000 (30%)	14 000 (20%)	21 000 (30%)	(70 000)	7 000 (10%)
4 Allocation of boiler house	1 400 (20%)	700 (10%)	2 100 (30%)	1 400 (20%)	1 400 (20%)	(7 000)
5 Allocation of canteen	140 (10%)	420 (30%)	280 (20%)	420 (30%)	(1 400)	140 (10%)
6 Allocation of boiler house	35 (20/80)	17 (10/80)	53 (30/80)	35 (20/80)		(140)
7 Allocation to production departments	228 575	532 137	346 433	442 855	–	–

Where this method is adopted the service department costs are repeatedly allocated in the specified percentages given in the question until the figures become too small to be significant. You can see from line 2 that the overheads of the boiler house are allocated according to the given percentages. As a result some of the overheads of the boiler house are transferred to the canteen. In line 3 the overheads of the canteen are allocated, which results in the boiler house receiving some further costs. The costs of the boiler house are again allocated and the canteen receives some further costs. This process continues until the costs become so small that any further detailed apportionments are unnecessary.

Simultaneous equation method
When this method is used, simultaneous equations are initially established as follows:

Let X be total overheads for canteen after boiler house charges have been allocated.
Let Y be total overheads for boiler house after canteen charges have been allocated.

The total overhead which is transferred into the boiler house and the canteen can be expressed as

$X = 50\,000 + 0.2Y$

$Y = 100\,000 + 0.1X$

Rearranging the above equations gives

$X - 0.2Y = 50\,000$ (1)

$-0.1X + Y = 100\,000$ (2)

> You can normally assume that you have reached the limit when the service department costs for reallocation are less than £500. Consequently the £140 in line 6 is apportioned to production departments only in the ratio 20:10:30:20. Note that in line 2 we allocated the boiler house overheads first, but you should arrive at the same answer if you apportion the canteen costs first in line 2.

We now multiply equation (1) by 5 and equation (2) by 1, giving

$5X - Y = 250\,000$

$-0.1X + Y = 100\,000$

Adding the above equations together, we have

$4.9X = 350\,000$

Therefore

$X = 71\,428.6\ (350\,000/4.9)$

Substituting this value for X in equation (1), we have

$71\,428.6 - 0.2Y = 50\,000$

$21\,428.6 = 0.2Y$

Therefore

$Y = 107\,143$

We now apportion the values of X and Y to the production departments in the agreed percentages:

	Production departments			
	1 £	2 £	3 £	4 £
Allocation as per overhead analysis	200 000	500 000	300 000	400 000
Allocation of canteen (£71 429)	7 143 (10%)	21 429 (30%)	14 286 (20%)	21 429 (30%)
Allocation of boiler house (£107 143)	21 429 (20%)	10 714 (10%)	32 143 (30%)	21 429 (20%)
	228 572	532 143	346 429	442 858

(b) The problems associated with apportioning service department costs to production departments are:

  (i) Difficulty in determining suitable bases for apportionment of service department costs to production. The base selected should be one that exerts a major influence on the costs of the service departments.

  (ii) When there are several service departments working for each other, the analysis can become complex. The simultaneous equation and repeated distribution methods cannot be used when complex interrelationships occur. Matrix algebra can be used for complex problems. Alternatively computers can easily deal with reciprocal service department apportionments.

Typical examination questions
The following are typical non-quantitative questions which have appeared in recent examination papers:

1. Explain why predetermined overhead absorption rates are preferred to overhead absorption rates calculated from factual information after the end of a financial period. (CIMA Cost Accounting I)
2. The production director of Bookdon PLC has suggested that 'as the actual overheads incurred and units produced are usually different from those budgeted, and as a consequence profits at each month end are distorted by over/under-absorbed overheads, it would be more accurate to calculate the actual overhead cost per unit each month end by dividing the total number of all units actually produced during the month into the actual overheads incurred.'

    Critically examine the production director's suggestion. (CACA Level 1 Costing)

4
Accounting entries for job costing and contract costing

4.1 Integrated and interlocking accounts

An *integrated cost accounting system* is an accounting system in which the cost and financial accounts are combined in one set of accounts. With a system of *interlocking accounts* a separate set of cost and financial accounts is maintained. An integrated cost accounting system is generally considered to be preferable to the interlocking system because the latter involves a duplication of accounting entries.

4.2 Control accounts

The recording system for interlocking and integrated accounts is based on a system of control accounts. A control account is a summary account, where entries are made from *totals* of transactions for a period. For example, the balance in the stores ledger control account will be supported by a voluminous file of stores ledger accounts which will add up to agree with the total in the stores ledger control account. If 100 items of materials were received for a period and totalled £100 000, then an entry for the total purchases of £100 000 would be recorded in the stores ledger control account. This will be supported by 100 separate entries in each of the individual stores ledger accounts. The total of these individual entries will add up to £100 000. The file for these individual ledger accounts supporting the total control account is called the *subsidiary ledger*.

Note that the entries in the control accounts form part of the system of *double entry*, whereas the separate entries in the individual accounts in the subsidiary ledger do not form part of the double entry system.

4.3 Accounting entries for an integrated cost accounting system

Purchase of raw materials
DR stores ledger control account   CR creditor control account

Issue of raw materials
DR WIP control account (for direct materials)   CR stores ledger control account
DR factory overhead control account (for indirect materials)   CR stores ledger control account

Payment of gross wages
DR wages control account CR wages accrued (for net wages)
  CR PAYE account
  CR National Insurance contributions account

Note that the total of the tax deductions and National Insurance deductions from the employees' wages are recorded as amounts owing in the PAYE account and NI account. The credit entries in the above accounts are cleared by cash payments – that is, DR wages accrued, PAYE and NI accounts, and CR cash.

Allocation of labour costs
DR WIP control account CR wages control account
  (for direct wages)
DR factory overhead control CR wages control account
  account (for indirect wages)

Manufacturing overheads incurred
DR manufacturing overhead CR expense creditors control
  control account account

Note that indirect materials and indirect labour will also have been debited to this account, as outlined for the accounting entries for labour and materials.

Allocation of manufacturing overheads
DR WIP control account CR manufacturing overhead control account

Note that manufacturing overheads are allocated to jobs using pre-determined overhead rates. The balance in the manufacturing overhead control account represents the under- or over-recovery of overhead which is transferred to the costing P & L account.

Non-manufacturing overheads
DR appropriate non-manufacturing CR expense creditors control
  overhead control account account

Note that non-manufacturing overheads should not be charged to WIP because they are period costs and not product costs. The non-manufacturing overhead control account is therefore cleared at the end of the period by a transfer to costing P & L account.

Cost of jobs transferred from WIP stock to finished goods stock
DR finished goods stock account CR WIP control account

Cost of finished goods sold
DR cost of sales account CR finished goods stock account

Note that at the end of the accounting period the cost of sales account is transferred to the costing P & L account.

Sales
DR Debtors CR Sales

You should note that some examination questions assume that creditors' accounts (that is, wages accrued, PAYE and N.I accounts) are not used for labour costs. Instead, all cash payments are recorded by debiting the wages control account and crediting cash. A credit balance on the wages control account represents accrued wages.

The employer also makes a payment for National Insurance contributions in respect of each employee. If the question does not specify the accounting treatment of employer's National Insurance contributions you should debit the manufacturing overhead control account and credit the National Insurance contributions account.

Some manufacturing overhead expenditure will not involve future cash commitments – for example, provision for depreciation. You should debit the manufacturing overhead control account and credit the provision for depreciation account with the annual provision for depreciation.

Typical examination question: integrated accounts

In the absence of the accountant you have been asked to prepare a month's cost accounts for a company which operates a batch costing system fully integrated with the financial accounts. The cost clerk has provided you with the following information, which he thinks is relevant.

	£
Balances at beginning of month:	
Stores ledger control account	24 175 (1)
Work in progress control account	19 210 (2)
Finished goods control account	34 164 (3)
Prepayments of production overheads brought forward from previous month	2 100 (4)
Transactions during the month:	
Materials purchased	76 150 (5)
Materials issued: to production	26 350 (6)
for factory maintenance	3 280 (7)
Materials transferred between batches	1 450 (8)

	Direct workers £	Indirect workers £
Total wages paid: net	17 646 (9)	3 342 (11)
employees' deductions	4 364 (10)	890 (12)

	£
Direct wages charged to batches from work tickets	15 236 (13)
Recorded non-productive time of direct workers	5 230 (14)
Direct wages incurred on production of capital equipment, for use in the factory	2 670 (15)
Selling and distribution overheads incurred	5 240 (16)
Other production overheads incurred	12 200 (17)
Sales	75 400 (18)
Cost of finished goods sold	59 830 (19)
Cost of goods completed and transferred into finished goods store during the month	62 130 (20)
Physical stock value of work in progress at end of month	24 360 (21)

The production overhead absorption rate is 150 per cent of direct wages and it is the policy of the company to include a share of production overheads in the cost of capital equipment constructed in the factory (22).

You are required to:

(a) Prepare the following accounts for the month:
    Stores ledger control account
    Work in progress control account
    Finished goods control account
    Production overhead control account
    Profit/loss account   (12 marks)

Accounting entries for job costing and contract costing   37

(b) Identify any aspects of the accounts which you consider should be investigated. (4 marks)
(CACA Level 1 Costing)

Answer

(a) The numbers in the parentheses in the question and answer have been added to represent the transaction numbers and give a clearer understanding of the entries relating to each transaction.

Stores ledger control account

	£		£
(1) Opening balances B/F	24 175	Materials issued:	
(5) Creditors: materials purchased	76 150	(6) Work in progress control	26 350
		(7) Production overhead control	3 280
		Closing stock C/F	70 695
	£100 325		£100 325

Work in progress control account

	£		£
(2) Opening balance B/F	19 210	(20) Finished goods Control: cost of goods transferred	62 130
(6) Stores ledger: materials issued	26 350		
(13) Wages control: direct wages	15 236		
(22) Production overhead Control: overhead absorbed (15 236 × 150%)	22 854	Closing stock C/F	24 360
P & L A/C: stock gain (see note (i))	2 840		
	£86 490		£86 490

Finished goods control account

	£		£
(3) Opening balance B/F	34 164	(19) P & L A/C: cost of sales	59 830
(20) Work in progress: cost of goods sold	62 130	Closing stock C/F (difference)	36 464
	£96 294		£96 294

Production overhead control account

	£		£
(4) Prepayments B/F	2 100	(22) Work in progress: overheads absorbed (15 236 × 150%)	22 854
(7) Stores ledger: materials issued for repairs	3 280		
(14) Wages control: idle time of direct workers	5 230	(22) Capital under construction A/C: overheads absorbed (2670 × 150%)	4 005
(11/12) Wages control: indirect workers' wages (3342 + 890)	4 232		
(17) Cash/creditors: other overheads incurred	12 200	P & L A/C: under-absorbed overhead (bal.)	183
	£27 042		£27 042

Profit and loss account

		£			£
(19)	Cost of goods sold	59 830	(18)	Sales	75 400
	Gross profit C/F	15 570			
		£75 400			£75 400
(16)	Selling and distribution overheads	5 240		Gross profit B/F	15 570
	Production overhead control: under- absorbed overhead	183		Stock gain: WIP control	2 840
	Net profit C/F	12 987			
		£18 410			£18 410

Notes and comments on (a)

(i) The stock gain in the WIP A/C represents a balancing figure. It is assumed that the stock gain arises from the valuation of closing stocks at the end of the period.

(ii) The value of materials transferred between batches (transaction 8) will be recorded in the subsidiary records but will not affect the control (total) accounts.

(iii) You might find it helpful if you prepare the wages control account:

Wages control account

		£			£
	Direct wages:		(13)	WIP	15 236
(9)	Wages accrued A/C	17 646	(15)	Capital equipment A/C	2 670
(10)	Employees' contributions A/C	4 364	(14)	Factory overhead (idle time)	5 230
	Indirect wages:		(11/12)	Factory overhead (indirect wages)	4 232
(11)	Wages accrued A/C	3 342			
(12)	Employees' contributions A/C	890			
	Balance (wages accrued A/C)	1 126			
		£27 368			£27 368

(iv) The opening balance (transaction 4) represents cash payments incurred last period for expenses due this period. Therefore there will be an opening debit balance of £2100 in the production overhead control account. The debit side of this account indicates that total overheads of £27 042 have been incurred and the credit side indicates that total overheads of £26 859 have been allocated. The balance of £183 represents an under-recovery of overheads which is charged to costing P & L account.

(v) Transaction 6 represents direct materials and transaction 7 indirect materials.

(vi) Transactions 9–12 in the wages control account indicate that total wage payments are £26 242. However, the credit side indicates that £27 368 labour costs have been allocated. It is assumed that the difference of £1126 represents labour costs owing.

(vii) Selling and distribution costs are debited to the selling and distribution overhead control account and transferred to costing profit and loss account as a period cost at the end of the accounting period.

(b) (i) Large increase in raw material stocks. Is this due to maintaining uneconomic stock levels, or is it due to an anticipated increase in production to meet future demand?
(ii) WIP stock gain.
(iii) Idle time is nearly 25 per cent of the total direct wages cost.
(iv) The gross direct wages are £22 010 (£17 646 + £4364) but the allocation amounts to £23 136 (£15 236 + £5230 + £2670).

4.4 Interlocking accounts

With a system of interlocking accounts, separate records of financial transactions (for example, entries in debtors' and creditors' accounts) are not maintained. To maintain the double entry records an account must be opened in the cost accounts to record the corresponding entry which, in an integrated accounting system, would normally be in one of the financial accounts (for example, debtors, creditors, wages accrued, PAYE, National Insurance contributions, expense creditors, and provision for depreciation). This account is called a *cost control* or *general ledger adjustment* account.

Typical examination question: interlocking accounts
At 1 July 1982 a manufacturing company had the following balances in the general ledger adjustment account in its cost ledger:

		£
Balance brought forward	CR	5625
Stores ledger control account		2125
Finished goods stock control account		1500
Work in progress control account		2000

You are required to open ledger accounts for the above items in the cost ledger, post the following items which occurred in the period up to 31 October 1982, and open up other accounts as considered necessary including a costing profit and loss account.

The question does not specify that interlocking accounts are required, but this is implied because a general ledger adjustment account is maintained.

Stock materials purchased	12 000
Stock materials issued to production	12 500
Stock materials issued to maintenance dept.	1 000
Wages: direct	10 830
Included in direct wages is indirect work	600
Factory overheads incurred	4 200
Factory overheads absorbed into production	5 800

Work transferred to finished stock, at cost		24 000
Factory cost of sales		22 500
Sales at selling price		28 750
Administrative and selling costs (to be written off against profits)		4 250
	(16 marks)	(AAT)

Answer

General ledger adjustment account

Note that corresponding entries are not made in financial accounts such as debtors' or creditors' account. The general ledger adjustment account is used to ensure that double entry records are maintained.

	£		£
Sales	28 750	Balance B/F	5 625
Balance C/D	10 155	Stores ledger control	12 000
		Wages control	10 830
		Overhead control	4 200
		Administration and selling	4 250
		Profit and loss account	2 000
	£38 905		£38 905
		Balance B/D	10 155

Stores ledger control account

	£		£
Balance B/F	2 125	Work in progress control	12 500
General ledger control	12 000	Factory overhead control	1 000
		Balance C/D	625
	14 125		14 125
Balance B/D	625		

Finished stock control account

	£		£
Balance B/F	1 500	Costing profit and	
Work in progress control	24 000	loss account	22 500
		Balance C/D	3 000
	£25 500		£25 500
Balance C/D	3 000		

Work in progress control account

	£		£
Balance B/F	2 000	Finished stock control	24 000
Stores ledger control	12 500	Balance C/D	6 530
Factory overhead control	5 800		
Wages control	10 230		
	£30 530		£30 530
Balance B/D	6 530		

Factory overhead control account

	£		£
Stores ledger control	1 000	Work in progress control	5 800
Wages control	600		
General ledger control	4 200		
	£5 800		£5 800

Wages control account

	£		£
General ledger control	10 830	Factory overhead control	600
		Work in progress control	10 230
	£10 830		£10 830

Costing profit and loss account

	£		£
Finished goods stock control account	22 500	Sales general ledger control	28 750
Administration and selling	4 250		
Net profit general ledger control	2 000		
	£28 750		£28 750

4.5 Contract costing

Contract costing is a system of job costing which is applied to jobs which normally take a considerable time to complete. Building and construction work, civil engineering and shipbuilding are some examples of industries where contract costing would be appropriate.

A contract account is maintained for each contract. Costs are debited and the contract price is credited to the contract account. Each contract account therefore becomes a small profit and loss account. Because of the considerable length of time which is taken to complete a contract the profit which is attributable to each accounting period must be determined. SSAP 9 provides the following guidance on the profit which should be taken up for a particular period:

The profit, if any, taken up needs to reflect the proportion of the work carried out at the accounting date and to take into account any known inequalities of profitability in the various stages of a contract. Many businesses, however, carry out contracts where the outcome cannot reasonably be assessed before the conclusion of the contract and in such cases it is prudent not to take up any profit. Where the business carries out contracts and it is considered that their outcome can be assessed with reasonable certainty before their conclusion, then the attributable profit should be taken up, but the judgement involved should be exercised with prudence.

You should be familiar with various terms which are used in contract costing questions. The estimate of the sales value of work carried out to date is called value of work certified. Progress payments represent payments made on account throughout the contract period by the customer to the contractor. Retention money represents a clause in the contract which entitles the customer to withhold a proportion of the value of work certified for a specified period after the end of the contract. During this period the contractor must make good all contractual defects. When the defects have been satisfactorily completed the customer will release the retention money.

Typical examination question: contract costing

A construction company is currently undertaking three separate contracts. Information relating to these contracts for the previous year, together with other relevant data, is shown below:

	Contract MNO £000	Contract PQR £000	Contract STU £000	Construction services dept overhead £000
Contract price	800	675	1100	
Balances brought forward at beginning of year:				
Cost of work completed	–	190	370	–
Material on site	–	–	25	–
Written down value of plant and machinery	–	35	170	12
Wages accrued	–	2	–	–
Profit previously transferred to profit and loss A/C	–	–	15	–
Transactions during year:				
Material delivered to sites	40	99	180	–
Wages paid	20	47	110	8
Payments to subcontractors	–	–	35	–
Salaries and other costs	6	20	25	21
Written down value of plant:				
issued to sites	90	15	–	–
transferred from sites	–	8	–	–
Balances carried forward at the end of year:				
Material on site	8	–	–	–
Written down value of plant and machinery	70	–	110	5
Wages accrued	–	5	–	–
Prepayments to subcontractors	–	–	15	–
Value of work certified at end of year	90	390	950	–
Cost of work not certified at end of year	–	–	26	–

The cost of operating the construction services department, which provides technical advice to each of the contracts, is apportioned over the contracts in proportion to wages incurred.

Contract STU is scheduled for handing over to the contractee in the near future and the site engineer estimates that the extra costs required to complete the contract in addition to those tabulated above will total £138 000. This amount includes an allowance for plant depreciation, construction services and for contingencies.

Accounting entries for job costing and contract costing

You are required to:

(a) Construct a cost account for each of the three contracts for the previous year and show the cost of the work completed at the year end. (9 marks)

(b) (i) Recommend how much profit or loss should be taken, for each contract, for the previous year. (7 marks)

(ii) Explain the reasons for each of your recommendations in (b)(i). (6 marks)

(CACA Level 1 Costing)

Answer
Contract accounts (for the previous year)

	MNO £000	PQR £000	STU £000		MNO £000	PQR £000	STU £000
Cost of contract to date B/F		190	370	Wages accrued B/F		2	
Materials on site B/F			25	Plant control A/C		8	
Plant on site B/F		35	170	Materials on site C/F	8		
Materials control A/C	40	99	180	Plant on site C/F	70		110
Wages control A/C	20	47	110	Prepayment C/F			15
Subcontractors A/C			35	Cost of work not			
Salaries	6	20	25	certified C/F			26
Plant control A/C	90	15		Cost of work certified			
Wages accrued C/F		5		(balance)	82	411	786
Apportionment of construction services	4	10	22				
	160	421	937		160	421	937
Cost of work certified B/F	82	411	786	Value of work certified	90	390	950
Profit taken this period			114	Loss taken		21	
Profit taken previous periods			15				
Profit not taken	8		35				
	90	411	950		90	411	950
Cost of work not certified B/F			26	Wages accrued B/F		5	
Materials on site B/F	8						
Plant on site B/F	70		110				
Prepayment B/F			15				

Note that the contract accounts are divided into three sections. The first section shows the costs which should be matched against the value of work certified so as to calculate the profit to date. The costs to be matched against sales are shown on the line 'cost of work certified' which is entered on the credit side of the account. Any unexpired costs (that is, future expenses) such as cost of work not certified and the written-down value of plant at the end of the period are carried forward from the first section to the third section of the account. You should regard the third section of the account as a future cost section.

In the second section of the account the cost of completed work is matched against the value of completed work so that the profit *to date* can be calculated. You can see that the profit (losses) for the contracts are:

If the question requires you to prepare contract accounts for more than one contract you can save time by preparing the accounts in columnar form.

Costs incurred by construction services department:

	£000
Plant depreciation	
(12 − 5)	7
Salaries	21
Wages paid	8
	36

Wages incurred by each contract are:

MNO	20
PQR	50 (47 + 5 − 2)
STU	110
	180

The costs apportioned to each contract are:

	£000	
MNO	4	|(20/180) £36|
PQR	10	|(50/180) £36|
STU	22	|(110/180) £36|
	36	

	£000
Contract MNO	8
Contract PQR	(21)
Contract STU	164

The profit *to be taken* for the year should be based on the principles outlined in SSAP 9. You are recommended to adopt the following guidelines:

(i) No profit should be taken if the contract is in its early stages (say less than 30 per cent complete) as the outcome cannot be assessed with reasonable certainty. For contract MNO the contract price is £800 000 but the value of work certified is only £90 000. It is therefore recommended that no profit is taken for this contract.

(ii) If a loss is incurred, the prudence concept should be applied and the loss (that is, £21 000) should be written off as soon as it is incurred.

(iii) When the contract is nearing completion the size of the eventual profit can normally be foreseen with reasonable certainty and a proportion of the anticipated profit should be taken. For contract STU the value of work certified is £950 000 and the contract price is £1 100 000, indicating that the contract is 86 per cent complete. The anticipated profit for contract STU is calculated as follows:

	£000
Cost of work certified	786
Cost of work not yet certified	26
Estimated costs to complete	138
	950
Contract price	1100
Anticipated profit	150

The profit taken to date is calculated using the following formula:

$$\frac{\text{cash received to date } (£950\,000)}{\text{contract price } (£1\,100\,000)} \times \text{anticipated profit } (£150\,000)$$

= £129 545 (say £129 000)

The profit for the current period is £114 000, consisting of the profit to date of £129 000 less the profit previously transferred to the profit and loss account of £15 000. You should note that more prudent approaches are sometimes used to calculate the profit earned to date.

(iv) Where a significant proportion of the contract has been completed (say 30–85 per cent) and the size of the eventual profit cannot be

---

Normally cash received to date is calculated by deducting the specified percentage for retention money from the value of work certified. As the question does not indicate the retention percentage it is assumed that no retention money is withheld by the customer. Therefore the cash received is assumed to be equal to the value of work certified.

foreseen with reasonable certainty, the following formula is often used to calculate the profit to date:

$$\frac{2}{3} \times \text{notional profit} \times \frac{\text{cash received}}{\text{value of work certified}}$$

The notional profit is the value of work certified to date minus the cost of work certified.

Balance sheet entries
The WIP valuation is calculated as follows:

	MNO £000	PQR £000	STU £000
Cost of work completed to date	82	411	812 (786 + 26)
Add profit (loss) taken to date		(21)	129
	82	390	941
Less progress payments received	81	351	855
	1	39	86

Other entries in the balance sheet will include:

	£000
Materials on site	8
Plant on site	180
Prepayments	15
Accruals	5

Most contracts include a clause withholding retention money. To illustrate the balance sheet entries it is assumed that a retention rate of 10 per cent of the value of work certified by the customer's architect has been agreed. The progress payments received are therefore calculated by deducting 10 per cent from the value of work certified.

5
Process costing

5.1 Job costing and process costing

Job costing is a costing system where costs are charged to each individual customer's order, because each order is unique and requires different amounts of labour, materials and overhead. A process costing system is *an average cost* system which is appropriate to an organization which produces many units of the *same* product during a period. The cost of an individual order for a single unit can be obtained by merely dividing the costs of production for a period by the units produced during that period. Examples of industries where a system of process costing is appropriate are chemicals, oil and textiles.

5.2 Accounting procedure for a process costing system

As production moves from process to process the costs are transferred with it. For example, the costs of process 1 are transferred to process 2; process 2 costs are then added to this cost and the resulting cost is transferred to process 3; process 3 costs are added to this cost; and so on. The last department's cost in the process determines the total cost to be transferred to finished goods stock. The cost per unit of output is the total cumulative cost recorded in the last process divided by the number of units produced.

5.3 Normal and abnormal losses

Normal losses are inherent in the production process and are not expected to be eliminated even under the most efficient operating conditions. Examples of normal losses include liquids which may evaporate or unavoidable losses of cloth lost when making a suit. Abnormal losses are avoidable losses which are not expected to occur under efficient operating conditions. Examples of abnormal losses include losses resulting from the incorrect cutting of cloth or the use of inferior materials.

The cost of a normal loss is absorbed by the production process, whereas the cost of an abnormal loss is removed from the process account and charged to an abnormal losses account. At the end of the accounting period the cost of the abnormal loss is written off to the profit and loss account as a period cost.

Remember that product costs are required based on normal production conditions. Stock valuation and product pricing should be based on normal costs, and abnormal costs should be excluded from the product costs.

5.4 Revenue received from process losses

Sometimes process losses can be sold for some small value. Sales value resulting from normal losses should be credited to the process for which the loss occurred and the corresponding debit will be made to the cash account. Sales revenue from abnormal losses should be credited to the abnormal losses account. Example 5.1 illustrates the accounting treatment of normal and abnormal losses.

Example 5.1

One thousand units were introduced into a process at a cost of £10 000. The output from the process was 850 units. A normal loss of 10 per cent is expected, and any units lost can be sold for £1 per unit.

The cost per unit is calculated by using the following formula:

$$\frac{\text{cost of production less scrap value of normal loss}}{\text{expected output}}$$

$$= \frac{£10\,000 - (100 \times £1)}{900 \text{ units}} = £11$$

Dividing by the expected output rather than actual output increases the unit cost and ensures that the normal loss is included in the unit cost.

The net cost of the process is £9850 (£10 000 − £150) and this cost is allocated as follows:

	£
Transferred to next process: 850 units at £11 per unit	9350
Abnormal loss:	
50 units at £11 per unit, less sales value of £50 from units lost	500
	9850

Completed production is 850 units and the normal loss is 100 units. The unaccounted output of 50 units represents the abnormal loss.

The accounting entries are as follows:

Process account

	Units	Unit cost	£		Units	Unit cost	£
Input costs	1000	10.0	10 000	Normal loss	100	–	100
				Abnormal loss	50	11.00	550
				Transferred to next process	850	11.00	9350
			10 000				10 000

Note that the sales value of the normal loss is credited to the process account and the cost of the abnormal loss is removed from the process account.

Abnormal loss account

	£		£
Process account	550	Cash sale for units lost	50
		Balance transferred to P & L A/C	500
	550		550

5.5 Abnormal losses and gains

Typical examination question: abnormal losses and gains

(a) In a process costing system, state what is meant by (i) normal loss, and (ii) abnormal loss, and indicate how you would treat these items in the cost accounts.

(b) A company makes one product which passes through two processes. From the data given below which relates to period 4, you are required to show the transactions which would appear in the two process accounts, finished goods account, abnormal loss account and the abnormal gain account:

Process 1
Material: 5000 kilograms at £0.5 per kilogram
Labour: £800
Production overhead 200 per cent on labour

Process 2
Materials: 4000 kilograms at £0.8 per kilogram
Labour: £1753
Production overhead 100 per cent on labour

Normal losses are 20 per cent of input in process 1 and 10 per cent of input in process 2, but without further processing any losses are able to be sold as scrap for £0.3 per kilogram from process 1 and £0.7 per kilogram from process 2.

The outputs for period 4 were:
3800 kilograms from process 1
7270 kilograms from process 2

There was no work in progress at the beginning or end of period 4 and no finished goods stock at the beginning of the period.

(20 marks) (CIMA Cost Accounting 1)

Answer for (b)

You can see from the process accounts on page 49 that actual output is greater than expected for process 2 and this results in an abnormal gain. The value of the gain is calculated in the same way as the abnormal loss, removed from the process account and transferred to the credit side of the profit and loss account at the end of the period. Because the units lost have a scrap value, the abnormal gain is reduced to reflect the fact that some scrap income is lost.

The abnormal gain is valued at the cost per unit of normal production. However, as 250 units were gained there is a loss of scrap sales of £175 (250 units at £0.70) and this lost income is offset against the abnormal gain of £375. The net gain of £200 is transferred to the profit and loss account.

Process 2 account is credited with the expected sales value of the normal loss of £546 (780 units at £0.70 per unit) as the objective is to record in the process account *normal* production costs. Because the normal loss of 780 units does not occur the company will not obtain the sales value of the

---

Total input to the process is 7800 units. The expected output is 7020 units (7800 − 780 units normal loss). Actual output is 7270 units and the difference represents an abnormal gain of 250 units.

normal loss of £546. This is dealt with by entering a corresponding debit of £546 in the normal loss account. This entry represents the amount due from the sale of scrap from the *expected* normal loss. The amount due (£546) is then reduced by £175 to reflect the fact that 250 units at 70 pence were not lost. You will see that the normal loss account is credited and the abnormal gain account is debited with £175. Therefore in respect of process 2 the normal loss account will show the amount of cash received from scrap income due (that is, £546 less £175 which represents 530 units actual loss at 70 pence).

Process 1

	kg	£ per kg	£		kg	£ per kg	£
Materials	5000	0.5	2500	Process 2	3800	1.15	4370
Labour			800	Normal loss	1000	0.30	300
Production overhead			1600	Abnormal loss	200	1.15	230
	5000		4900		5000		4900

$$\text{Cost per unit} = \frac{\text{cost of production less scrap value of normal loss}}{\text{expected output}}$$

$$= \frac{£4900 - £300}{4000 \text{ kg}} = £1.15 \text{ per kg}$$

Process 2

	kg	£ per kg	£		kg	£ per kg	£
Transferred from				Finished goods			
process 1	3800	1.15	4370	stock	7270	1.50	10 905
Materials	4000	0.80	3200	Normal loss	780	0.70	546
Labour			1753				
Production overhead			1753				
			11 076				
Abnormal gain	250	1.50	375				
	8050		11 451		8050		11 451

$$\text{Cost per unit} = \frac{£11\,076 - £546}{7800 - 780} = £1.50$$

Finished goods stock account

	£		£
Process 2	10 905		—

Process costing 49

Abnormal loss account

	£		£
Process 1	230	Normal loss A/C	
		(200 × £0.30)	60
		P & L A/C	170
	230		230

Abnormal gain account

	£		£
Normal loss A/C (250 × £0.70)	175	Process 2 A/C	375
P & L A/C	200		
	375		375

Normal loss account (income due)

	£		£
Process 1 (normal loss)	300	Abnormal gain	175
Process 2 (normal loss)	546	Balance or cash received	731
Abnormal loss	60		
	906		906

5.6 Closing work in progress and equivalent production

So far we have assumed that there were no stocks of partly completed production (WIP). Where stocks of WIP exist, output consists of fully and partly completed production. It is therefore incorrect to add unlike items together to calculate the cost per unit. To overcome this problem, WIP is expressed in terms of fully complete units. For example, 1000 units 50 per cent complete are equivalent to 500 fully complete units. The term *equivalent production* is used to refer to the finished equivalents of partly completed production.

It would be incorrect to add say 2000 fully complete units to 1000 units which are half complete because the units of output are not homogeneous.

Typical examination question: work in progress and equivalent production
A cleansing agent is manufactured from the input of three ingredients. At 1 December there was no work in progress. During December the ingredients were put into the process in the following quantities:

A 2000 kg at 80p/kg
B 3000 kg at 50p/kg
C 6000 kg at 40p/kg

Additionally, labour working 941 hours and being paid £4 per hour was incurred, and overheads were recovered on the basis of 50 per cent of labour cost. There was no loss in the process. Output was 8600 kg. The remaining items in work in progress were assessed by the company's works manager as follows:

(a) Complete so far as materials were concerned
(b) One-quarter of the items were 60 per cent complete for labour and overheads
(c) Three-quarters were 25 per cent complete for labour and overheads.

You are required to produce a cleansing agent process account, showing clearly the cost of the output and work in progress carried forward.

(16 marks) (AAT)

Answer

If the question includes WIP stocks you should prepare a statement showing the calculation of the cost per unit. The statement should include separate columns for completed units and WIP equivalent production. WIP equivalent production is calculated by multiplying the number of units in progress by the percentage degree of completion. Materials are normally used at the start of the process and will therefore be 100 per cent complete. Sometimes materials are introduced at the end of the process and then zero should be entered in the WIP column, as WIP will not have reached the point where materials are added.

Most examination questions include only one batch of WIP.

Calculation of cost per unit

	1	2	3	4	5	6	7	8
	Total cost £	Comp. units	Equiv. WIP1	Equiv. WIP2	Total equiv. units	Cost per unit £	WIP1 value £	WIP2 value £
Materials	5500	8600	600	1800	11 000	0.50	300	900
Labour	3764	8600	360	450	9 410	0.40	144	180
Overheads	1882	8600	360	450	9 410	0.20	72	90
	11 146					1.10	516	1170

Value of WIP (£516 + £1170)   £1 686
Value of completed production (8600 × £1.10)   9 460
     11 146

The arrow indicates that you can check if your calculations are correct. The cost of the output should agree with the cost of the input.

Note that 11 000 kg were put into the process and 8600 kg were completed. Therefore WIP is 2400 kg, consisting of two batches – one batch (WIP1) of 600 units 60 per cent complete, and the second batch (WIP2) of 1800 units 25 per cent complete for labour and overhead. You can see that the cost per unit is calculated by dividing the total cost (column 1) by the total equivalent units (column 5). The WIP valuations (columns 7 and 8) are obtained by multiplying the cost per unit (column 6) by the WIP equivalent production (columns 3 and 4).

Materials are assumed to be 100 per cent complete for both batches.

Cleansing agent process account

		kg	£		kg	£
Ingredient:	A	2 000	1 600	Completed production	8 600	9 460
	B	3 000	1 500	WIP C/F	2 400	1 686
	C	6 000	2 400			
Wages			3 764			
Overhead			1 882			
		11 000	11 146		11 000	11 146
WIP B/F		2 400	1 686			

5.7 Equivalent production and normal and abnormal losses at the end of the process

Most examination questions state that losses occur at inspection point, which is normally assumed to be the end of the process. Therefore the cost of the normal loss should be allocated only to those units which have reached the end of the process (that is, completed units). However, if the loss occurs before the end of the process and the WIP has passed this point, then the loss should be allocated to completed production and closing WIP.

Typical examination question: equivalent production and losses
A chemical compound is manufactured as a result of two processes. The details for the second process – process B – for the month of July are as follows:

Opening work in process	nil
Materials transferred from process A	10 000 kg valued at £40 500
Labour cost	1000 hours paid at £5.616 per hour
Overheads	50 per cent of labour cost
Output transferred to finished goods	8000 kg
Closing work in process	900 kg

Quality control checks at the end of the process of manufacture normally lead to a rejection rate of 10 per cent.

Closing work in process is 100 per cent complete for material content, and 75 per cent complete for both labour and overheads.

You are required to prepare the process B account for July. Clearly show your workings. (13 marks)
(AAT)

Answer
It is unclear from the question whether the normal loss is 10 per cent of the process input (10 per cent of 10 000 kg) or 10 per cent of the output reaching the final inspection point (10 per cent of 10 000 kg introduced less the closing WIP of 900 kg). It is assumed that the question implies the latter. It is also assumed that the loss occurs at the end of the process so that none of the normal loss will be allocated to closing WIP. The normal loss

is therefore 910 kg (10 per cent of 9100) and the abnormal loss is the balance of 190 kg (10 000 − (8000 + 900 + 910)).

Calculation of cost per unit

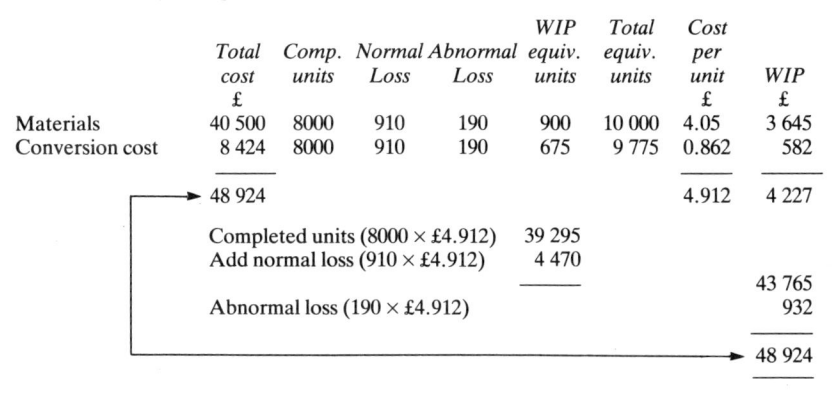

	Total cost £	Comp. units	Normal Loss	Abnormal Loss	WIP equiv. units	Total equiv. units	Cost per unit £	WIP £
Materials	40 500	8000	910	190	900	10 000	4.05	3 645
Conversion cost	8 424	8000	910	190	675	9 775	0.862	582
	48 924						4.912	4 227

Completed units (8000 × £4.912)   39 295
Add normal loss (910 × £4.912)   4 470
                                  ────── 43 765
Abnormal loss (190 × £4.912)   932
                                         ────── 48 924

If the question does not clearly state where the loss occurs or whether the loss is a percentage of input or output then state the assumptions which you have made in your answer to the question.

The term 'conversion cost' refers to the total of direct labour, direct expenses and overhead. Normally these items are subject to the same degree of completion and you can save time by grouping all expenses (other than materials) together and referring to them as conversion cost.

Note that in the above statement additional columns are added for normal and abnormal losses and the cost of the normal loss has been allocated to completed production.

Process B account

	kg	£		kg	£
Transferred from process A	10 000	40 500	Normal loss	910	–
Labour		5 616	Completed production to finished stock	8 000	43 765
Overheads		2 808	Abnormal loss A/C	190	932
			WIP C/F	900	4 227
	10 000	48 924		10 000	48 924
WIP B/F	900	4 227			

5.8 Equivalent production and losses part way through a process

Example 5.2

The following data relates to a process:

Opening WIP	nil
Materials introduced at the start (16 000 units)	£47 600
Direct labour	£4880
Direct expenses	£4270
Overhead absorbed	250 per cent of direct labour
Output	8000 units
Closing WIP (75 per cent complete)	5600 units

The normal loss is 15 per cent of process input and is detected at the inspection point which is at the 75 per cent stage of completion. Closing WIP has just passed the inspection point.

Answer

Input is 16 000 units and the output consists of 8000 completed units plus 5600 units WIP plus 2400 units normal loss. Because the input is fully accounted for there is no abnormal loss.

Calculation of cost per unit

	£	Completed units	Normal loss	Closing WIP	Total equiv. units	Cost per unit £	WIP value £
Materials	47 600	8000	2400	5600	16 000	2.975	16 660
Conversion cost	21 350	8000	1800	4200	14 000	1.525	6 405
	68 950					4.50	23 065

The conversion cost is given by

direct labour (£4880) + direct expenses (£4270) + overhead (250% × £4880)

Note that the 2400 spoilt units will not be processed any further once the loss is detected at the 75 per cent completion stage. Therefore 1800 units equivalent production (2400 × 75 per cent) is entered in the normal loss column for conversion cost equivalent production. Because materials are introduced at the start of the process they will be fully complete when the loss is detected. The cost of the normal loss is:

	£
Materials (2400 × £2.975) =	7140
Conversion cost (1800 × £1.525) =	2745
	9885

Because the WIP has reached the point at which the loss is detected, the normal loss is apportioned between completed units and WIP in the ratio of completed units and WIP equivalent units as follows:

If WIP had not reached the inspection point (say it was 60 per cent complete) then all of the normal loss would be charged to completed production. Theoretically, it is preferable to apportion the normal loss in the ratio of completed units and incomplete units in progress. However, most examination questions assume that the method specified in the answer will be adopted.

Completed units		WIP	
Materials 8000/13 600 × £7140 = £4200		5600/13 600 × £7140 = £2940	
Conversion cost 8000/12 200 × £2745 = £1800		4200/12 200 × £2745 = £ 945	
	£6000		£3885

The cost of completed units and WIP is as follows:

		£	£
Completed units: (8000 × £4.50)		36 000	
	Share of normal loss	6 000	
			42 000
WIP:	Original allocation	23 065	
	Share of normal loss	3 885	
			26 950
			68 950

You should note that where the normal loss is to be apportioned between completed production and WIP an alternative and simpler approach is not to include the normal loss in the unit cost statement. The calculation is as follows:

	£	Comp. units	Closing WIP	Total equiv. units	Cost per unit £	WIP £
Materials	47 600	8000	5600	13 600	3.50	19 600
Conversion cost	21 350	8000	4200	12 200	1.75	7 350
					5.25	26 950
			Completed units (8000 × £5.25)			42 000
						68 950

If the question is unclear then state your assumption regarding the point at which you assume the loss occurs. If you assume it occurs at the end of the process then calculate the amount of normal loss and charge all of it to completed production. Alternatively you might assume that it occurs throughout the process and share it between completed production and WIP. In this situation it is suggested you adopt the alternative method – that is, do not include the normal loss in the unit cost calculations.

5.9 Opening work in progress: FIFO method

When opening stocks of WIP exist there are two alternative methods of allocating the opening stocks to the current accounting period for calculating unit costs – the FIFO method and the weighted average method. The FIFO method assumes that the opening WIP is the first group of units to be processed and completed during the current period. The opening WIP is charged separately to completed production, *and the cost per unit is based on the current period costs and production*. The closing WIP is assumed to consist of part of the cost of the output of the *current* period.

Typical examination question: FIFO method
Shown below is the previous month's operating data for process 3, the final manufacturing operation in the production of standard sized insulation blocks.

Work in process:
   Opening stock 400 blocks, total cost £1000
   Closing stock 500 blocks

The degree of completion of both opening and closing stocks of work in process was:
   Previous process costs   100 per cent
   Process 3 materials   80 per cent
   Conversion costs   60 per cent

During the month 4500 blocks were transferred from process 2 at a total cost of £9000. Other costs charged to process 3 during the month were:
   Materials   £4360
   Labour and overhead   £2125

Process inspection occurs when process 3 materials are 60 per cent complete and conversion costs 30 per cent complete, and normally no losses are expected at this stage. However, during the month 300 blocks were rejected at inspection and sold as scrap for £1 each.

The company operates the first in, first out method of charging opening stock to production.

You are required to:

(a) Prepare the process 3 account and an abnormal loss account recording the data shown above. Include a detailed working paper showing all your calculations. (17 marks)

(CACA Foundation Costing)

Answer

(a) You are recommended initially to produce a statement of physical input and output whenever you answer process costing questions.

Input	Blocks	Output	Blocks
Opening WIP	400	Closing WIP	500
Transfer from previous process	4500	Abnormal loss	300
		Completed units (balance)	4100
	4900		4900

Statement of equivalent production and calculation of cost and completed production: FIFO method

	Current costs	Completed units less opening WIP equiv. units	Abnormal loss	Closing WIP equiv. units	Current total equiv. units	Cost per unit £
Previous process costs	9 000	3700 (4100 − 400)	300	500	4500	2.0
Materials	4 360	3780 (4100 − 320)	180 (60%)	400 (80%)	4360	1.0
Labour and overhead	2 125	3860 (4100 − 240)	90 (30%)	300 (60%)	4250	0.50
	15 485					3.50

Previous process cost represents the transferred cost from the previous process. It should be treated as a separate element of cost. Note that previous process cost will always be fully complete when calculating equivalent production.

	£	£
Cost of completed production		
Opening WIP (given)	1000	
Previous process cost (3700 × £2)	7400	
Materials (3780 × £1)	3780	
Labour and overhead (3860 × £0.50)	1930	
		14 110
Cost of closing WIP		
Previous process cost (500 × £2)	1000	
Materials (400 × £1)	400	
Labour and overhead (300 × £0.50)	150	
		1 550
Cost of abnormal loss		
Previous process cost (300 × £2)	600	
Materials (180 × £1)	180	
Labour and overhead (90 × £0.50)	45	
		825

You can see from the above statement that the cost per unit is calculated by dividing the *current period* costs by the *current* period's equivalent production. Note that the latter figure excludes the equivalent production for the opening WIP as this was not produced in the current period. The closing WIP equivalent production is multiplied by the current period's cost per unit and does not therefore include any share of the opening WIP. The objective is to ensure that the opening WIP of £1000 is allocated to completed production and not included in the unit cost calculations which are used as the basis for valuing WIP.

Process 3 account

	Blocks	£		Blocks	£
Opening WIP	400	1 000	Abnormal loss	300	825
Transfer from process 2	4500	9 000	Completed production transferred to		
Current cost:			finished stock	4100	14 110
Materials		4 360	Closing WIP	500	1 550
Labour and overhead		2 125			
		16 485			16 485

Abnormal loss account

	£		£
Process 3 A/C	825	Cash/bank	300
		Profit and loss A/C	525
	825		825

5.10 Opening WIP: weighted average method

The weighted average method assumes that the units and value of opening WIP are merged with the current period costs and production to calculate the average cost per unit for the current period. The previous question is used to illustrate the weighted average method. However, this method requires an analysis of the opening WIP of £1000 by elements of cost. Assume opening WIP consists of £600 previous process cost, £300 materials and £100 for labour and overhead.

The question should indicate which method (FIFO or weighted average) should be used. If it does not, then state your assumption and use the method which you prefer.

Calculation of cost per unit

	Opening WIP £	Current cost £	Total cost £	Comp. units	Abnormal loss	Closing WIP	Total equiv. units	Cost per unit £	WIP £
Previous process costs	600	9000	9 600	4100	300	500	4900	1.959	979
Materials	300	4360	4 660	4100	180	400	4680	0.996	398
Labour and overhead	100	2125	2 225	4100	90	300	4490	0.496	148
			16 485					3.451	1 525

Completed units (4100 × £3.451)   14 149
Abnormal loss:
  Previous process cost (300 × £1.959) 588
  Materials   (180 × £0.996) 178
  Labour and overhead (90 × £0.496)   45
                                                       811
                                                    16 485

You can see from the above statement that the opening value of WIP is included as part of the total cost for the period and the completed units column includes the completion of the 400 units opening WIP. In other words, the opening WIP is merged with the production of the current period to form one homogeneous batch of production.

6
Joint product and by-product costing

6.1 Joint products and by-products

Joint products and by-products arise in situations where the production of one product makes inevitable the production of other products. Joint products and by-products are not identifiable as different individual products until they emerge from a joint production process. The production process for joint products and by-products is illustrated in Figure 6.1. You will see from this illustration that after the joint process, joint products X and Y and by-product Z all emerge, and that it is not possible to allocate the costs of the joint process directly to the joint products or to by-products. After joint processing the separate products emerge (this stage in the production process is called the *split-off point*) and

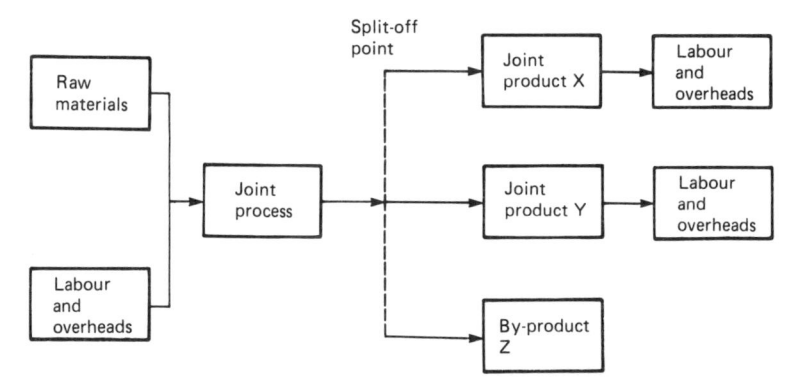

Figure 6.1 Production process for joint products and by-products

further processing costs are added to the joint products before sale. Note that the further processing costs can be specifically identified with the joint products. By-products are products which have minor sales value and emerge incidentally from the production of the joint products. The objective is to produce joint products X and Y, but by-product Z also emerges from the joint production process.

6.2 Apportionment of joint costs

For financial accounting purposes, stock valuations for individual joint products should include a share of joint product costs plus any directly attributable additional costs of further processing. It is therefore necessary to apportion the costs of the joint production process to the joint products so as to meet the requirements of financial accounting. You should note, however, that joint cost apportionments should not be used for decision-making. Joint costs can be apportioned on the basis of *physical measures* of output or *market value* of the output.

Typical examination question: apportionment of joint costs

(a) Products A, B, C and D are produced jointly from a base material. In month 3 the base material input into the process cost £1 800 000. The following production and sales occurred in the month:

	Production kg	Sales kg	Selling price per kg
A	14 000	12 000	£50
B	20 000	17 000	£60
C	25 000	21 000	£20
D	1 000	nil	£100

There were no stocks in hand at the beginning of the month.
You are required to find:

(i) The value of the stock at the end of the month using the sales value of production and physical output methods of valuation
(ii) The operating profit and loss for the month. (14 marks)

(b) The directors are considering a proposal to further process products A, B and C only. Market research has evaluated that by converting A, B and C into X, Y and Z the selling price of each new product would be £60, £70 and £30 respectively.
Further costs would arise as follows:

	X	Y	Z
Variable conversion costs per kg	£7	£9	£8
Monthly hire of new machinery (£000)	28	40	25

You are required to produce an evaluation of the proposal.
(14 marks)
(AAT adapted)

Answer for (a)

Apportionment: sales value of production method

	1	2	3	4	5
Product	Sales value of production £	Proportion to total	Joint costs apportioned £	Cost per kg £	Stock valuation £
A	700 000	7/25	504 000	36.00	72 000
B	1 200 000	12/25	864 000	43.20	129 600
C	500 000	5/25	360 000	14.40	57 600
D	100 000	1/25	72 000	72.00	72 000
	2 500 000		1 800 000		331 200

When this method is used, production is expressed in terms of market value and the joint costs of £1 800 000 are then apportioned to products in proportion to their sales value (that is, £1 800 000 is multiplied by the proportions in column 2). The joint cost per kg in column 4 is calculated by dividing the apportioned joint costs (column 3) by the number of kg produced. The stock valuation is ascertained by multiplying the number of kg in stock by the cost per kg.

Apportionment: physical output method

Product	Production in kg	Proportion to total	Joint costs apportioned £	Cost per kg £	Stock valuation £
A	14 000	14/60	420 000	30	60 000
B	20 000	20/60	600 000	30	90 000
C	25 000	25/60	750 000	30	120 000
D	1 000	1/60	30 000	30	30 000
	60 000		1 800 000		300 000

Normally joint products will be subject to further processing and the cost per unit of further processing should be added to the joint process unit cost for stock valuations.

An alternative approach would be to calculate the cost per kg (£30) by dividing the joint costs of £1 800 000 by the total output of 60 000 kg.

Profit statement: sales value of production method

	A £	B £	C £	D £	Total £
Joint production costs	504 000	864 000	360 000	72 000	1 800 000
Less closing stock	72 000	129 600	57 600	72 000	331 200
Cost of sales	432 000	734 400	302 400	–	1 468 800
Sales	600 000	1 020 000	420 000	–	2 040 000
Profit	168 000	285 600	117 600	–	571 200

Profit statement: physical output method

	A	B	C	D	Total
Joint production costs	420 000	600 000	750 000	30 000	1 800 000
Less closing stock	60 000	90 000	120 000	30 000	300 000
Cost of sales	360 000	510 000	630 000	–	1 500 000
Sales	600 000	1 020 000	420 000	–	2 040 000
Profit (loss)	240 000	510 000	(210 000)		540 000

You can see that different methods of apportionment result in different profit calculations and stock valuations. The physical output method assumes that the joint cost per unit of output is the same for each of the products. This assumption results in some products showing very high profits and others showing very low profits (for example, product C) when the market prices of the products differ widely. Also the product stock valuations using the physical output method bear no relationship to the revenue-producing ability of the individual profits. For example, product C is valued at £30 per kg but the selling price for this product is £20. This is not in accordance with the lower of cost or market value principle which is required for financial accounting purposes. Apportionments based on market values are preferable because they do not suffer from these disadvantages.

Net realizable value of production method of apportionment

Frequently joint products are not in a saleable condition at the split-off point and further processing is necessary before the products can be sold. Therefore market values cannot be ascertained at the split-off point and the net realizable values must be estimated. Net realizable value is ascertained by deducting the further processing costs after the split-off point from the selling price of the product after further processing. In part (b) of the previous question the selling prices of products X, Y and Z are £60, £70 and £30 respectively. Further processing costs are:

	A converted to X £	B converted to Y £	C converted to Z £
Variable cost	7	9	8
Machinery hire cost	2	2	1
	9	11	9

This method should only be used if market values at the split-off point cannot be ascertained.

Note that the unit hire cost is calculated by dividing the monthly hire cost by the monthly production. The net realizable value for product X is £51 (£60 – £9), for product Y £59 (£70 – £11), and for product Z £21 (£30 – £9). The net realizable value of the total production is ascertained and the joint costs are apportioned in these proportions.

6.3 Joint product costs and decision-making

The apportionment of joint costs to products is necessary for stock valuation, but product costs which include joint cost apportionments should not be used for decision-making. If you refer to the profit statement which was prepared using the physical output method of apportioning joint costs you will see that product C shows a loss of £210 000. Should product C be dropped? The answer is no because the joint costs would still be incurred if product C is not produced. The company would lose the sales revenue of £420 000 from product C and total profits would therefore decline by £420 000.

The joint process costs of £750 000 apportioned to product C would have to be reapportioned to products A, B and D if production of product C ceased.

The relevant costs and revenues which should be used for decision-making purposes are the additional costs and revenues which a product incurs; that is, those costs and revenues which will be eliminated if the product is not made. Most examination questions on this topic will require you to recommend whether joint products should be subject to further processing. The previous question is used to illustrate the relevant information which should be presented for such a decision.

Answer for (b)

The joint costs of £1 800 000 will be incurred irrespective of which decision is taken, and are not relevant for this decision. The information required for this decision is a comparison of the additional costs with the additional revenues. Assuming that monthly sales remain unchanged, the comparison is as follows:

	X	Y	Z
Additional selling price per kg	£10	£10	£10
Additional variable cost per kg	£ 7	£ 9	£ 8
Contribution per kg	£ 3	£ 1	£ 2
Sales volume (kg)	14 000	20 000	25 000
Total contribution	£42 000	£20 000	£50 000
Hire of machinery (fixed cost)	£28 000	£40 000	£25 000
Additional profit contribution	£14 000	(£20 000)	£25 000

The term 'contribution' is explained in Chapter 8.

Products A and C should be converted into X and Z because they provide additional contributions to profit. However, product B should not be converted to product Y because the additional costs exceed the additional revenues.

It is possible that monthly sales volume will decline in the future. Because the hire costs are fixed there is a possibility that future sales volume will not be sufficient to generate sufficient contribution to cover fixed costs. Management should therefore be informed how many units should be sold in order to justify further processing.

	X	Y	Z
Contribution per kg	£3	£1	£2
Hire of machinery	£28 000	£40 000	£25 000
Break-even point (kg)	9 333	40 000	12 500

The logic underlying the calculation of the break-even points is explained in Chapter 8.

The number of units that must be sold to justify further processing (that is, the break-even point) is calculated by dividing the fixed hire costs by the contribution per kg. If management anticipates that monthly sales volume will exceed the break-even point then further processing should be undertaken.

6.4 Accounting for by-products

Joint production costs should not be apportioned to by-products because the objective is to produce the joint products; the by-products emerge incidentally from the production of the joint products. Any further by-product processing costs after the split-off point should be charged to the by-product (That is, DR by-product A/C and CR Cash). The estimated revenue due from the by-product at split-off point should be deducted from the joint production costs before they are allocated to the individual joint products (That is, DR by-product A/C and CR Joint product WIP A/C). For an illustration of this approach see answer to Question 5.1 in Part 3.

7 Absorption and variable costing systems

7.1 Absorption and variable costing

With an absorption costing system, fixed manufacturing overheads are apportioned to the products and included in the stock valuation. With a variable costing system, only variable manufacturing costs are allocated to the products; fixed manufacturing costs are regarded as period costs and written off to the profit and loss account. Both variable and absorption costing treat non-manufacturing overheads as period costs (that is, non-manufacturing overheads are not allocated to products and included in stock valuations). Note that absorption costing is sometimes called *full* costing, and other terms used to describe a variable costing system are *marginal* costing or *direct* costing.

Note that Chapters 3–6 described the accounting procedures for an absorption costing system.

7.2 Internal and external reporting

It is important that companies use similar approaches when valuing stocks and measuring profits. Inter-firm comparisons would be difficult if some companies valued stocks on an absorption costing basis and others did so on a variable costing basis. To ensure consistency SSAP 9 requires companies to use absorption costing when preparing the published external annual accounts.

Management requires internal profit statements at frequent intervals to measure the performance of each major segment of the business. For internal reporting management does not have to comply with SSAP 9, and they should select the costing system which provides the more meaningful information.

Typical examination question: variable and absorption costing
Bittern Ltd manufactures and sells a single product at a unit selling price of £25. In constant price-level terms its cost structure is as follows:

Variable costs:	production materials	£10 per unit produced
	distribution	£1 per unit sold
Semi-variable costs:	labour	£5000 per annum, plus £2 per unit produced
Fixed costs:	overheads	£5000 per annum

For several years Bittern has operated a system of variable costing for management accounting purposes. It has been decided to review the system and to compare it for management accounting purposes with an absorption costing system.

As part of the review you have been asked to prepare estimates of Bittern's profits in constant price-level terms over a three-year period in three different hypothetical situations, and to compare the two types of system generally for management accounting purposes.

You are required:

(a) In each of the following three sets of hypothetical circumstances, to calculate Bittern's profit in each of years t_1, t_2 and t_3, and also in total over the three-year period t_1 to t_3, using first a variable costing system, and then a full cost absorption costing system with fixed cost recovery based on a normal production level of 1000 units per annum:

(i) Stable unit levels of production, sales and inventory:

	t_1	t_2	t_3
Opening stock	100	100	100
Production	1000	1000	1000
Sales	1000	1000	1000
Closing stock	100	100	100

(5 marks)

(ii) Stable unit level of sales, but fluctuating unit levels of production and inventory:

	t_1	t_2	t_3
Opening stock	100	600	400
Production	1500	800	700
Sales	1000	1000	1000
Closing stock	600	400	100

(5 marks)

(iii) Stable unit level of production, but fluctuating unit levels of sales and inventory:

	t_1	t_2	t_3
Opening stock	100	600	400
Production	1000	1000	1000
Sales	500	1200	1300
Closing stock	600	400	100

(5 marks)

Note: all the data in (i)–(iii) are volumes, not values.

(b) To write a short comparative evaluation of variable and absorption costing systems for management accounting purposes, paying particular attention to profit measurement, and using your answer to (a) to illustrate your arguments if you wish. (10 marks)

(ICAEW Management Accounting)

Answer for (a)

The product cost calculation is as follows:

	£
Materials	10
Labour	2
Variable production cost	12
Variable distribution cost	1
Total variable cost	13
Fixed overhead (£10 000/1000 units)	10
Total cost	23

The product costs for stock valuation purposes are:

Variable costing   £12 (variable production cost)
Absorption costing   £22 (variable production cost + fixed manufacturing overhead)

Note that the fixed manufacturing overhead is calculated by dividing the total manufacturing overhead by the normal production level of 1000 units. You should also note that the variable distribution cost varies with units sold and not units produced.

In Chapter 3 it was explained why predetermined overhead rates should be used. The estimated activity level should be the anticipated average normal level of activity over a period of years.

(i) *Profit statements*

	Variable costing			Absorption costing		
	t_1	t_2	t_3	t_1	t_2	t_3
	£	£	£	£	£	£
Opening stock	1 200	1 200	1 200	2 200	2 200	2 200
Production	12 000	12 000	12 000	22 000	22 000	22 000
	13 200	13 200	13 200	24 200	24 200	24 200
Closing stock	1 200	1 200	1 200	2 200	2 200	2 200
Cost of sales	12 000	12 000	12 000	22 000	22 000	22 000
Fixed manufacturing costs	10 000	10 000	10 000	–	–	–
Total cost	22 000	22 000	22 000	22 000	22 000	22 000
Sales	25 000	25 000	25 000	25 000	25 000	25 000
Gross profit	3 000	3 000	3 000	3 000	3 000	3 000
Distribution costs	1 000	1 000	1 000	1 000	1 000	1 000
Net profit	2 000	2 000	2 000	2 000	2 000	2 000
Total profit		6 000			6 000	

With the variable costing system the product cost is £12 per unit (that is, variable production cost only). In periods t_1–t_3 stocks and production are valued at £12 per unit. The fixed costs of £10 000 per period are not included in the product costs but are charged as a separate lump sum to each accounting period.

When the absorption costing system is used the fixed manufacturing overheads are allocated to individual products and included in the stock valuation. Therefore stocks and production are valued at £22 per unit total manufacturing cost. With absorption costing the fixed manufacturing cost of £10 000 is charged to products and included in the production cost figure (that is, 1000 units at £10 per unit fixed cost). With variable costing the fixed manufacturing cost of £10 000 is charged separately and is not included in the product costs. Both systems therefore charge to production £10 000 fixed overheads per period.

(ii) *Profit statements*

	Variable costing			Absorption costing		
	t_1 £	t_2 £	t_3 £	t_1 £	t_2 £	t_3 £
Opening stock	1 200	7 200	4 800	2 200	13 200	8 800
Production	18 000	9 600	8 400	33 000	17 600	15 400
Under (over) recovery				(5 000)	2 000	3 000
	19 200	16 800	13 200	30 200	32 800	27 200
Closing stock	7 200	4 800	1 200	13 200	8 800	2 200
Cost of sales	12 000	12 000	12 000	17 000	24 000	25 000
Fixed manufacturing costs	10 000	10 000	10 000	–	–	–
Total cost	22 000	22 000	22 000	17 000	24 000	25 000
Sales	25 000	25 000	25 000	25 000	25 000	25 000
Gross profit	3 000	3 000	3 000	8 000	1 000	–
Distribution costs	1 000	1 000	1 000	1 000	1 000	1 000
Net profit (loss)	2 000	2 000	2 000	7 000	–	(1 000)
Total profit		6 000			6 000	

The same principles as those applied in (i) have been used to calculate the profits. Because stocks fluctuate, the opening and closing stock valuations differ. For example, with the variable costing system the opening stock valuation for period t_1 is £1200 (100 units at £12 manufacturing variable cost) and the closing stock valuation is £7200 (600 units at £12) – a stock increase of £6000. When the absorption costing system is used, the opening stock valuation is £2200 (100 units at £22 total manufacturing cost) and the closing stock valuation is £13 200 (600 units at £22) – a stock increase of £11 000. The difference between the stock increases (£6000 for variable costing and £11 000 for absorption costing) explains the difference in profits of £5000 between the two systems.

With absorption costing the fixed overhead charged to production will not equal the fixed overhead incurred whenever actual production differs from the estimated production used to calculate the predetermined fixed overhead rate. For example, in period t_1 production is 1500 units, and £15 000 fixed overheads (1500 × £10) are included in the production cost of £33 000. Fixed overheads of £10 000 are incurred, so £5000 too much has been charged. This over-recovery of fixed costs is recorded as a period cost adjustment in the absorption costing profit calculations. In period t_2 800 units were produced at a cost of £17 600, which includes fixed overheads of £8000 (800 × £10). Hence there is an under-recovery of £2000, which is written off as a period cost.

If you do not understand under/over-recovery of fixed overheads you should refer back to Chapter 3.

(iii) The profit calculations for each method are:

	Variable costing			Absorption costing		
	t_1	t_2	t_3	t_1	t_2	t_3
Profit (loss)	(£4000)	£4400	£5600	£1000	£2400	£2600
Total profit		£6000			£6000	

Both systems yield different profits because of the fluctuating stock levels. Note that actual production is equal to the estimated normal production level which was used to calculate the fixed overhead rate. Under- or over-recoveries of fixed overheads will not therefore arise.

7.3 Differences in profit calculations

Whenever *production equals sales*, stock levels will remain unchanged. The opening and closing stock valuations will thus cancel out and so the fixed overheads included in the stock valuations will also cancel out. Consequently with an absorption costing system the fixed overhead charged as an expense for the period will be equal to the fixed overhead incurred. Thus whenever sales are equal to production the profits will be the same for both the absorption costing and variable costing systems. You can see that in part (a)(i) of the previous question production equals sales for all three periods and the profits calculated for both systems are identical.

Whenever *production exceeds sales* stocks are increasing and so the absorption costing system will produce higher profits. This is because a greater amount of fixed overhead in the closing stocks is being deducted from the expenses of the period than is being brought forward in the opening stock for the period. In period t_1 (see part (a)(ii) of the question) production exceeds sales by 500 units and stocks increase from 100 to 600 units. The opening stock valuation includes £1000 fixed overhead (100 units × £10), which is charged as an expense for the period. The closing

Note that the fixed overhead included in the production cost plus any under-recovery (or minus any over-recovery) will equal the amount of fixed overheads incurred (that is £10 000).

stock valuation includes £6000 fixed overhead (600 units × £10), which is deducted from the expenses for the period. The overall effect of the stock movement is that the fixed overhead charge is reduced by £5000 – from £10 000 to £5000 for the period. With the variable costing system the fixed overhead incurred of £10 000 is charged as an expense. Consequently absorption costing profits are £5000 greater than variable costing profits in period t_1.

A system of variable costing will yield the higher profits whenever *sales exceed production* (that is, stocks are decreasing). Whenever stocks decline and an absorption costing system is used, a greater amount of fixed overheads will be brought forward as an expense in the opening stock than is being deducted in the closing stock adjustment. Hence the amount of fixed overhead which is charged as an expense will be greater than the amount of fixed overhead which is incurred. You can see that in period t_2 for part (a)(ii) of the question, sales exceed production and variable costing shows the higher profit.

Note that profits for periods t_1–t_3 total £6000 for all the situations described in the question. This is because the opening stock in period t_1 is equal to the closing stock in period t_3. Over the whole life of a business, absorption costing and variable costing systems will produce the same *total* profits but the profits attributed to each period will differ.

7.4 Arguments supporting variable costing

Absorption costing can produce some strange profit calculations

Profits fluctuate with the absorption costing system because stock changes result in different amounts of fixed overhead being charged in each period.

With this change, the closing stock valuation will be zero and sales revenue and variable distribution cost will increase by £2500 and £100 respectively.

It is assumed that costs and selling prices remain unchanged.

If you refer to the profit calculations for (a)(ii) you will see that profits are £7000 (t_1), zero (t_2) and a loss of £1000 (t_3). Sales volume and costs per unit throughout the three periods have not changed and yet profits fluctuate. With the variable costing system, profits are constant at £2000. Consider the profit calculations for period t_3 assuming that sales were 1100 units (instead of 1000 units). Absorption costing will show a loss of £800 and variable costing will show a profit of £3200. A manager whose performance is being judged in period t_3 using the absorption costing system will have little confidence in an accounting system which shows a decline in profits when sales volume has increased and the cost structure and selling price has not changed. By contrast, the variable costing profit calculations show that when sales volume increases profit also increases. The reason for these differences is that, with a system of variable costing, profit is a function of sales volume only, whereas profit is a function of sales volume *and* production volume with absorption costing.

Absorption costing motivates managers to increase stocks

Internal profit statements are often used as a basis for measuring managerial performance. When an absorption costing system is used managers may deliberately alter stock levels to influence profits; for example, it is possible for a manager to deliberately defer some of the fixed overhead charge by unnecessarily increasing stocks over successive periods.

Variable costing provides more useful information for decision-making

You will see in Chapter 9 that fixed costs are often irrelevant for short-term decisions. There is a danger with an absorption costing system that total costs will be used for decision-making and this can lead to incorrect decisions. With a system of variable costing the analysis of variable and fixed costs is highlighted, thus ensuring that relevant cost information is provided for decision-making.

7.5 Arguments supporting absorption costing

Fixed costs are not ignored

There is a danger that decisions based on a variable costing system may concentrate solely on sales revenue and variable costs and ignore the fact that fixed costs must be met in the long run. For example, if variable costs are used as a basis for setting selling prices then total sales revenue may not cover *all* costs.

Absorption costing is theoretically superior to variable costing

The production of goods is not possible if fixed manufacturing costs are not incurred. It is therefore argued that fixed manufacturing costs should be charged to units produced and included in the stock valuation.

8
Cost-volume-profit analysis

8.1 Cost-volume-profit (CVP) analysis

CVP analysis is concerned with examining the relationship between changes in the level of activity and changes in total sales revenue, expenses and net profit. CVP analysis is based on the relationship between sales, costs and profit in the short run. The *short run* is defined as a period in which the output of a firm is restricted to that available from the current operating capacity. In the short run additional materials and labour can normally be obtained at short notice, but it takes time to expand the capacity of plant and machinery. Output is therefore normally limited in the short run because plant facilities cannot be expanded.

8.2 CVP analysis: comparison of accountants' model with economic theory

An understanding of the underlying assumptions, uses and limitations of the accountants' model requires an understanding of economic theory. The following is a recent examination question on this topic.

Typical examination question

Figure 8.1 shows cost-volume-profit relationships as they are typically represented in (a) management accounting and (b) economic theory. In each graph TR is total revenue, TC is total cost, and P is profit.

You are required to compare these different representations of cost-volume-profit relationships, identifying, explaining and commenting on points of similarity and also differences.   (15 marks)

(ICAEW Management Accounting)

Economic theory

Economic theory assumes that the firm is only able to sell increasing quantities of output by reducing the selling price per unit and this results in the total revenue line rising less steeply, and eventually beginning to decline. The assumption results in a curvilinear total revenue line.

Between points A and B in Figure 8.1, total costs rise rather steeply at first because the firm is operating at lower levels of output. Within this output range, the plant is being operated at less than maximum efficiency and the firm is unable to obtain the full benefits of bulk buying and the

---

The original examination question did not include letters A, B, C and D. These items have been added to provide you with a clearer understanding of the differences between the two diagrams.

The lines marked with the letter P represent the profits at various output levels. The discussion focuses on the total cost and revenue lines because an explanation of the shape of the total cost and revenue functions also provides an explanation of the shape of the profit lines.

This is because the adverse effect of price reductions outweighs the benefits of increased sales volume.

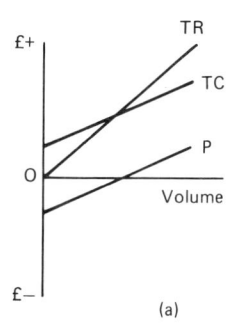

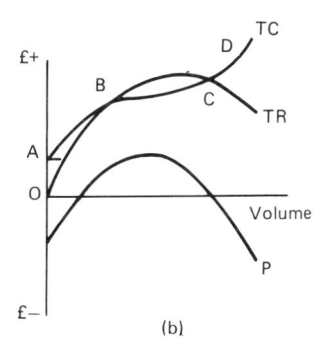

Figure 8.1 CVP relationships: (a) management accounting (b) economic theory

specialization of labour. Between points B and C the total cost line rises less steeply and levels out. Within this output range the plant is operating at maximum efficiency and the firm is able to take full advantage of specialization of labour and bulk purchasing discounts. Between points C and D, cost per unit increases and the total cost line rises more steeply. This is because the plant is operating beyond the activity level for which it was designed; bottlenecks develop and plant breakdowns begin to occur. Note that the total revenue line crosses the total cost line at two points; hence there are two break-even points.

Economic theory describes this situation as decreasing returns to scale.

Accountants' model

The management accountants' model assumes a variable cost and a selling price which are constant per unit; this results in a linear relationship for total cost and total revenue with volume changes. Consequently there is only one break-even point in the diagram, and the profit area widens as volume increases. The most profitable output level is therefore at maximum capacity.

Relevant range

The objective of the accountants' model is to represent the behaviour of total cost and total revenue over the range of output at which a firm expects to be operating in the future. This range of output is called the relevant range and is represented by the output range between points A and B in Figure 8.2. You can see that between points A and B the accountants' total cost line bears a close relationship to the economists' total cost line. The accountants' diagram is not intended to provide an accurate representation of total cost and total revenue throughout all ranges of output. The objective is to provide a good approximation of cost and revenue behaviour only within the relevant range of production. Within this range of output the accountant assumes that the total cost and revenue lines are linear. (Note that several empirical studies support the assumption that the total cost line is approximately linear within the relevant range.) It is unwise, however, to assume that the total cost line is linear outside the relevant range.

Therefore CVP analysis will only be correct within the normal production range. It is dangerous to rely on projections outside the relevant range.

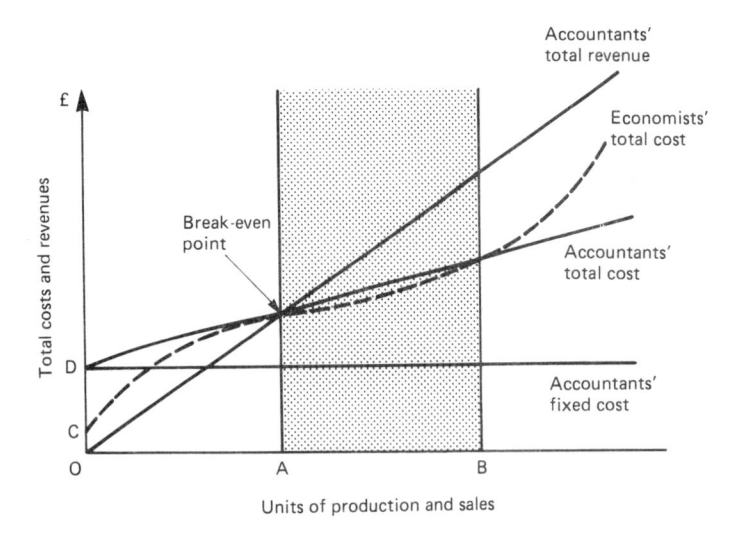

Figure 8.2 Accountants' CVP diagram

Sales revenue
Firms will set selling prices which maximize profits. Alternatively they may have no choice but to accept the going market price. Once the pricing decision has been made it is difficult to change it in the short run. The accountant therefore assumes a constant selling price per unit. Beyond the relevant range, increases in sales volume may only be possible by offering substantial reductions in price. Because it is the intention of firms to operate within the relevant range, the accountant makes no attempt to produce accurate revenue functions outside this range.

It is assumed that the adverse effect of the price reduction outweighs the benefits of increased sales volume outside the relevant range. Profits will therefore decline if a firm operates outside the relevant range.

8.3 Cost-volume-profit analysis assumptions

It is essential when interpreting CVP information that you are aware of the assumptions on which the analysis is based. If these assumptions are not recognized, wrong conclusions may be drawn from the analysis. The following is a typical question.

Typical examination question
Identify and critically examine the underlying assumptions of CVP analysis and consider whether such analyses are useful to the management of an organization. (CACA Level 1 Costing)

Answer
All other variables remain constant The analysis assumes that all variables other than activity remain constant. For example, changes in other variables such as sales mix, production methods and efficiency will influence sales revenue and costs. CVP analysis will be incorrect if significant changes in these other variables occur. If such changes do occur it will be necessary to alter the analysis to reflect the changes.

Linearity and relevant range The analysis assumes that unit variable cost and selling price are constant, but this assumption is appropriate only for decisions taken within the relevant production range. It is incorrect to project cost and revenue figures outside the relevant range.

Profits are calculated on a variable costing basis The analysis assumes that fixed costs incurred during a period are charged as an expense for the period. In other words, variable costing profit calculations are assumed. With an absorption costing system the analysis will be correct only when production equals sales.

Costs can be correctly categorized as either fixed or variable Many costs are neither purely fixed nor purely variable. The extent to which these costs can be accurately categorized will significantly affect the accuracy of the analysis. You should note that an explanation of how total costs can be analysed by their fixed and variable elements is shown in the answer to Question 8.1 in Part 3 and Chapter 11 (section 11.8).

Single product or constant sales mix The analysis assumes that either a single product is sold or, if a range of products is sold, a predetermined sales mix will be maintained.

8.4 A numerical approach to CVP analysis

Instead of a diagram to present CVP information, a numerical approach can be used. The numerical approach is quicker and more flexible than the graphical approach for producing the appropriate information. The following formula should be used:

$$\text{break-even point in units} = \frac{\text{fixed costs}}{\text{contribution per unit}}$$

If the question does not specify that the graphical approach should be used, you should always use the numerical approach. The graphical presentation is time consuming and you can save time by using the numerical approach.

Contribution = selling price − variable cost.

This formula is multiplied by the selling price to calculate the break-even point in terms of sales value. If the variable cost and selling price per unit are not given but details of *total* variable costs and sales revenue *are* given, then the break-even point can be calculated as follows:

$$\text{break-even point in sales value} = \frac{\text{fixed costs}}{\text{total contribution}} \times \text{total sales}$$

$$\text{units sold for desired profit} = \frac{\text{fixed costs + desired profit}}{\text{contribution per unit}}$$

Profit–volume ratio

This ratio is the contribution expressed as a percentage of sales. For example, if the contribution is £15 per unit and the selling price is £30 per unit, the profit–volume ratio is 50 per cent. Given an estimate of total sales revenue, the profit–volume ratio can be used to estimate total contribution

The profit–volume (PV) ratio is assumed to remain constant because unit selling price and variable cost are also assumed to remain constant. It is unwise to rely on PV ratio calculations outside the relevant range.

for output levels within the normal production range. For example, if total sales revenue is estimated to be £500 000 the total contribution will be £250 000 (50% × £500 000). Profit can be calculated by deducting fixed costs from the total contribution.

Typical examination question

The summarized profit and loss statement for Exewye PLC for the last year is as follows:

	£000	£000
Sales (50 000 units)		1000
Direct materials	350	
Direct wages	200	
Fixed production overhead	200	
Variable production overhead	50	
Administration overhead	180	
Selling and distribution overhead	120	
	—	1100
Profit/(loss)		(100)

At a recent board meeting the directors discussed the year's results, following which the chairman asked for suggestions to improve the situation.

You are required, as management accountant, to evaluate the following alternative proposals and to comment briefly on each:

(a) Pay salesmen a commission of 10 per cent of sales and thus increase sales to achieve break-even point. (5 marks)
(b) Reduce selling price by 10 per cent, which it is estimated would increase sales volume by 30 per cent. (3 marks)
(c) Increase direct wage rates from £4 to £5 per hour, as part of a productivity/pay deal. It is hoped that this would increase production and sales by 20 per cent, but advertising costs would increase by £50 000. (4 marks)
(d) Increase sales by additional advertising of £300 000, with an increased selling price of 20 per cent, setting a profit margin of 10 per cent. (8 marks)

(CIMA P2 Cost Accounting 2)

Answer

Workings:	£000
Sales	1000
Variable costs	600
Contribution	400
Fixed costs	500
Profit (loss)	(100)

Unit selling price = £20 (£1 m/50 000)

Unit variable cost = £12 (600 000/50 000)
Unit contribution = £8

(a) Sales commission will be £2 per unit, thus reducing the contribution per unit to £6. The break-even point will be 83 333 units (£500 000/£6) or £1 666 666 sales value. This requires an increase of 67 per cent on previous sales, and the company must assess whether or not sales can be increased by such a high percentage.

(b) A 10 per cent decrease in selling price will reduce the selling price by £2 per unit and the revised unit contribution will be £6.

	£
Revised total contribution (65 000 × £6)	390 000
Less fixed costs	500 000
Profit (loss)	(110 000)

The estimated loss is worse than last year and the proposal is therefore not recommended.

(c) Wages will increase by 25 per cent – that is, from £200 000 to £250 000 – and this will cause output to increase by 20 per cent.

	£	£
Sales		1 200 000
Direct materials and variable overheads	480 000	
Direct wages	250 000	730 000
Contribution		470 000
Less fixed costs		550 000
Profit (loss)		(80 000)

This represents an improvement of £20 000 on last year's loss of £100 000.

(d) The revised selling price is £24. Let x be the revised sales volume. Then

sales revenue − (variable costs + fixed costs) = profit
$$24x - (12x + 800\,000) = 0.1(24x)$$
$$9.6x = 800\,000$$
$$x = 83\,333 \text{ units}$$

Clearly this proposal is preferable since it is the only proposal to yield a profit. However, the probability of increasing sales volume by approximately 67 per cent plus the risk involved from increasing fixed costs by £300 000 must be considered.

When calculating profits you should multiply the contribution per unit by the sales volume and deduct the fixed costs. Many students perform two calculations – first the selling price and then the variable cost are multiplied by the units sold. This approach is time consuming. Some students also multiply the fixed cost per unit by various activity levels in the question and ignore under/over-recoveries. It is recommended that you adopt a variable costing approach; that is, contribution − fixed costs = profit.

8.5 CVP analysis: a graphical approach

Examination questions occasionally require you to prepare break-even charts. There are three alternative forms of presentation – a break-even graph, a contribution graph and a profit–volume graph.

Typical examination question

(a) From the following information you are required to construct

    (i) A break-even chart, showing the break-even point and the margin of safety
    (ii) A chart displaying the contribution level and the profit level
    (iii) A profit–volume chart.

Sales	6000 units at £12 unit =	£72 000
Variable costs	6000 units at £ 7 unit =	£42 000
Fixed costs	=	£20 000

    (9 marks)

(b) State the purposes of each of the three charts in (a) above. (6 marks)
(c) Outline the limitations of break-even analysis. (5 marks)
(d) What are the advantages of graphical presentation of financial data to executives? (2 marks)

(AAT)

Answer

(a)(b) It is suggested that you list the relevant information for three different activity levels: zero; an intermediate range of activity; and maximum activity. The following provides the necessary information to construct the graphs:

Activity level	Fixed cost £	Variable cost £	Total cost £	Sales	Profit (loss) £
0	20 000	0	20 000		(20 000)
3000	20 000	21 000	41 000	36 000	(5 000)
6000	20 000	42 000	62 000	72 000	10 000

The three graphs are shown as Figure 8.3.

(i) *Break-even chart* The fixed cost line is plotted first as a single horizontal line at a level of £20 000. Variable costs are added to the fixed costs to enable the total cost line to be plotted. Note that at zero activity level total costs are £20 000 (that is, total costs will be equal to the fixed costs). The sales line is drawn at the rate of £12 per unit. The question requires the *margin of safety* to be shown on the graph. The margin of safety indicates by how much sales may decrease before a company will suffer a loss. In other words it is the difference between the expected sales of 6000 units and the break-even point of 4000 units. Sometimes the margin of safety is expressed in percentage form using the following ratio:

% margin of safety

$$= \frac{\text{expected sales (6000 units)} - \text{break-even sales (4000 units)}}{\text{expected sales (6000 units)}}$$

$$= 33.3 \text{ per cent}$$

By plotting three points you can check whether all the points fall on a straight line. You should always prepare calculations for the maximum level of activity given in the question because this gives you the maximum range which should be plotted on the horizontal and vertical axis of your graph.

Besides showing the break-even point on the graph you should supplement this by providing a more precise answer using the numerical approach (that is, break-even point = fixed cost/contribution per unit).

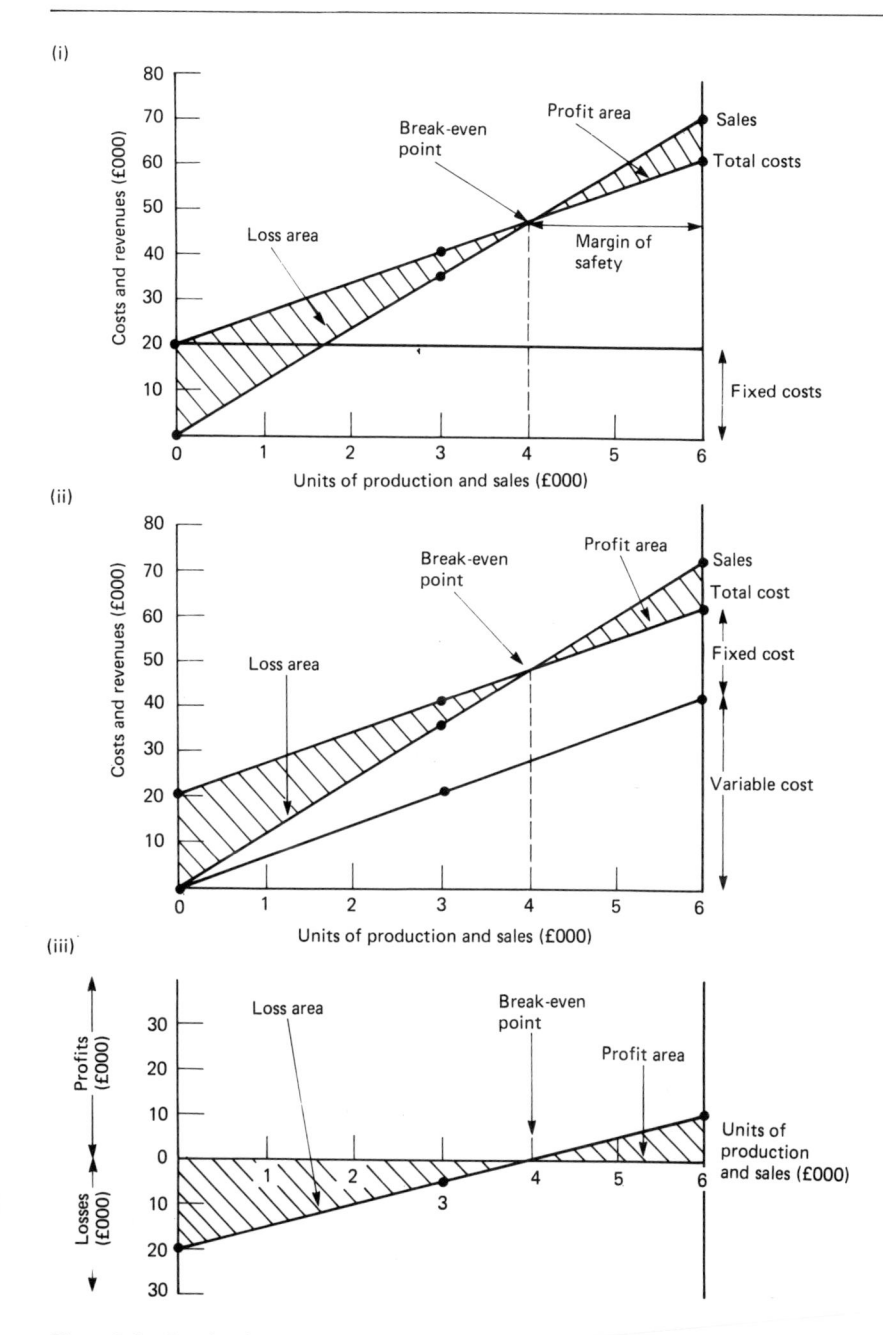

Figure 8.3 Graphical CVP analysis: (i) break-even chart (ii) contribution graph (iii) profit–volume graph

(ii) *Contribution graph* You can see that the variable cost line is drawn first. The total cost line should then be drawn parallel to the variable cost line. This is because fixed costs are assumed to be constant at £20 000 throughout the entire output range. Therefore the difference between the total cost line and the

Note that contribution is represented by the distance between the sales and variable cost lines.

variable cost line represents the fixed costs. The advantage of this form of presentation is that total contribution is emphasized in the graph.

(iii) *Profit–volume graph* You will see from the diagram that the horizontal axis represents the various levels of sales volume and the profits and losses for the period are recorded on the vertical scale. The profits and losses are plotted for each of the various sales levels and these points are connected by a profit line. The break-even point occurs at the point where the profit line intersects the horizontal line at an output level of 4000 units. Note that if sales are zero, the maximum loss will be equal to the fixed costs of £20 000. The advantage of this form of presentation is that profit or losses are highlighted at different output levels, whereas with break-even and contribution graphs it is necessary to examine the difference between the total cost and total revenue lines in order to ascertain the profit or loss figures.

(c) The major limitations are:
   (i) Costs and revenue may only be linear within a certain output range.
   (ii) In practice it is difficult to separate fixed and variable costs and the calculations will represent an approximation.
   (iii) It is assumed that profits are calculated on a variable costing basis.
   (iv) The analysis assumes that a single product is sold or a constant sales mix is maintained.

(d) The advantages are:
   (i) The information can be absorbed at a glance without the need for detailed figures.
   (ii) Essential features are emphasized.
   (iii) The graphical presentation can be easily understood by non-accountants.

9
Accounting information for decision-making

9.1 Relevant costs and revenues

A decision involves a choice between various alternative courses of action. Those costs and revenues which are common to all alternatives are not relevant to the decision. For example you might have two alternative means of travelling to college – by car or public transport. Assuming that you already own a car, you should not include a portion of the road fund licence when comparing the costs of the two alternatives. This is because you will incur the cost of the licence irrespective of which alternative you select. The relevant financial information for decision-making purposes consists of future cash flows which will differ between the various alternatives being considered. In other words, only incremental cash flows should be taken into account, and cash flows which will be the same for all alternatives are irrelevant.

When you are trying to establish which costs are relevant to a particular decision you may find that some costs are relevant in one situation but irrelevant in another situation. For example, a firm might be negotiating a price for a job with a customer. If the company has a temporary excess supply of direct labour and wishes to maintain the labour force in the short term then the additional direct labour cost of undertaking the job will be zero. On the other hand the company might hire additional labour on a temporary basis to meet the customer's order. In this situation the customer's order will result in future cash outflows increasing by the amount of the labour cost. The direct labour cost incurred will therefore be the relevant cost for this decision.

Note that for this situation the relevant labour cost is zero.

You can see that the identification of relevant costs for an alternative depends on the circumstances. It is not therefore possible to provide a list of costs which would be relevant in particular situations. You should follow the principle that the relevant costs are future cash outflows or loss of future cash inflows that will differ among alternatives.

You will find that examination questions require the application of the principle of relevant costs to the following decision-making problems:

(a) Discontinuing a segment
(b) Special selling price decisions
(c) Make or buy decisions
(d) Limiting factors.

9.2 Discontinuing a segment

A segment consists of a product, type of customer, geographical region or any other part of a firm that can be considered for expansion or reduction. In the following example the segments of the business are represented by the various traffic routes.

Example 9.1

As assistant to the accountant of a passenger transport authority you have been asked to comment on a proposal that route 3 should be discontinued. The following are estimates of profits/(losses) for the next year:

	Route 1 £000		Route 2 £000		Route 3 £000	
Revenue from passengers		220		296		116
Direct costs (variable)	150		200		80	
Specific fixed costs	36		48		24	
Apportioned fixed costs (garage maintenance and administration)	24	210	32	280	20	124
Profit (loss)		10		16		(8)

Examples of specific fixed costs include hire of vehicles and the fixed wages of drivers. It is assumed that the drivers for a particular route would be made redundant and no redundancy costs would occur if a route was discontinued.

The company hires all its vehicles and the hire costs are included within the specific fixed costs.

Answer

If route 3 is discontinued the sales revenue, direct variable costs and the fixed costs which are specific to the vehicles will be eliminated. These costs are therefore relevant because they will differ depending on whether or not route 3 is operated. The garage maintenance and administration fixed costs are apportioned costs and these costs will still be incurred if the route is discontinued. These costs are therefore *irrelevant* for this decision. The relevant costs and revenues for the decision are:

		£000
Sales revenue		116
Less relevant costs: direct variable costs	80	
specific fixed costs	24	104
Excess of relevant revenues over relevant costs		12

You can see from this calculation that future cash flows will decline by £12 000 if route 3 is discontinued. This is because the authority will lose a contribution of £12 000 towards the general fixed costs (that is, garage maintenance and administration). Whenever a segment of a business can provide a contribution towards meeting common and unavoidable (general) fixed costs it should not be discontinued, always assuming that the facilities have no alternative use which would yield a higher contribution, and that the sales in the other segments are unaffected by the decision.

Students often assume that all fixed costs should be ignored for decision-making. The above answer indicates that some fixed costs may change when a particular alternative is being considered (that is, discontinue route 3). These specific fixed costs should therefore be included as relevant costs for the decision. You should note, however, that common and unavoidable fixed costs which are apportioned to segments are not relevant for decision-making purposes.

Always remember to consider qualitative factors if the financial analysis suggests that a segment should be discontinued. Examples of qualitative factors for this question include the effect on employees' morale if some employees are made redundant, and the social implications and the effect on customer goodwill if a bus service was not offered to all members of the community. This might encourage customers to use other forms of transport even on the profitable routes. Qualitative factors are discussed in Section 9.3.

9.3 Special selling price decisions

Typical examination question

Your company has been invited to supply sub-components for a period of one year at a price of £10 000. The costing department has produced the following data and estimates relating to the manufacture of the sub-components:

(a) Material A is in stock and cost £2000. It was originally intended for use in a product line which has now been discontinued. The material can now only be used for the manufacture of the sub-components or disposed of, the latter incurring transport and other costs of £700.

(b) Material B will have to be ordered, the current price of which is £1400.

(c) Skilled men will be required to help manufacture the sub-component, receiving pay totalling £4000. They will be transferred from another department which will have to recruit labour as replacements, at an estimated total cost of £5000 including pay and recruitment costs.

(d) It is intended to extend the duties of a foreman currently employed elsewhere in the factory to include the supervision of the production process relating to the manufacture of the sub-components. Approximately 10 per cent of the foreman's time will be devoted to the sub-components: the foreman is paid £8000 p.a.

(e) Machinery currently lying idle will be used to manufacture the sub-components. Details of the machinery are:

	£
Original cost 5 years ago	10 000
Estimated life 10 years	
Current realizable value	2 000
Estimated realizable value in one year's time after use on the order	500

(f) General overheads are to be allocated on the basis of 100 per cent of labour cost.

You are required to present a report to management which recommends whether or not to supply the sub-component, clearly explaining your reasoning.

Your answer should also indicate any other factors which you consider might be relevant before a decision is finally taken. (25 marks)
(AAT Pilot Paper)

Answer

When the company has completed the order the stock valuation will consist of the following costs:

This information is not required to answer the question. The information is presented to emphasize that costs accumulated for stock valuation purposes should not be used for decision-making purposes.

		£
Materials (£2000 + £1400)		3 400
Skilled labour	4000	
Foreman's salary	800	4 800
Share of general overheads (100% × £4800)		4 800
		13 000

It is assumed that allocated overheads include a share of depreciation. At first sight it would appear that the company should reject the offer as the above cost of £13 000 is in excess of the proposed selling price. However, *costs used for stock valuation purposes should not be used for decision-making purposes*. For example, common and unavoidable fixed costs have been allocated to the product but these costs will still continue if the sub-components are not produced. The relevant information for decision-making purposes is a comparison of relevant costs with relevant revenues.

Relevant costs and revenue of producing sub-components

	£
Material A	(700)
Material B	1 400
Skilled labour	5 000
Loss in sale value of machinery	1 500
	7 200
Selling price	10 000
Excess of relevant revenues over relevant costs	2 800

If materials are already in stock and are regularly used then the decision to use materials on a particular job will necessitate their replacement. The relevant cost of materials which are regularly used is the replacement cost. If materials have no alternative use and can be sold then the relevant cost of using them on a particular job will be the lost sales value.

Material A The original purchase price is a sunk cost and cannot be changed whatever decision is taken. The materials will not be replaced and if they are not used for the manufacture of the sub-components they will be disposed of at a *cost* of £700. Therefore if the components are produced future cash outflows will be *reduced* by £700.

Material B The relevant cost is £1400 because future cash outflows will increase by this amount if the sub-components are produced.

Skilled labour Future cash outflows of the company will increase by £5000 if the order is accepted.

Foreman's salary It is assumed that the salary will remain unchanged whatever decision is taken. Therefore future cash flows will not change and the relevant cost is zero.

Machinery It is assumed that the machinery will be sold now if the components are not produced or one year later if they are produced. Therefore future cash inflows will decline by £1500 if the sub-components are produced.

The lost cash inflow represents an opportunity cost of producing the components.

Overheads will not change as a result of producing the components and the relevant cost is zero.

Net future cash flows of the company will increase by £2800 if the order is accepted. However, not all the important factors affecting decisions can be expressed in monetary terms. Those factors which cannot easily be expressed in monetary terms are classified as *qualitative factors*. Qualitative factors must be brought to the attention of management – otherwise there is a danger that the wrong decision will be taken. The qualitative factors to be considered for this question are:

(i) Will a selling price based on covering relevant short-run costs but which does not cover long-run fixed costs induce competitors to adopt similar pricing policies? This might result in a decline in market prices for the company's products.
(ii) What will happen to the recruited labour once the contract is completed? Can they be laid off? Will this have a harmful effect on labour relations?
(iii) What will be the foreman's reaction to the increased workload without any extra payment?

9.4 Make or buy decisions

Typical examination question
The management of Springer PLC is considering next year's production and purchase budgets.

One of the components produced by the company, which is incorporated into another product before being sold, has a budgeted manufacturing cost as follows:

	£
Direct material	14
Direct labour (4 hours at £3 per hour)	12
Variable overhead (4 hours at £2 per hour)	8
Fixed overhead (4 hours at £5 per hour)	20
Total cost	54 per unit

Trigger PLC has offered to supply the above component at a guaranteed price of £50 per unit.

You are required to carry out the following:

(a) Considering cost criteria only, advise management whether the above component should be purchased from Trigger PLC. Any calculations should be shown and assumptions made, or aspects which may require further investigation should be clearly stated.

(6 marks)

(b) Explain how your above advice would be affected by each of the following two separate situations:
  (i) As a result of recent government legislation, if Springer PLC continues to manufacture this component the company will incur additional inspection and testing expenses of £56 000 per annum, which are not included in the above budgeted manufacturing costs. (3 marks)
  (ii) Additional labour cannot be recruited, and if the above component is not manufactured by Springer PLC the direct labour released will be employed in increasing the production of an existing product which is sold for £90 and which has a budgeted manufacturing cost as follows:

	£
Direct material	10
Direct labour (8 hours at £3 per hour)	24
Variable overhead (8 hours at £2 per hour)	16
Fixed overhead (8 hours at £5 per hour)	40
	90 per unit

All calculations should be shown. (4 marks)

(c) The production director of Springer PLC recently said: 'We must continue to manufacture the component as only one year ago we purchased some special grinding equipment to be used exclusively by this component. The equipment cost £100 000, it cannot be resold or used elsewhere, and if we cease production of this component we will have to write off the written-down book value which is £80 000.'

Draft a brief reply to the production director commenting on his statement. (4 marks)
(CACA Level 1 Costing)

Answer

Always remember to state your assumptions if the facts are not clearly stated in the question.

(a) It is assumed that the company has sufficient spare capacity to produce the components. It is also assumed that fixed overheads apportioned to the product will still be incurred if the company purchases the component from Trigger PLC. Fixed overheads are therefore irrelevant in deciding which alternative to choose. Assuming that the company will not incur the direct labour, material and variable overhead costs if the component is purchased, then these costs will be different depending on which decision is taken. The relevant costs are:

	£
Purchase price of component from supplier	50
Additional cost of manufacture (variable cost only)	34
Saving if the component is manufactured	16

The component should therefore be manufactured.

(b) (i) The inspection costs represent additional costs which the company will incur if the components are manufactured. Inspection costs are therefore relevant to the decision. The relevant costs of manufacturing the component are variable costs of £34 per component produced plus a fixed sum of £56 000 per annum. The company makes a saving of £16 for each unit manufactured but incurs additional fixed costs of £56 000. The break-even point is 3500 units (fixed costs of £56 000/£16 per unit saving). If the quantity of components manufactured per year is less than 3500 units then it will be cheaper to purchase them from the outside supplier.

(ii) The company no longer has any spare capacity. Hence it is necessary to take into account the work which will be carried out using the productive facilities if the component is *not* manufactured. If the component is manufactured then production of the existing product will have to be reduced, resulting in a lost contribution. This lost contribution represents the *opportunity cost* of manufacturing the component.

The existing product requires 8 *scarce* labour hours and yields a contribution of £40 (£90 selling price − £50 variable cost). The component requires 4 *scarce* labour hours. Therefore for every two components produced a contribution of £40 will be lost from the reduced production of the existing product. The lost contribution (that is, opportunity cost) if one component is manufactured is £20. Hence the relevant cost of manufacturing a component is £54, consisting of £34 variable cost plus a lost contribution or opportunity cost of £20. The component should be purchased from the supplier.

(c) The book value of the equipment is a sunk cost and is not relevant to the decision whether the company should purchase or continue to manufacture the components. If the company ceases production now, the written-down value will be written off in a lump sum, whereas if it continues production, the written-down value will be written off over a number of years. Future cash outflows on the equipment will not be affected by the decision to purchase or continue to manufacture the components. The original purchase cost or the written-down value of the equipment is therefore not relevant for decision-making purposes.

For this question, capacity is measured in terms of labour hours.

Whenever a factor of production is scarce, opportunity costs must be included as part of the relevant cost for the alternative under consideration.

Remember to qualify your answer by drawing attention to the qualitative factors. For example, will the quality of the components and the delivery service be satisfactory? There is a danger that future sales might decline if the product quality and delivery are not maintained.

Note that if the equipment has a realizable value then this value will be lost if it is used for a particular alternative. This opportunity cost represents a relevant cost for the course of action being considered.

9.5 Limiting factors

Sometimes sales demand is in excess of the company's productive capacity and future profits will be restricted by the company's ability to increase output. For example, output might be restricted by the shortage of labour, materials, equipment or factory space. The factors responsible for limiting output are called *scarce or limiting factors*. Where a limiting factor exists it is important that the greatest possible contribution to profit is obtained each time that the limiting factor is used.

It is assumed that profits are equivalent to net cash inflows.

Typical examination question: limiting factors
A glazing company has the following standard costs per square metre for its product range:

	Replacement windows £	Patio doors £	Secondary glazing £
Materials:			
Glass	4.00	6.00	3.50
Frames	1.34	1.37	0.90
Labour:			
Constructors	5.46	7.98	3.36
Installers	4.50	9.00	1.00
Selling prices are	40.00	50.00	20.00
Sales quantities expected (m^2)	7800	3800	8000

Fixed costs are £300 000 per period.

The constructors are currently paid £4.20 per hour and are in short supply. It is forecast that only 18 440 hours are available from them to meet the sales demand.

(a) You are required to produce a statement to show the most profitable course of production. (15 marks)
(AAT)

Answer (a)

(a)
	Windows	Doors	Glazing
Product contribution per m^2	£24.70	£25.65	£11.24
Construction hours required	1.3	1.9	0.8
Contribution per construction hour	£19.00	£13.50	£14.05
Ranking	1	3	2

Note that the construction hours are calculated by dividing the constructor's labour cost by the hourly rate of £4.20.

The company's ability to increase its output and profits/net cash inflows is limited by the availability of constructors' hours. At first glance it might appear that the company should give top priority to producing doors, since doors yield the highest contribution per unit sold, but this assumption is incorrect. To produce doors, 1.9 scarce hours are required whereas windows and glazing only use 1.3 and 0.8 hours respectively. For example, if only 247 hours were available, 190 (m^2) windows could be produced (247/1.3 hours) yielding a contribution of £4693, or 130 (m^2) doors could be produced (247/1.9 hours) yielding a contribution of £3334. Windows should therefore be produced in preference to doors as long as labour hours are the limiting factor.

The way in which you should determine the production plan which maximizes profits is to calculate the contribution per limiting factor for each product and then to rank the products in order of profitability based on this calculation. You should now allocate the 18 440 scarce constructors' hours in accordance with the above rankings. The first choice should be to produce as many windows as possible. The maximum sales are 7800 (m^2) and production of this quantity will require 10 140 hours (7800 × 1.3 hours), thus leaving 8300 hours. The second choice is to concentrate on secondary glazing. Maximum secondary glazing sales will require 6400 hours (8000 × 0.8 hours). This leaves a balance of 1900 hours, which will enable 1000 patio doors (1900/1.9 hours) to be produced. The allocation of the scarce hours and the profit calculation is as follows:

Production	Hours used	Contribution
		£
7800 (m^2) windows	10 140	192 660 (7800 × £24.70)
8000 (m^2) glazing	6 400	89 920 (8000 × £11.24)
1000 (m^2) doors	1 900	25 650 (1000 × £25.65)
		308 230
	Less fixed costs	300 000
	Profit	8 230

10 Capital investment appraisal

10.1 Distinguishing feature of capital investment decisions

Capital investment involves an initial cash outflow followed by a stream of cash inflows in future years. Capital investment decisions are different from short-term decisions because of the time element. With short-term decisions a short time elapses from the commitment of funds to the receipt of the benefits. With capital investment decisions the cash inflows will probably be received over a period of several years and it may take a considerable time before the initial investment is recouped. Because of this time factor it is necessary to incorporate an interest cost into the analysis.

Capital investment appraisal is not examined until stage 3 of the CIMA, level 2 of the CACA and P2 of ICAEW examinations. This topic is included in the examinations of some of the A level bodies and the AAT. You should check whether capital investment/discounting is included in your examination syllabus.

10.2 Opportunity cost of an investment

Investors can invest funds in building societies, banks and traded securities of companies in exchange for an annual return on the funds invested. Assume you can earn an annual return of 10 per cent on an investment. You would therefore be prepared to invest your funds in a company only if the management of the company can find capital projects which will yield a return in excess of 10 per cent. If they cannot find projects which yield returns in excess of 10 per cent then you would prefer the company to return the funds to you so that you can invest the funds yourself at 10 per cent. This 10 per cent minimum rate of return which you require is known as the *opportunity cost of capital* or the *discount rate*.

The company should invest the funds to earn a return in excess of 10 per cent. The return will be repaid to you in the form of cash dividends. Alternatively the return may be reinvested by the company, thus resulting in the share price increasing. You can then sell your shares at a profit which will result in a return in excess of 10 per cent.

10.3 Compounding and discounting

Suppose you invest £1000 at 10 per cent payable at the end of each year. Table 10.1 shows that if your interest is reinvested your investment will accumulate to £1331 by the end of year 3. Period 0 in the first column of Table 10.1 means that no time has elapsed, or the time is *now*; period 1 means one year later; and so on.

The values in Table 10.1 can also be obtained by using the following compound interest formula:

$$FV_n = V_0(1+K)^n$$

Table 10.1 The value of £1000 invested at 10 per cent, compounded annually for three years

End of year	Interest earned £	Total investment £
0		1000
	0.10 × £1000	100
1		1100
	0.10 × £1100	110
2		1210
	0.10 × £1210	121
3		1331

where FV_n denotes the future value of an investment in n years, V_0 denotes the amount invested at the beginning of the period, K denotes the rate of return on the investment and n denotes the number of years for which the money is invested. The calculation of £1000 invested at 10 per cent for two years is

$$FV_2 = £1000 (1 + 0.10)^2 = £1210$$

In Table 10.1 all of the year end values are equal in terms of the time value of money. For example, £1210 received at the end of year 2 is equivalent to £1000 received today because money received today can be invested at 10 per cent to accumulate to £1210 by the end of year 2. The implication of this is that £1 received in the future is not equivalent to £1 received today. It is therefore necessary to convert future cash flows into the value at the present time. The process of converting cash to be received in the future into a value at the present time is termed *discounting* and the resulting present value is the *discounted present value*.

The compound interest formula can be rearranged to produce the following discounted present value formula:

$$V_0 \text{ (discounted present value)} = \frac{FV_n}{(1+K)^n}$$

Therefore the present value (*PV*) of £1210 received in year 2 is

$$PV = \frac{£1210}{(1+0.10)^2} = £1000$$

Using the above formula the *PV* of £1 received in two years time is £0.8264 (£1/(1.10)²). The *PV* of £1 received in one year's time is £0.9091 (£1/1.10). Your examination paper will include tables showing the value of £1 received in *x* years time. These values are called *discount factors*. So if you are required to calculate the *PV* of £1210 which is received in year 2, you multiply £1210 by the discount factor of 0.8264. The answer is £1000 – the same as the formula method.

You are recommended to calculate PV using the discount tables (which will normally be reproduced and included in examination questions) rather than using the formula. Always show your workings – that is, cash flows × discount factor = PV.

10.4 Net present value

The objective is to invest in projects which yield returns in excess of the rate of return available to investors (that is, the opportunity cost of capital). You can check whether a project meets this objective by calculating its net present value (*NPV*). This is the *PV* of the net cash inflows less the project's investment cost. If the rate of return on the project is greater than the opportunity cost of capital, the *NPV* will be positive. Alternatively, if the rate of return is lower the *NPV* will be negative. The decision rule is therefore to accept projects with positive *NPV*s and reject projects with negative *NPV*s.

Net cash flows = cash inflow – cash outflow.

Remember: NPV = PV *of net cash inflows less the investment cost.*

Typical examination question: net present value
The management of an hotel group is deciding whether to scrap an old but still serviceable machine bought five years ago to produce fruit pies, and replace it with a newer type of machine.

It is expected that the demand for the fruit pies will last for a further five years only and will be as follows:

	Produced and sold number of pies
Year 1	40 000
Year 2	40 000
Year 3	30 000
Year 4	20 000
Year 5	20 000

The fruit pies are currently sold for £3 per pie.

Each machine is capable of meeting these requirements. Data for the two machines are as follows:

	Existing machine	New machine
Capital cost	£320 000	£150 000
Operating costs:	per unit	per unit
Direct labour	£0.6	£0.40
Materials	£0.6	£0.60
Variable overheads	£0.3	£0.25
Fixed overheads:		
Depreciation	£0.8	£1.00
Allocated costs (100% direct labour costs)	£0.6	£0.40
	£2.9	£2.65

Unit operating costs, fixed overhead costs and selling price are expected to remain constant throughout the five-year period.

You are required to:

(a) Using data relating *only* to the new machine
    (i) Calculate the payback period of the new machine.

(ii) Calculate the net present value of the new machine.
NB The hotel group expects that its cost of capital will be 20 per cent p.a. throughout the period. (10 marks)
(b) Assume that the existing machinery could be sold for £130 000 immediately, if it was replaced. Show, using present value calculations, whether the existing machine should be replaced by the new machine.

Note: PV   20 per cent
      Year 1   0.833
      Year 2   0.694
      Year 3   0.579
      Year 4   0.482
      Year 5   0.402 (8 marks)
(AAT)

Answer

(a) (i) For the answer to this question see Section 10.6.
(ii) This part of the question requires you to consider only the new machine. You should note that depreciation should never be included in *NPV* calculations. This is because the investment cost is deducted from the *PV* of cash inflows. Therefore including annual depreciation costs would result in the double counting of the investment cost. The allocated costs will consist of a share of the common and unavoidable fixed costs which will still continue if the machine is not purchased. These costs are not relevant to the decision. The net cash inflow per unit is £1.75 (£3 selling price − £1.25 variable cost). The calculation of the *NPV* is as follows:

Year	Net cash inflow £	Discount factor	Present value £
1	70 000 (40 000 × £1.75)	0.833	58 310
2	70 000 (40 000 × £1.75)	0.694	48 580
3	52 500 (30 000 × £1.75)	0.579	30 398
4	35 000 (20 000 × £1.75)	0.482	16 870
5	35 000 (20 000 × £1.75)	0.402	14 070
			168 228
	Less investment cost		150 000
	Net present value		18 228

The principle of relevant cost and revenues explained in Chapter 9 should also be applied to capital investment appraisal.

If you are very short of time show the net cash flows, discount factors and the deduction of the investment cost. Include a note in your answer that you would multiply the net cash inflow by the discount factor but you have insufficient time to do this.

The new machine should be purchased because it yields a positive *NPV*.
(b) This part of the question requires a decision on whether the existing machine should be replaced by a new machine. With replacement decisions output and sales will normally be the same for both

94 Cost Accounting Revision Guide

machines. If output and sales remain unchanged you can save time by excluding sales revenue from the analysis. The analysis should consist of a comparison of the cost savings from operating the new machine (plus any sale proceeds from the old machine) with the investment cost of the new machine. Note that the cost savings will increase future cash flows and can thus be regarded as cash inflows. The calculation of NPV is as follows:

You will still arrive at the correct answer if you include sales as a cash inflow for both alternatives and then deduct the actual cash outflows for each alternative. This approach should be followed when the output and sales for each machine are not identical.

Year	Net cash inflow £	Discount factor	Present value £
0	130 000	1.000	130 000
1	10 000	0.833	8 330
2	10 000	0.694	6 940
3	7 500	0.579	4 342
4	5 000	0.482	2 410
5	5 000	0.402	2 010

	154 032
Less investment cost	150 000
NPV	4 032

Note that the net cash inflows consist of £130 000 from the sale of the old machine and the savings from operating the new machine (that is, £0.25 difference in variable cost multiplied by the number of units produced). Because the new machine has a positive NPV it should be purchased.

10.5 Internal rate of return

IRR tends not to be included in the AAT and A level examinations

The internal rate of return (*IRR*) is an alternative technique for appraising capital projects which takes into account the time value of money. The *IRR* represents the return which an investment earns over its life. The decision rule is that a project should be accepted if the project yields a return which is in excess of the opportunity cost of capital. The *IRR* is calculated by finding the discount rate which will cause the *NPV* of an investment to be zero.

An easier way to calculate the IRR is to use the interpolation method.

The discount factors for the discount rates used in this chapter are:

Year	10 per cent	26 per cent	30 per cent
1	0.9091	0.7937	0.7692
2	0.8264	0.6299	0.5917
3	0.7513	0.4999	0.4552
4	0.6830	0.3968	0.3501
5	0.6209	0.3149	0.2693
6	0.5645	0.2499	0.2072
7	0.5132	0.1983	0.1594

The NPV of £18 228 was calculated for the answer to the typical examination question following Section 10.4.

Consider the previous typical examination question. The *IRR* can be found by trial and error by using a number of discount factors until the *NPV* equals zero. For example, if you use a 30 per cent discount factor you should get a negative *NPV* of approximately £9160. The *NPV* using a discount factor of 20 per cent is £18 228. Therefore the *NPV* will be zero somewhere between 20 and 30 per cent. Continuing this process of trial and error you will find that the *IRR* is approximately 26 per cent, as indicated in the following calculation:

Year	Net cash inflow £	Discount factor at 26%	Present value £
1	70 000	0.7937	55 559
2	70 000	0.6299	44 093
3	52 500	0.4999	26 245
4	35 000	0.3968	13 888
5	35 000	0.3149	11 022
			150 807
		Less investment cost	150 000
		NPV	807

The *IRR* is 26 per cent and the opportunity cost of capital is 20 per cent. Therefore the new machine should be purchased.

The NPV using a discount rate of 27 per cent is – £1804. Therefore the correct IRR is between 26 and 27 per cent. An approximate calculation is sufficient for decision-making purposes.

10.6 Payback method

The payback period is defined as the length of time it takes for the initial investment outlay to be recovered. For example, if a machine cost £100 000 and was expected to produce annual net cash inflows of £25 000 for six years, then the investment cost would have been recovered by the end of year 4. In other words the payback period is four years. Let us now calculate the payback period for the previous question.

The cumulative net cash inflows are £70 000 in year 1, £140 000 by the end of year 2 and £192 500 by the end of year 3. Therefore the payback period is between two and three years. By the end of year 2, £140 000 is recovered and the balance of the investment cost to be recovered is £10 000. Assuming that the £52 500 accrues evenly throughout year 3 then it will take 0.19 years to recover the remaining £10 000 in year 3 (that is £10 000/£52 500 × 1 year). Therefore the payback period is 2.19 years.

Management normally sets payback target periods and accepts only those projects which fall within the target period. For example, if a payback period of three years is set then a project with a payback period of 2.19 years should be accepted. Using the payback method can lead to incorrect decisions. Consider Example 10.1.

Example 10.1

The cash flows and *NPV* calculations for two projects are as follows:

	Project X £	Project Y £
Initial cost	75 000	75 000
Net cash inflows: year 1	15 000	15 000
2	30 000	15 000
3	30 000	15 000
4	30 000	30 000
5	15 000	45 000
6	–	45 000
7	–	45 000
	120 000	210 000
NPV (at 10% cost of capital)	15 770	59 227

The payback period is three years for project X and four years for project Y. However, project Y has a higher *NPV* and the payback method incorrectly ranks project X in preference to project Y.

You should note that the payback method has two deficiencies. First, it does not take into account cash flows which are earned after the payback date, and, second, it ignores the timing of the cash flows prior to the payback date. The payback method ignores the fact that future cash receipts cannot be validly compared with an initial outlay until they are discounted to their present values.

Examiners frequently ask for a discussion of the limitations of payback and an explanation of why it is frequently used in practice.

Nevertheless a recent survey indicated that the payback method is the most frequently used method of investment appraisal. The main attraction of the payback method is that it provides a rough indication of risk in the sense that the longer the payback period, the greater the risk that future cash flows may not be obtained. The payback method is appropriate in situations where risky investments are made in uncertain markets which are subject to fast design and product changes. It is also appropriate for companies which have a weak cash and credit position and which require a fast repayment of investments.

10.7 Accounting rate of return

The accounting rate of return is calculated by dividing the average annual profits from a project into the average investment cost. The average annual profits are calculated by dividing the difference between the additional revenues and costs resulting from the project by the estimated life of the project. Note that the additional costs will include either the net investment cost or the total depreciation charges, these figures being identical. The average investment cost is one-half of the amount of the initial investment plus the scrap value at the end of the project's life. The accounting rate of return for each project in Example 10.1 is

For an explanation of why the full amount of the scrap value is added, see the answer to Question 10.1 in Part III.

	Project X	*Project Y*
$\dfrac{\text{average annual profits}}{\text{average investment}} =$	$\dfrac{£9\,000}{£37\,500} = 24 \text{ per cent}$	$\dfrac{£19\,286}{£37\,500} = 51.4 \text{ per cent}$

The total profit for project X over its five-year life is £45 000, giving an average annual profit of £9000. For project Y, the total profit over its seven-year life is £135 000, giving an average annual profit of £19 286. The average investment cost is half of the initial cost of £75 000.

The profit of £45 000 is calculated by deducting the investment cost of £75 000 from the net cash inflows of £120 000.

The decision rule is to accept those projects with an accounting rate of return which is in excess of the target set by the management of a company. The accounting rate of return ignores the time value of money and for this reason cannot be recommended.

11
Budgeting and budgetary control

11.1 Definition of a budget

A budget is a plan, usually quantified in monetary terms, that covers a specified period, normally one year. Budgets are formulated for the organization as a whole, and for the individual segments within the firm.

11.2 Objectives of budgetary planning and control systems

Planning The budgeting process forces management to think ahead, and to consider how conditions in the next year might change and what steps they should take now to respond to these changed conditions.

Co-ordination Without a budget, managers will tend to focus only on the activities of their own departments and fail to consider how the activities relate to other departments and the organization as a whole. The budget serves as a vehicle through which the actions of the different parts of an organization can be brought together and reconciled into a common plan.

Motivation A budget provides targets which under certain circumstances provide a challenge and motivate managers to strive to achieve the organization's goals. The setting of targets in the form of budgets is more likely to motivate than a situation of vagueness and uncertainty.

Communication A budget communicates plans to those managers who are responsible for carrying them out and ensures that all members of the organization are clearly aware of what is expected of them during the forthcoming budget period.

Control By comparing the actual results with the budget amounts for different categories of expenses, managers are provided with information on costs which do not conform with the budget and which require their attention. By investigating the reasons for the deviations and taking corrective action, managers can ensure that the inefficiencies are not repeated.

11.3 Organization required for the preparation of budgets

Budget period

The budget is normally prepared for one year. For control purposes the annual budget should be divided into monthly or weekly periods so that actual results can be compared with the monthly/weekly budgets at frequent intervals. Sometimes the annual budget is updated at quarterly intervals so that a twelve-month budget is always available. This approach is known as *continuous* or *rolling* budgets. The alternative approach is to prepare an annual budget once per year.

The budget committee

The budget committee should consist of the chief executive and senior managers representing the major segments of the business. The budget committee should be responsible for authorizing the budgets and ensuring that they are co-ordinated satisfactorily.

The budget officer and budget staff

The budget staff are responsible for the direction and supervision of the budget process. They should assist managers in the preparation of the budgets by offering advice; for example, by providing past information which will help in preparing budgets, and ensuring that managers submit their budgets on time.

The budget manual

The manual should describe the objectives and procedures involved in the budget process. In particular the manual should set out the responsibilities of individuals involved in the budget process and the forms and records to be used. In addition, the manual may include a timetable which specifies the order in which the budgets should be prepared and the dates when they should be presented to the budget committee.

Typical examination question
Outline:

(a) The objectives of budgetary planning and control systems. (7 marks)
(b) The organization required for the preparation of a master budget.
(10 marks)
(CACA Level 1 Costing)

11.4 Stages in the budget process

Setting policy and guidelines

Top management determines the objectives and policies for implementing them. Policies and guidelines must be communicated to those who are responsible for preparing the budgets. Policy effects might include planned changes in the sales mix and expansion of sales territories. Guidelines must also be communicated; for example, the allowances which should be made for price and wage increases.

Identifying the limiting factor

There will always be some factor which restricts the profit performance of an organization during a particular period. If sales demand exceeds production capacity then profits will be restricted by production capacity. In most organizations the factor which restricts profit performance is the limitation on sales demand. It is important that the limiting factor is identified prior to the start of the budget process, as this factor determines the point at which the annual budget process should begin.

The sales budget

Sales demand is normally the factor which restricts output and determines the level of a company's operation. Consequently the sales budget will be the most important budget. A number of approaches may be used when preparing the sales budget. The simplest approach is to produce estimates for each product for each sales territory based on the opinions of the sales managers. An alternative approach is to estimate sales demand by using statistical techniques which incorporate market conditions and past growth in sales.

Preparation of the budgets

The managers who are responsible for achieving the budgeted performance should prepare the budget for those areas for which they are responsible. Past data are often used as the starting-point for producing the budget, but changes in future conditions must also be taken into account. In addition, managers will rely on the guidelines provided by top management for determining the content of the budgets.

Examples of functional budgets include the sales budget, the production budget, the distribution budget and the administration budget.

Budget preparation should start at the lowest level of management. The managers at this level should submit their budget to their superiors for approval. The superior will then incorporate this budget with other budgets for which he is responsible and then submit this budget for approval to his superior. This process will continue until a budget emerges for each major function of the business. At each of these stages the budgets will be negotiated between the budgetees and their supervisors until they reach agreement. It is important that budgetees should participate in the preparation of the budget rather than the budget being imposed on them by their superiors. It is unlikely that managers will be motivated to achieve a budget unless they have been able to participate in the setting of the budget.

Some writers argue that if lower level managers are allowed to participate in the budget process then both motivation and performance will increase.

Co-ordination and approval of the budgets

As the individual budgets move up the organization hierarchy in the negotiation process they are examined in relation to each other so that they are in harmony. Functional budgets emerge from this process and these are submitted to the budget committee for approval. The committee will ensure that the functional budgets are also in harmony with each other.

Budgeting and budgetary control

The functional budgets are then summarized into a master budget which will consist of a budgeted profit and loss account, a balance sheet and a cash budget.

11.5 Preparation of functional budgets

Typical examination question
You are required, from the data given below, to prepare next year's budgets for (a) production, (b) purchases, and (c) production cost.
Standard cost data are as follows:

		Product	
		Aye £	Bee £
Direct materials:			
X	24 kg at £2.0	48	
	30 kg at £2.0		60
Y	10 kg at £5.0	50	
	8 kg at £5.0		40
Z	5 kg at £6.0	30	
	10 kg at £6.0		60
Direct wages:			
Unskilled	10 hours at £3.0 per hour	30	
	5 hours at £3.0 per hour		15
Skilled	6 hours at £5.0 per hour	30	
	5 hours at £5.0 per hour		25

Production overhead is absorbed on a basis of direct labour hours, while other overhead is recovered on the basis of 20 per cent of production cost. Profit is calculated at 20 per cent of sales price.

The budgeted data for the year are as follows:

		Material		
		X £	Y £	Z £
Stock at standard price				
1 January		60 000	125 000	72 000
31 December		70 000	135 000	75 000
Production overhead	£900 000			
Labour hours	75 000			

	Product	
	Aye £	Bee £
Finished goods stock at production cost:		
Opening stock	152 000	256 000
Closing stock	190 000	352 000
Sales at standard sales price	1 368 000	1 536 000

(25 marks)
(CIMA Cost Accounting 2)

Most examination questions on budgeting require the preparation of functional budgets or a cash budget. The examiners normally require you to prepare any one of the following budgets – sales, production, production cost, purchasing, materials usage, wages. See Question 11.2 in Part III for a further question on the preparation of functional budgets.

Answer

The calculation of the standard cost and selling price for each product is as follows:

	Aye £	Bee £
Direct material cost	128	160
Direct wages	60	40
Production overhead (W1)		
16 hours at £12	192	
10 hours at £12		120
Production cost	380	320
Other overheads	76	64
Total cost	456	384
Profit margin [20/(100 − 20)] × total cost	114	96
Selling price	570	480

> Do not be put off if you have difficulty in calculating the profit margin. If your calculation is wrong then the examiner will award you marks if you have followed the correct approach with the remaining part of the answer.

(W1) Production overhead absorption rate = £900 000/75 000 hours = £12 per hour

> Production budgets are prepared in both physical and monetary terms. If you are unsure which budget is required then state your assumption. Remember to add closing stock and deduct opening stock when ascertaining the number of units to be produced during a period.

(a) *Production budget (units)*

	Aye	Bee
Sales	2400 (£1 368 000/£570)	3200 (£1 536 000/£480)
plus		
Closing stocks	500 (£190 000/£380)	1100 (£352 000/£320)
	2900	4300
less		
Opening stocks	(400)(£152 000/£380)	(800)(£256 000/£320)
Production required	2500	3500

(b) *Purchases budget*

Materials	X kg	Y kg	Z kg
Production:			
Aye 2500 units	60 000	25 000	12 500
Bee 3500 units	105 000	28 000	35 000
	165 000	53 000	47 500
plus			
Closing stocks	35 000	27 000	12 500
	200 000	80 000	60 000

less Opening stocks	(30 000)	(25 000)	(12 000)
Purchases required (kg)	170 000	55 000	48 000
Cost per kg	£2	£5	£6
Purchases cost	£340 000	£275 000	£288 000
Total purchases		£903 000	

(c) *Production cost budget*

	Aye	Bee	Total
Production (units)	2500	3500	–
	£	£	£
Direct materials:			
X at £2 per kg	120 000	210 000	330 000
Y at £5 per kg	125 000	140 000	265 000
Z at £6 per kg	75 000	210 000	285 000
	320 000	560 000	880 000
Direct wages:			
Unskilled at £3 per hour	75 000	52 500	127 500
Skilled at £5 per hour	75 000	87 500	162 500
	150 000	140 000	290 000
Production overhead:			
Direct labour hour rate (£12 per hour)	480 000	420 000	900 000
Production cost	950 000	1 120 000	2 070 000

11.6 Cash budgets

Typical examination question

(a) Discuss the importance of the cash budget to a manufacturing company. (6 marks)
(CACA Level 1 Costing)

Answer

(a) It is possible for a firm to make profits but to have insufficient cash to meet its commitments. If a company runs out of cash and cannot borrow at short notice then it may have to cease operations. It is therefore of vital importance that a company prepares a cash budget so as to ensure that sufficient cash is available at all times to meet the level of operations which are outlined in the various budgets. The preparation of cash budgets enables cash deficiencies to be identified in advance so that steps can be taken to ensure that borrowing can be arranged to meet the deficiencies. Alternatively cash budgets can help a firm identify cash balances which are surplus to requirements. Management can then take steps in advance to invest the surplus cash. Cash budgeting enables a firm to attain maximum cash availability and maximum interest income on any idle funds.

Typical examination question: preparation of cash budgets
G. T. Urnside PLC, a company which manufactures pressed steel fitments, commenced trading on 1 December 1981. Summarized below is the profit statement and balance sheet after the first year of trading.

G. T. Urnside PLC
Summarized profit statement for the year ended 30 November 1982

	£000	£000
Sales		240
Cost of sales:		
Direct materials	60	
Direct labour	48	
Variable overhead	30	
Fixed overhead	70	
	—	208
Net operating profit		£32
Proposed dividends to ordinary shareholders		15
Retained profit		17
		£32

G. T. Urnside PLC
Summarized balance sheet as at 30 November 1982

	£000	£000	£000
Issued share capital			
108 000 £1 ordinary shares			108
Reserves			
Retained profit			17
Shareholders' fund			
			£125
Represented by:			
Fixed assets:			
Plant and machinery (at cost on 1 December 1981)	120		
less Depreciation	24		
	—		96
Current assets:			
Stocks of materials	8		
Debtors	40		
Cash	1		
	49		

less Current liabilities			
Creditors	5		
Dividend	15		
	—	20	
Net working capital		—	29
Net assets employed			£125

Shown below are relevant data extracted from the company's budget for the year ended 30 November 1983:

Sales 1st quarter £66 000   3rd quarter £90 000
   2nd quarter £78 000   4th quarter £84 000

The weekly sales in each quarter will be constant and, on average, debtors pay eight weeks after goods have been despatched. The selling prices and product mix will remain the same as the previous year.

Materials The price of materials will be 20 per cent lower than the previous year. The weekly purchases of materials in each quarter will be constant, except for the budgeted stock increase in the third quarter shown below. Material suppliers are paid on average four weeks after the goods have been received.

Direct labour Wages will be paid at the 1981–2 level of £12 000 per quarter plus the following changes:

(i) All direct operatives have been awarded a 15 per cent rate of pay increase with effect from 1 December 1982.
(ii) One additional direct operative will be recruited at the beginning of the second quarter, and another direct operative will be recruited at the beginning of the third quarter. Both operatives will be paid £100 per week and will continue to be employed for the remainder of the year.

Wages are paid at the end of the week in which they are earned.

Overheads Variable overheads vary directly with production activity and there will be no price increases from the previous year. Fixed overheads will increase by £12 000 p.a. and the total amount will be incurred evenly throughout the year. All relevant overheads are paid in cash immediately they are incurred.

Stocks Stocks of work in progress and finished goods will not be carried. However, stocks of raw materials will increase by £3000 in the first week of the third quarter and remain at £11 000 throughout the remainder of the year.

Capital expenditure Additional equipment costing £20 000 will be purchased and paid for during the second quarter of the year. Depreciation on this equipment will not commence until the following year.

Dividends The dividends outstanding will be paid in the first quarter of the year.

You are required to prepare the company's quarterly cash budgets for the year ended 30 November 1983.

Note: It should be assumed there are 12 weeks in each quarter. Any other assumptions which you consider to be necessary should be clearly stated.

(22 marks)
(CACA Level 1 Costing)

Answer

Quarterly cash budget for year ending 30 November 1983

	Qtr 1 £000	Qtr 2 £000	Qtr 3 £000	Qtr 4 £000
Receipts from debtors (note 1)	62.00	70.00	82.00	88.00
Payments:				
Creditors (note 2)	13.80	14.80	20.20	17.20
Direct labour (note 4)	13.80	15.00	16.20	16.20
Variable overhead (note 5)	8.25	9.75	11.25	10.50
Fixed overhead *less* Depreciation (note 6)	14.50	14.50	14.50	14.50
Capital expenditure		20.00		
Dividends	15.00			
Total cash outflow	65.35	74.05	62.15	58.40
Net movement in cash during quarter	−3.35	−4.05	+19.85	+29.60
Cash balance at beginning of quarter	+1.00	−2.35	−6.40	+13.45
Cash balance at end of quarter	−2.35	−6.40	+13.45	+43.05

Notes

	Qtr 1 £000	Qtr 2 £000	Qtr 3 £000	Qtr 4 £000
1 Calculation of receipts from debtors				
Opening balance	40			
4 weeks current quarter sales (4/12)	22	26	30	28
8 weeks previous quarter sales (8/12)	–	44	52	60
	62	70	82	88

2 *Calculation of payments to creditors*
   Materials purchased (20% of sales – see note 3) 13.2 15.6 18.0 16.8

Opening balance	5.0			
8 weeks current quarter purchases (8/12)	8.8	10.4	12.0	11.2
4 weeks previous quarter purchases (4/12)	–	4.4	5.2	6.0
Stock increase			3.0	
	13.8	14.8	20.2	17.2

3 Direct materials are 25 per cent of sales for year ending 30 November 1982. For year ending 30 November 1983 the prices of materials are 20 per cent lower. Therefore materials are 20 per cent (80 per cent × 25 per cent) of sales for 1983. It is assumed that material usage remains unchanged.

4

	Qtr 1	Qtr 2	Qtr 3	Qtr 4
	£000	£000	£000	£000
Existing employees (£12 000 + 15%)	13.8	13.8	13.8	13.8
Additional operations		1.2	2.4	2.4
	13.8	15.0	16.2	16.2

5 For year ending 30 November 1982, variable overheads are 12.5 per cent of sales. Quarterly variable overheads are assumed to be 12.5 per cent of quarterly sales for 1983.

6

	£
Fixed overheads for 1982	70 000
Less depreciation	24 000
	46 000
Add increase for 1983	12 000
Total fixed overheads for 1983	58 000
Quarterly fixed overheads	14 500

Remember that depreciation is a non-cash expense which does not involve a cash outflow.

11.7 Responsibility accounting

The budget process should not stop when the budgets have been agreed. Periodically the actual results should be compared with the budgeted results. This will enable managers to identify items which are not proceeding according to plan. The system which provides reports that compare budget performance with actual performance is known as responsibility accounting.

A responsibility centre is defined as a segment of an organization where an individual manager is held accountable for the segment's performance. Responsibility accounting is the process of presenting detailed control information on short-term operating activities and is implemented by issuing performance reports at frequent intervals. Details of the deviations from the budget for various items of expense are highlighted in the performance reports. It is important to distinguish in the performance reports between controllable and uncontrollable costs. The system will break down if managers are held accountable for expenses which they cannot control.

Direct labour and materials are examples of controllable expenses. Apportioned overheads are uncontrollable expenses.

If performance reports are used as punitive post-mortem devices then there is a danger that managers may resort to such activities as trying to obtain over-generous budgets at the planning stage or contriving lower performance to ensure that easily attainable budgets are obtained in the future. It is therefore important that managers see performance reports as a device to help them and not as a device for undertaking recriminatory post-mortems.

11.8 Flexible budgeting

It is necessary to take into account the variability of costs when preparing performance reports. For example, if the actual level of activity is greater than the budgeted level of activity then those costs which vary with the level of activity will be greater than the budgeted costs purely because of changes in activity. For example, if the budget for a variable item of expense was set at £5000 (5000 units at £1 per unit) and actual expenditure was £5200 for an output of 5500 units, then it would be incorrect to compare the actual expense with the original budget of £5000. This would incorrectly suggest an over-spending of £200. It is incorrect to compare actual costs at one level of activity with budgeted costs at another level of activity. The original fixed budget must be adjusted (that is, flexed) to the actual level of activity so as to compare like with like. The correct comparison is as follows:

The original budget is called a fixed budget.

Budgeted expenditure   Actual expenditure
(flexed to 5500 units)   (5500 units)
£5500   £5200

A comparison of the actual expenditure with the flexible budget indicates that the manager has incurred £300 less expenditure than would have been expected for the activity level of 5500 units. A favourable variance should therefore be recorded on the performance report, and not an adverse variance of £200 which would have been recorded if the original budget had not been adjusted.

Typical examination question: flexible budgeting

(a) Explain what is meant by the terms 'fixed budget' and 'flexible budget' and state the main objective of preparing flexible budgets.
(5 marks)

(b) (i) Prepare a flexible budget for 1986 for the overhead expenses of a production department at the activity levels of 80, 90 and 100 per cent, using the information listed below. (12 marks)

1 The direct labour hourly rate is expected to be £3.75.
2 100 per cent activity represent 60 000 direct labour hours.
3 Variable costs:
   Indirect labour   £0.75 per direct labour hour
   Consumable supplies   £0.375 per direct labour hour
   Canteen and other   6 per cent of direct *and* indirect
     welfare services   labour costs
4 Semi-variable costs are expected to correlate with the direct labour hours in the same manner as for the last five years, which was:

Year	Direct labour hours	Semi-variable costs £
1981	64 000	20 800
1982	59 000	19 800
1983	53 000	18 600
1984	49 000	17 800
1985	40 000 (estimate)	16 000 (estimate)

5 Fixed costs:

	£
Depreciation	18 000
Maintenance	10 000
Insurance	4 000
Rates	15 000
Management salaries	25 000

6 Inflation is to be ignored.

(ii) Calculate the budget cost allowance for 1986 assuming that 57 000 direct labour hours are worked. (3 marks)
(CIMA Cost Accounting 1)

Answer

(a) A fixed budget refers to a budget which is designed to remain unchanged irrespective of the level of activity, whereas a flexible budget is a budget which adjusts the expense items for different levels of activity. See Section 11.8 for an explanation of the objectives of flexible budgeting.

(b) (i) *Flexible budget (overhead expenditure)*

Activity levels	80%	90%	100%
Direct labour hours	48 000	54 000	60 000
	£	£	£
Variable costs:			
Indirect labour at £0.75 per direct labour hour	36 000	40 500	45 000
Consumable supplies at £0.375 per direct labour hour	18 000	20 250	22 500

If actual activity is at the 90 per cent level then this budget will be used to compare with actual performance. If the actual level of activity is 57 000 hours (95 per cent) then actual results for each item of expense will be compared with 95 per cent of the budgeted expense items (see answer (b) (ii) for an illustration).

Canteen and other welfare services at 6% of direct plus indirect wages		12 960	14 580	16 200
Semi-variable: variable (W1)		9 600	10 800	12 000
		76 560	86 130	95 700
Semi-variable: fixed (W1)		8 000	8 000	8 000
Fixed costs:				
Depreciation		18 000	18 000	18 000
Maintenance		10 000	10 000	10 000
Insurance		4 000	4 000	4 000
Rates		15 000	15 000	15 000
Management salaries		25 000	25 000	25 000
		156 560	166 130	175 700

Workings

(W1) Obtained by using high and low points method:

			£
High	64 000	Direct labour hours	20 800
Low	40 000	Direct labour hours	16 000
Difference	24 000	Difference	4 800

$$\frac{£4\,800}{24\,000} = £0.20 \text{ per direct labour hour}$$

Variable costs 64 000 × £0.20	£12 800
Total costs	£20 800
Therefore	
Fixed costs	£8 000

(ii)
	£
Variable cost	90 915 (57 000/60 000 × £95 700)
Fixed costs	80 000
Budgeted cost allowance	170 915

The variable element is found by comparing the costs for the highest level of activity with the costs for the lowest level of activity. The difference in costs represents the change in variable costs. The variable cost per unit is calculated by dividing the change in costs by the change in activity. For any level of activity (say 64 000 DLHs) the fixed cost can be ascertained by deducting the variable cost for the selected level of activity (64 000 DLHs) from the total cost.

12 Standard costing

12.1 Standard costs and budgeted costs

Standard costs are target costs which should be incurred under efficient operating conditions. They are not the same as budgeted costs. A standard cost relates to cost expectations *per unit* of activity, whereas a budget provides the expected cost for the *total activity*.

12.2 Setting standard costs

The standard cost for an operation consists of the sum of the target costs for labour, materials and overheads. The standard cost for each element of expense is determined by multiplying the standard quantity by the standard price. A detailed study of each operation is required to set *quantity* targets. For example, time and motion study is used to determine the standard quantity of labour hours required. The most efficient operating methods are established and this is followed by time measurements which are made to determine the number of standard hours which are required to complete the operation. Target *prices* should also be established. For example, standard material prices are set based on the selection of a supplier who can supply the required quantity of sound quality materials at the best price.

12.3 Standard hours produced

Where a department produces several different products it is not possible to measure *total* output by adding together the production of the different products. This problem is overcome by establishing the amount of time it should take to make each product. This time calculation is called standard hours produced. For example, product A requires 5 standard hours and product B requires 3 standard hours. Assuming that 100 units of both products are produced, then output can be expressed as 800 standard hours. Standard hours thus act as a common denominator for adding together the production of unlike items.

Remember that standard hours are a measure of output. The number of hours actually worked is likely to differ from the 800 standard hours of output.

12.4 Types of cost standards

Ideal standards are standards which are set based on perfect performance. Ideal standard costs are the minimum costs which are possible under the most efficient operating conditions. Because the standards are extremely difficult to achieve they may cease to represent a target. For this reason they are rarely used.

Basic cost standards are left unchanged over long periods. This enables actual costs to be compared with the same standard over a period of years. It is therefore possible to observe trends in efficiency. The disadvantage with using basic standards is that they do not represent current target costs.

Currently attainable standards are standards which are difficult but not impossible to achieve. Attainable standards include allowances for normal spoilage, machine breakdowns and lost time. Currently attainable standards are most frequently used in practice because they provide a fair base from which to measure deviation from targets.

12.5 Variance analysis

A standard costing system enables a detailed analysis of variances to be presented. For example, variances for each responsibility centre can be identified by each element of cost and analysed according to the price and quantity content. This detailed analysis pinpoints areas for further investigation by the responsibility centre manager. The manager should ascertain the reasons for the variance and take appropriate remedial action to prevent any inefficiencies recurring.

The following question is used as an illustration throughout the chapter.

Typical examination question: variance analysis
Bronte Ltd manufactures a single product, a laminated kitchen unit, which has a standard cost of £80 made up as follows:

		£
Direct materials	15 m^2 at £3 per m^2	45
Direct labour	5 hours at £4 per hour	20
Variable overheads	5 hours at £2 per hour	10
Fixed overheads	5 hours at £1 per hour	5
		80

The standard selling price of the kitchen unit is £100. The monthly budget projects production and sales of 1000 units. Actual figures for the month of April are as follows:

Sales 1200 units at £102
Production 1400 units
Direct materials 22 000 m^2 at £4 per m^2
Direct wages 6800 hours at £5
Variable overheads £11 000
Fixed overheads £6000

You are required to prepare a trading account reconciling actual and budgeted profit and showing all appropriate variances. (13 marks)
(ICAEW Accounting Techniques)

12.6 Material variances

Material price variance

The standard price is £3 per square metre but the actual price paid was £4. Consequently there is an adverse variance of £1 per square metre. However, to ascertain the full effect of this it is necessary to multiply the difference between the standard price and the actual price by the quantity purchased. Therefore the total amount of the variance is £22 000 adverse. In formula terms:

material price variance

$$= \text{(standard price} - \text{actual price)} \times \textbf{actual quantity}$$

Note that actual quantity should be defined as quantity purchased rather than quantity used. For example, assume 12 000 units of a material were purchased at an excess price of £1 per unit and used at the rate of 2000 units per month. An adverse variance of £2000 will be reported each month for the next six months if the variance is calculated based on quantity used. It is preferable to base the calculation on quantity purchased and report the full price variance of £12 000 in the period in which it is incurred. This approach enables the full amount of the variance to be speedily reported to management. Possible causes of adverse material price variances include a general increase in market prices or a failure by the purchasing department to seek the most advantageous source of supply. A favourable price variance might be due to the purchase of inferior quality materials, but this may lead to more wastage and an adverse materials usage variance. Any excess wastage due to the purchase of inferior quality materials should be charged to the purchasing department.

The amount of the material price variance which is due to changes in market prices should be regarded as uncontrollable.

Material usage variance

The material usage variance compares the standard quantity which should have been used with the actual quantity used. The standard usage for one unit of the product is 15 m². As 1400 units were produced, 21 000 m² (1400 units × 15 m²) should have been used; however, 22 000 m² are used, which means there has been an excess usage of 1000 m². The variance is expressed in monetary terms by multiplying the excess usage by the standard price per square metre. The material usage variance is therefore £3000 adverse (1000 m² × £3). In formula terms:

material usage variance

$$= \left(\begin{array}{c} \text{standard quantity for} \\ \text{actual production} \end{array} - \begin{array}{c} \text{actual quantity} \\ \text{used} \end{array} \right) \times \begin{array}{c} \text{standard} \\ \text{price} \end{array}$$

Note that standard price and not actual price is used. If the actual price is used the usage variance will be affected by the efficiency of the purchasing department, as any excess purchase price will be assigned to the excess usage. Multiplying by the standard price avoids any price effects being included in the usage variance calculation.

Note that the calculations of quantity variances should be based on the standard quantity required for actual production and not budgeted production. Basing the calculations on actual production ensures that you are following the principles of flexible budgeting.

The material usage variance is normally controllable by the production foreman. Common causes of material usage variances include excess wastage due to careless handling of materials by production personnel, changes in methods of production, pilferage and purchase of inferior quality materials.

Total material variance

It is unlikely that the examiner will require you to calculate total variances for labour, materials, overhead and sales. You should not waste time in calculating these variances. The total variances are presented to give you a better understanding of variance analysis.

This variance is the total variance before it is analysed into the price and usage elements. An output of 1400 units should cost £63 000 (1400 × £45) but the actual cost incurred was £88 000 (22 000 m^2 × £4), and therefore the variance is £25 000 adverse. The price variance of £22 000 plus the usage variance of £3000 agrees with the total variance. In formula terms:

total materials variance

= **standard cost for actual production − actual cost**

12.7 Labour variances

Wage rate variance

This variance is calculated by comparing the standard price per hour with the actual price paid per hour. The standard hourly wage rate is £4 and the actual hourly rate is £5, giving an adverse variance of £1 per hour. To determine the total amount of the variance the difference between the standard price and the actual price is multiplied by the number of labour hours worked. Therefore the total amount of the variance is £6800 adverse. The formula is:

wage rate variance

$$= \left(\begin{array}{c} \text{standard hourly} \\ \text{wage rate} \end{array} - \begin{array}{c} \text{actual hourly} \\ \text{wage rate} \end{array} \right) \times \textbf{actual hours worked}$$

The wage rate variance tends not to be subject to control by management. In most cases the variance is due to a negotiated increase in the wage rate which is not reflected in the standard wage rate. The variance may also be due to highly skilled labour being assigned to operations which are normally performed by unskilled workers. In this situation the variance can be regarded as controllable.

Labour efficiency variance

The labour efficiency variance compares the number of hours which should have been used with the actual number of hours worked. The standard time for producing one unit of the product is 5 hours. As 1400 units are produced, it should have taken 7000 hours (1400 units × 5 hours); however, 6800 hours were worked, which means that 200 hours were saved. The hours saved are multiplied by the standard wage rate to

The 7000 hours represents the standard hours produced.

calculate the variance. This gives a favourable variance of £800 (200 hours at £4). The formula is:

labour efficiency variance

$$= \left(\begin{array}{c} \text{standard hours for} \\ \text{actual production} \end{array} - \begin{array}{c} \text{actual hours} \\ \text{worked} \end{array} \right) \times \text{standard wage rate}$$

The labour efficiency variance is normally controllable by the departmental foreman. Possible causes include: use of different grades of labour or inferior materials; the introduction of new equipment or tools; failure to maintain machinery in proper condition; and changes in methods of production.

Total labour variance

An output of 1400 units should cost £28 000 (1400 × £20) but the actual cost incurred was £34 000 (6800 hours × £5). The variance is £6000 adverse, consisting of a £6800 adverse wage rate variance and a favourable labour efficiency variance of £800. The formula is:

total labour variance

$$= \textbf{standard cost for actual production} - \textbf{actual cost}$$

12.8 Fixed overhead variances

You will remember from Chapter 3 that predetermined overhead rates are used and that the fixed overhead rate is calculated as follows:

$$\text{fixed overhead rate} = \frac{\text{budgeted fixed overhead expenditure}}{\text{budgeted activity}}$$

If actual expenditure is different from budgeted expenditure, or if actual activity is different from budgeted activity, there will be an under/over-recovery of fixed overheads. The fixed overhead variance is equivalent to this under/over-recovery.

Details of budgeted fixed overhead expenditure and activity are required to calculate fixed overhead variances. Budgeted production is 1000 units. Therefore budgeted fixed overheads are £5000 (1000 units × £5) and budgeted activity is 5000 direct labour hours (1000 units × 5 hours). The budgeted fixed overhead rate is £1 per hour.

Total fixed overhead variance

Actual production is 1400 units or 7000 standard hours when measured in hours of output. The fixed overhead charged to production is £7000 (7000 hours at £1 per hour, or 1400 units at £5 per unit) and the actual fixed overheads incurred is £6000. This over-recovery of fixed overhead of £1000 represents the total fixed overhead variance. In formula terms:

You can calculate the total fixed overhead variance and the volume variance by measuring production in units produced or standard hours produced. Remember to use the fixed overhead rate per unit if you express output in units produced. Alternatively you should use the fixed overhead rate per hour if you measure output in standard hours produced.

total fixed overhead variance

$$= \frac{\text{standard fixed overhead cost}}{\text{for actual production}} - \frac{\text{actual fixed}}{\text{overheads}}$$

We have noted that the under/over-recovery of fixed overheads may be due to actual expenditure or activity being different from budget. These two reasons relate to the two sub-variances of the total fixed overhead variance – that is, the fixed overhead expenditure variance and the volume variance.

Fixed overhead expenditure variance

This variance is also called the fixed overhead spending variance.

This variance identifies that portion of the total fixed overhead variance which is due to the actual fixed overhead expenditure differing from the budgeted fixed overhead expenditure. The standard fixed overhead rate is calculated on the basis of budgeted fixed overhead expenditure of £5000, but actual fixed overhead expenditure is £6000. The fixed overhead expenditure variance is therefore £1000 adverse. In formula terms:

fixed overhead expenditure variance

= **budgeted fixed overheads − actual fixed overheads**

To ascertain the cause of this variance it is necessary to compare actual with budget for individual items of fixed overhead. Generally, the difference is likely to be due to a change in the market prices, and this variance is therefore likely to be uncontrollable.

Fixed overhead volume variance

This variance identifies that part of the total fixed overhead variance which is due to actual production being different from budgeted production. The budgeted fixed overhead rate is calculated on the basis of a budgeted production of 1000 units (or 5000 standard hours), but actual production is 1400 units (or 7000 standard hours). Because actual production is 400 units (or 2000 standard hours) greater than the budgeted production, an extra £2000 (400 units at £5 fixed overhead per unit, or 2000 standard hours at £1 fixed overhead rate per hour) fixed overheads will be recovered. The formula is:

volume variance

$$= \left(\begin{array}{c} \text{actual} \\ \text{production} \end{array} - \begin{array}{c} \text{budgeted} \\ \text{production} \end{array} \right) \times \textbf{standard fixed overhead rate}$$

When the favourable volume variance of £2000 is added to the adverse expenditure variance of £1000, the result is equal to the total fixed overhead favourable variance of £1000. *The reasons for the volume variance can be ascertained by analysing the variance into two further sub-variances – the volume efficiency and the capacity variances.*

Volume efficiency variance

This variance seeks to explain how much of the volume variance is due to the level of the labour efficiency being different from the level of efficiency anticipated in the budget. Actual direct labour hours are 6800, but actual production is 7000 standard hours. Consequently an additional 200 standard hours of output are produced and this has resulted in the absorption of an additional £200 fixed overheads. The formula is:

volume efficiency variance

$$= \left(\begin{array}{c}\text{standard hours for}\\ \text{actual production}\end{array} - \begin{array}{c}\text{actual hours}\\ \text{worked}\end{array}\right) \times \begin{array}{c}\text{standard fixed}\\ \text{overhead rate}\end{array}$$

Note that volume efficiency and variable overhead efficiency are based on labour efficiency. Consequently the same formula is used to calculate the labour, volume efficiency and variable overhead efficiency variances.

The reasons for this variance are the same as those described for the labour efficiency variance.

Volume capacity variance

The budget is based on the assumption that the direct labour hours of input will be 5000 hours, but actual hours of input are 6800 hours. The company has utilized an additional 1800 hours of capacity. Consequently an additional £1800 fixed overheads is absorbed. Hence the capacity variance is £1800 favourable. The formula is:

It is assumed that the additional 1800 hours of capacity used are utilized at the standard level of efficiency.

volume capacity variance

= (actual hours − budgeted hours) × standard fixed overhead rate

Possible reasons for an adverse capacity variance include material shortages, machine breakdowns, poor production scheduling and a reduction in sales demand.

Summary of fixed overhead variances

A summary of the fixed overhead variances is shown in Figure 12.1.

12.9 Variable overhead variances

Total variable overhead variance

The variable overhead expenses for an actual output of 1400 units should be £14 000 (1400 units × £10). Actual expenditure is £11 000, giving a favourable variance of £3000. The formula is:

total variable overhead variance

$$= \begin{array}{c}\text{standard variable overhead cost}\\ \text{for actual production}\end{array} - \begin{array}{c}\text{actual variable}\\ \text{overheads}\end{array}$$

The total variable overhead variance can be analysed into two sub-variances – the variable overhead expenditure variance and the variable overhead efficiency variance.

```
                    Total variance (£1000F)
                    ┌───────────┴───────────┐
              Expenditure              Volume
              variance                 variance
              (£1000A)                 (£2000F)
                                    ┌─────┴─────┐
                               Efficiency    Capacity
                                (£200F)      (£1800F)
```

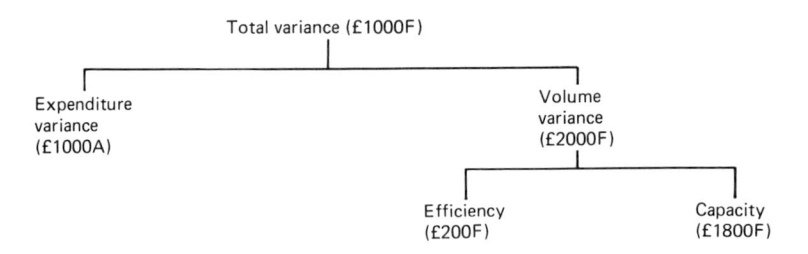

Figure 12.1 Summary of fixed overhead variances for Bronte Ltd (F favourable, A adverse)

Variable overhead expenditure variance

It is generally assumed that variable overheads vary with direct labour hours worked. Because spending will vary depending on activity, it is incorrect to compare actual spending with the original fixed budget. It is necessary to flex the budget on the basis of direct labour hours. Actual overhead spending is £11 000, resulting from 6800 direct labour hours. For this level of activity variable overheads of £13 600 (6800 direct labour hours at £2) should have been spent. Spending is £2600 less than budgeted for this activity level and this results in a favourable variance. The formula is:

variable overhead expenditure variance

= **budgeted flexed variable overheads − actual variable overheads**

To ascertain the reasons for the variance it is necessary to compare the flexed budget with the actual expenditure for each individual item of expense.

Variable overhead efficiency variance

This variance arises because 7000 direct labour hours should have been used to produce 1400 units of output, but only 6800 hours were actually worked. Because variable overheads are assumed to vary with hours worked, the saving of 200 hours should reduce variable overhead spending by £400 (200 hours at £2). The formula is:

variable overhead efficiency variance

$$= \left(\begin{array}{c} \text{standard hours for} \\ \text{actual production} \end{array} - \begin{array}{c} \text{actual hours} \\ \text{worked} \end{array} \right) \times \begin{array}{c} \text{standard variable} \\ \text{overhead} \end{array}$$

The reasons for the variance will be the same as those described for the labour efficiency variance.

12.10 Sales margin variances

Note that the sales variances are calculated in terms of profit margins and not sales values.

Sales variances are not part of the syllabus for some examining bodies. You should check whether or not sales variances are included in the syllabus for the examinations for which you are studying.

Total sales margin variance

This variance explains the influence which the sales function has on the difference between budgeted and actual profit. The budgeted profit is £20 000 (1000 units at a profit per unit of £20). This is compared with the profit from the actual sales volume of 1200 units. Because the sales function is accountable for sales revenue but not manufacturing costs, the standard cost of sales and not the actual cost of sales is deducted from the actual sales revenue. Therefore for the purpose of calculating the total sales margin variance the actual profit calculation is:

actual sales (1200 units at £102)
  − standard cost of sales (1200 units at £80) = £26 400

The total variance is therefore £6400 favourable. The formula is:

total sales margin variance

  = **actual profit − standard profit**

It is possible to analyse the total sales margin variance into two sub-variances − a sales margin price variance and a sales margin volume variance.

Sales margin price variance

The actual selling price is £102 and the budgeted selling price is £100. With a standard unit cost of £80, the change in selling price has led to an increase in profit margin from £20 to £22 per unit. Multiplying by the actual sales volume of 1200 units gives a favourable sales margin price variance of £2400. The formula for calculating the variance is:

sales margin price variance

  = **(actual profit margin − standard profit margin) × actual sales volume**

Sales margin volume variance

Budgeted sales are 1000 units but actual sales are 1200 units. The extra sales generates an additional profit of £4000 (200 units × £20 profit margin). Note that the standard margin is used so that the variance is not affected by any changes in the selling price. The formula is:

sales margin volume variance

  = $\left(\begin{array}{c}\text{actual sales} \\ \text{volume}\end{array} - \begin{array}{c}\text{budgeted sales} \\ \text{volume}\end{array}\right)$ × **standard profit margin**

Note that standard cost is deducted from both the budget and actual selling prices in order to calculate budgeted and actual profit margins. Deducting standard cost ensures that the production variances do not distort the sales variances. An alternative formula for calculating the sales margin price variance is:

Sales margin price variance = (actual selling price − budgeted selling price) × actual sales volume

12.11 Reconciliation of budgeted and actual profits

The actual profit for Bronte Ltd for the period is calculated as follows:

	£	£
Sales (1200 units × £102)		122 400
Production costs: Materials	88 000	
Labour	34 000	
Fixed overhead	6 000	
Variable overhead	11 000	
	139 000	
less Closing stock at standard cost	16 000	123 000
Actual loss		(600)

Note that the closing stock is valued at standard cost. Therefore the variances are charged as an expense in the current accounting period and not included in the stock valuation.

The reconciliation of the budgeted and the actual profit is as follows:

	Adverse £	Favourable £	£
Budgeted profit			20 000
Sales margin price		2 400	
Sales margin volume		4 000	
Material price	22 000		
Material usage	3 000		
Wage rate	6 800		
Labour efficiency		800	
Fixed overhead expenditure	1 000		
Fixed overhead efficiency		200	
Fixed overhead capacity		1 800	
Variable overhead expenditure		2 600	
Variable overhead efficiency		400	
	32 800	12 200	
Net adverse variance			20 600
Actual profit (loss)			(600)

Note that the reconciliation indicates that the material price and wage rate variances have significantly reduced the profit. These variances should be investigated, but the differences are likely to be due to an increase in the market price of materials and labour.

12.12 Control ratios

It can be argued that it is not very meaningful to measure the fixed overhead volume variance and the volume sub-variances in monetary terms. This is because fixed overhead expenditure has already been incurred and fixed overhead spending will not change because of changes in efficiency and capacity. It may be preferable to restate the three variances in non-monetary terms using the following control ratios:

$$\text{production volume ratio} = \frac{\text{standard hours of actual output (7000)}}{\text{budgeted hours of output (5000)}} \times 100$$

$$= 140 \text{ per cent}$$

$$\text{efficiency ratio} = \frac{\text{standard hours of actual output (7000)}}{\text{actual hours worked (6800)}} \times 100$$

$$= 102.9 \text{ per cent}$$

$$\text{capacity ratio} = \frac{\text{actual hours worked (6800)}}{\text{budgeted hours of input (5000)}} \times 100$$

$$= 136 \text{ per cent}$$

These ratios can be interpreted in the same way as their equivalent monetary variances.

12.13 Accounting entries for a standard costing system

The previous question is used to illustrate the accounting entries.

The ledger accounts are shown at the end of this section. The following abbreviations are used:

AQ	actual quantity
AP	actual price
SP	standard price
SQ	standard quantity

Purchase of materials

	£	£
DR stores ledger control account (AQ × SP)	66 000	
DR material price variance account	22 000	
CR creditors control account (AQ × AP)		88 000

Usage of materials

	£	£
DR WIP (SQ × SP)	63 000	
DR material usage variance	3 000	
CR stores ledger control account (AQ × SP)		66 000

Direct labour

The actual wages cost is initially recorded:

	£	£
DR wages control account	34 000	
CR wages accrued account		34 000

The wages control account is cleared as follows:

DR WIP (SQ × SP)	28 000	
CR wages control account		28 000
DR wage rate variance	6 800	
CR labour efficiency variance		800
CR wages control account		6 000

You can see that the wages control account is initially debited with the actual cost. The standard cost is credited and the WIP control account is debited. The difference between the actual cost and standard cost in the wages control account represents the sum of the wage rate and labour efficiency variances. The difference is transferred to the appropriate variance accounts.

Manufacturing overhead

The actual overhead incurred is initially recorded:

	£	£
DR factory fixed overhead control account	6 000	
DR factory variable overhead control account	11 000	
CR expense creditors		17 000

The manufacturing fixed overhead control account is cleared as follows:

DR WIP control account (SQ × SP)	7 000	
CR factory fixed overhead control account		7 000
DR fixed overhead expenditure variance account	1 000	
CR volume variance account		2 000
DR factory fixed overhead control account	1 000	

You will see that the standard fixed overhead cost of £7000 is credited to the fixed factory overhead control account. The difference between the actual overheads of £6000 and the standard fixed overhead costs of £7000 represents the sum of the expenditure and volume variances. The difference is transferred to the appropriate variance accounts.

The variable fixed overhead control account is cleared as follows:

DR WIP control account (SQ × SP)	14 000	
CR factory variable overhead account		14 000
DR factory variable overhead control account	3 000	
CR variable overhead expenditure account		2 600
CR variable overhead efficiency account		400

Completion of production

You can see that the total amount recorded on the debit side of the WIP account is £112 000. This represents 1400 completed units at a standard cost per unit of £80. The WIP is transferred to finished goods stock (DR finished goods stock and CR WIP).

Sales

Actual sales are recorded in the accounts and therefore sales variances are not recorded. The cost of goods sold consists of 1200 units at a standard cost of £80. This is recorded in the accounts by debiting the cost of sales and crediting the finished goods stock account. The closing stock of 200 units is shown as a closing balance in the finished goods stock account.

Calculation of profit

You can see that the standard cost of sales and the net total of adverse variances are transferred to the costing profit and loss account. Actual sales are credited and the difference represents the profit (loss) for the period.

The ledger accounts are as follows.

Ledger accounting entries for a standard costing system

Stores ledger control account

Creditors	66 000	WIP	63 000
		Material usage variance	3 000
	66 000		66 000

WIP control account

Stores ledger	63 000	Finished goods stock	112 000
Wages control	28 000		
Fixed factory overhead	7 000		
Variable factory overhead	14 000		
	112 000		112 000

Wages control account

Wages accrued account	34 000	WIP	28 000
Labour efficiency variance	800	Wager rate variance	6 800
	34 800		34 800

Fixed factory overhead account

Expense creditors	6 000	WIP	7 000
Volume variance	2 000	Expenditure variance	1 000
	8 000		8 000

Variable factory overhead account

Expense creditors	11 000	WIP	14 000
Expenditure variance	2 600		
Efficiency variance	400		
	14 000		14 000

Finished goods stock

WIP	112 000	Cost of sales	96 000
		Closing stock C/F	16 000
	112 000		112 000

Cost of sales account

Finished goods stock	96 000	Costing P & L A/C	96 000

Variance accounts

Creditors	22 000	Wages control (labour efficiency)	800
Stores ledger (material usage)	3 000	Fixed overhead (volume)	2 000
Wages control (wage rate)	6 800	Variable overhead (expenditure)	2 600
Fixed overhead (expenditure)	1 000	Variable overhead (efficiency)	400
		Costing P & L A/C (balance)	27 000
	32 800		32 800

Costing P & L account

Cost of sales	96 000	Sales	122 400
Variance account (net variances)	27 000	Loss for period	600
	123 000		123 000

Part Three
Past Examination Questions and Worked Answers

Questions for Chapter 1

1.1
Mrs Johnston has taken out a lease on a shop for a down payment of £5000. Additionally, the rent under the lease amounts to £5000 per annum. If the lease is cancelled, the initial payment of £5000 is forfeit. Mrs Johnston plans to use the shop for the sale of clothing, and has estimated operations for the next twelve months as follows:

	£	£
Sales	115 000	
less Value added tax (VAT)	15 000	
		100 000
Cost of goods sold	50 000	
Wages and wage-related costs	12 000	
Rent including the down payment	10 000	
Rates, heating, lighting and insurance	13 000	
Audit, legal and general expenses	2 000	
		87 000
Net profit before tax		13 000

In the figures no provision has been made for the cost of Mrs Johnston, but it is estimated that one half of her time will be devoted to the business. She is undecided whether to continue with her plans because she knows that she can sub-let the shop to a friend for a monthly rent of £550 if she does not use the shop herself.

You are required to:

(a) (i) Explain and identify the 'sunk' and 'opportunity' costs in the situation depicted above;
    (ii) State what decision Mrs Johnston should make according to the information given, supporting your conclusion with a financial statement; (11 marks)
(b) Explain the meaning and use of 'notional' (or 'imputed') costs and quote *two* supporting examples. (4 marks)

(CIMA Foundation Cost Accounting 1, May 1985)

For an explanation of sunk and opportunity costs see section 1.5. Note that the £5000 sunk cost is not included in the opportunity cost calculation. However, a further rental payment of £5000 will be necessary if the shop is sub-let, and this future cash outlay must be included in the opportunity cost calculation.

Answer

(a) (i) The down payment of £5000 represents a sunk cost. This payment represents the cost of a resource which has already been acquired. Hence this cost will be unaffected by the choice between the various alternatives. If Mrs Johnston runs the shop she will forgo a contribution of £1600 per annum ((£550 × 12) − £5000). This represents the benefit sacrified (that is, the opportunity cost) if the shop is used for the sale of clothing.

(ii) The relevant information for running the shop is:

	£
Net sales	100 000
Costs (£87 000 − £5000 sunk cost)	82 000
	18 000
Less opportunity cost from sub-letting	1 600
Profit	16 400

This calculation indicates that £16 400 additional profits will be obtained from using the shop for the sale of clothing. It is assumed that Mrs Johnston will not suffer any other loss of income if she devotes half her time to running the shop.

(b) The CIMA terminology defines a notional cost as 'a hypothetical cost taken into account in a particular situation to represent a benefit enjoyed by an entity in respect of which no actual expense is incurred'. Examples of notional costs include:
(i) Interest on capital to represent the notional cost of using an asset rather than investing the capital elsewhere
(ii) Including rent as a cost for premises owned by the company so as to represent the lost rent income resulting from using the premises for business purposes.

1.2
(a) Describe the role of the cost accountant in a manufacturing organization. (8 marks)
(b) Explain whether you agree with each of the following statements:
  (i) 'All direct costs are variable.'
  (ii) 'Variable costs are controllable and fixed costs are not.'
  (iii) 'Sunk costs are irrelevant when providing decision-making information.' (9 marks)
(CACA Level 1 Costing, December 1984)

Answer
(a) Your answer should stress that the cost accountant provides financial information for stock valuation purposes and also presents relevant information to management for decision-making and planning and cost control purposes. Financial accounting requires that we match costs with revenues to calculate profit. Therefore any unsold finished

goods stock or WIP must be deducted from production costs so as to calculate the cost of sales. In an organization which produces a wide range of different products or jobs it will be necessary, for stock valuation purposes, to charge the costs to each individual job. The total value of the stocks of completed jobs and WIP plus any unused raw materials forms the basis for the stock valuation to be deducted from the current period's costs when calculating profits. Costs are therefore allocated to each individual job or product to provide the necessary information for financial accounting reports.

The cost accountant also assists management in their planning and decision-making activities. Because decisions are concerned with future events, management requires estimates of the relevant future costs and revenues of alternative courses of action, for example: What would be the effect on profits if we reduce our selling price and sell more units? Should we manufacture a component internally or should we purchase it from an outside supplier? By providing relevant financial information on alternative courses of action the cost accountant can help managers to make better decisions. Budgeting is the process by which decisions are implemented. The cost accountant is responsible for establishing budget procedures, assisting managers in preparing the budgets and co-ordinating the budgets to ensure that they are in harmony with each other.

The accountant also assists management in controlling the activities for which they are responsible by providing comparisons of actual expenditure with budgeted expenditure so that deviations from the budget can be immediately identified and corrective action taken.

Note that actual expenses are compared with budgeted expenses for various expense categories. This enables managers to identify trouble spots and frees them from an unnecessary concern with those expenses which are adhering to the plans. The process of concentrating action only on those activities which are not proceeding according to plan is called management by exception.

(b) (i) Direct costs are those costs which can be traced to a cost objective. If the cost objective is a sales territory then *fixed* salaries of salesmen will be a direct cost. Alternatively, if the cost objective is a product then the hire of machinery used exclusively in the manufacture of that product would be a direct cost. Therefore the statement is incorrect.

(ii) Whether a fixed cost is controllable depends on the level of authority and time span being considered. For example, a departmental foreman may have no control over the number of supervisors employed in his department, but this decision may be made by his superior. In the long term such costs are controllable by the superior.

(iii) This statement is correct; see 'sunk costs' in Section 1.5 (Chapter 1) for an explanation of why this statement is correct.

1.3
(a) Explain what you understand by the term 'cost behaviour', why it is important in the context of cost and management accounting, and what behaviour patterns may be encountered. (8 marks)
(b) What factors influence the behaviour of costs in response to changes in an organization's level of activity? (9 marks)
(CACA Level 1 Costing, June 1986)

Answer

(a) The term 'cost behaviour' refers to the relationship between changes in the level of activity and changes in total costs. An awareness of how costs change in response to changes in activity is important for decision-making and cost control. For example, decisions on whether to expand or reduce capacity or to reduce selling prices in order to increase demand requires estimates of costs and revenues at different activity levels. For cost control it is necessary to compare actual costs estimated costs at different activity levels. This process is called flexible budgeting.

Cost behaviour patterns which may be encountered include variable costs, fixed costs, semi-variable costs and semi-fixed costs. You will find an explanation of these cost behaviour patterns in Section 1.5.

(b) Factors which influence cost behaviour include:

Level of activity in relation to available capacity If the firm is operating at very low levels of activity then it may not be obtaining the full benefits of bulk purchasing discounts and the division of labour. Expansion of output may enable the firm to obtain economies of scale and thus reduce unit variable costs. On the other hand, if a firm is operating at near full capacity an expansion of output might result in the purchase of additional plant and machinery, thus increasing fixed costs.

Level of capital employed The greater the level of capital intensity the greater will be the proportion of fixed costs as an element of total costs.

Redundancy policy The policy regarding redundancy of labour when output declines will determine whether labour will be a variable or a fixed cost. If the policy is to maintain a stable labour force then labour costs will be predominantly fixed.

Management decisions A large proportion of non-manufacturing costs are of a discretionary nature. In respect of such costs management has some significant range of discretion as to the amount it will spend for the particular activity in question. An example of a discretionary cost is advertising. Management policy might be to spend a fixed amount on advertising. Alternatively the policy might be to spend a fixed percentage of sales revenue. If this policy is adopted advertising will vary with sales revenue.

Period under consideration In the long run all costs are variable, whereas in the short run a large proportion of costs will be fixed.

Questions for Chapter 2

2.1
(a) It has been said that the LIFO method of charging stock items to production is the best method since it is always related as closely as possible to current price levels.

Note that in addition to Chapter 1 this question requires a knowledge of cost-volume-profit analysis (see Chapter 8) and flexible budgeting (see Chapter 11). You are therefore recommended to read Chapters 1, 8 and 11 prior to answering this question.

(i) Discuss the above statement by describing the application of LIFO in stores accounting.
(ii) How does this conform to current accountancy practice?
(11 marks)

(b) The controller of an organization is convinced that inefficiencies are occurring in the management of the stocks and has called upon you for advice, requesting a prompt reply.

The principal item of stock is a small electric motor, and you ascertain the following for last month:

Unit cost	£5
Opening stock counted by stores staff	200 units
Closing stock counted by you	300 units
Creditors at beginning of month	£2500
Creditors at end of month	£1500
Amount paid to creditors during month	£6500
Issues recorded during month	£4500

Draft a reply to the controller showing your calculations and conclusions.
(11 marks)
(AAT, June 1985)

Answer

(a) You will find the answer to this question in Section 2.3. Your answer should illustrate that issues based on LIFO are more closely related than FIFO and average prices to current prices. In the second part of your answer you should stress that SSAP 9 states that LIFO is unacceptable for financial accounting.

(b) *Calculation of purchases*
Creditors account:

	£		£
Cash paid	6500	Opening balance	2500
Closing balance	1500	Purchases (difference)	5500
	8000		8000

1100 units of £5 were purchased during the month.

Report content

The report should indicate that opening stock of 200 units plus purchases of 1100 units less issues of 900 units should result in a closing stock of 400 units. The actual closing stock count is 300 units, thus resulting in a loss of 100 units. The report should explain possible reasons for the stock loss and draw attention to the fact that the loss may have occurred in an earlier period. The report should stress the need for a system of perpetual inventory – that is, a system which involves the recording of each stock movement on a bin card or computerized record so that the balance of every item in stock is always available. Materials should be issued only against a stores requisition which is countersigned by authorized personnel. The materials should be stored in a secure location which minimizes the possibility of theft. At frequent intervals stocks should be counted and compared with book records. Any differences should be investigated and causes ascertained.

2.2

On 1 January Mr G started a small business buying and selling a special yarn. He invested his savings of £40 000 in the business and, during the next six months, the following transactions occurred:

Yarn purchases

Date of receipt	Quantity boxes	Total cost £
13 January	200	7 200
8 February	400	15 200
11 March	600	24 000
12 April	400	14 000
15 June	500	14 000

Yarn sales

Date of despatch	Quantity boxes	Total value £
10 February	500	25 000
20 April	600	27 000
25 June	400	15 200

The yarn is stored in premises that Mr G has rented, and the closing stock of yarn, counted on 30 June, was 500 boxes.

Other expenses incurred, and paid in cash, during the six-month period amounted to £2300.

You are required to
(a) Calculate the value of the material issues during the six-month period, and the value of the closing stock at the end of June, using the following methods of pricing:
  (i) First in, first out
  (ii) Last in, first out
  (iii) Weighted average (calculations to two decimal places only).
(10 marks)
(b) Calculate and discuss the effect that each of the three methods of material pricing will have on the reported profit of the business, and examine the performance of the business during the first six-month period. (12 marks)
(CACA Level 1 Costing, June 1984)

Answer

(a) FIFO

2100 boxes were purchased and 1500 boxes were issued to production, leaving a balance of 600 boxes. Actual closing stock is 500 boxes, resulting in a stock loss of 100 boxes. The closing stock will be valued at the latest purchase price, i.e. £28 per unit (£14 000/500):

Closing stock valuation = £14 000 (500 × £28)
Cost of sales (including stock loss) = £60 400
  (total purchase cost £74 400 − £14 000)

If the question does not require you to prepare a stores ledger account, you are recommended for the FIFO method to follow the approach shown in this answer. First calculate the closing stock in units. With the FIFO method the closing stock will be valued at the latest purchase prices. You can calculate the cost of sales as follows: cost of sales = opening stock + purchases − closing stock

LIFO

Date	Issue	Cost £
10 February	400 units	15 200
	100 units at £7200/200	3 600
		18 800
20 April	400 units	14 000
	200 units at £24 000/600	8 000
		22 000
25 June	400 units at £14 000/500	11 200
30 June	100 units (stock loss) at £14 000/500	2 800
	Total cost of issues	54 800

Closing stock = purchase cost £74 400 − issue cost £54 800
            = £19 600

The weighted average issue price is calculated by dividing the total amount in stock by the total quantity in stock. For example, the issue price on 8 February is calculated by dividing £22 400 by 600 boxes.

Weighted average method

	Receipts			Issues			Closing balance	
Date	Quantity	Total cost	Date	Quantity	Total cost	Quantity	Cost	Weighted at issue price
	boxes	£		boxes	£	boxes	£	£
13 January	200	7 200				200	7 200	36.00
8 February	400	15 200				600	22 400	37.33
			10 February	500 at £37.33	18 665	100	3 735	37.35
11 March	600	24 000				700	27 735	39.62
12 April	400	14 000				1100	41 735	37.94
			20 April	600 at £37.94	22 764	500	18 971	37.94
15 June	500	14 000				1000	32 971	32.97
			25 June	400 at £32.97	13 188	600	19 783	32.97
			30 June	100 at £32.97	3 297	500	16 486	32.97
					57 914			

(b) *Profit calculations*

	FIFO £	LIFO £	Weighted average £
Sales	67 200	67 200	67 200
Cost of sales and stock loss	(60 400)	(54 800)	(57 914)
Other expenses	(2 300)	(2 300)	(2 300)
Profit	4 500	10 100	6 986

The purchase cost per box is £36 (January), £38 (February), £40 (March), £35 (April) and £28 (June).

The use of FIFO results in the lowest profit because prices are falling and the higher earlier prices are charged to production, whereas with LIFO the later and lower prices are charged to production. The use of the weighted average method results in a profit calculation between these two extremes. There are two items of concern regarding the performance of the business:

(i) The large purchase at the highest purchase price in March. This purchase could have been delayed until April so as to take advantage of the lower price.
(ii) The stock loss should be investigated. A materials control procedure should be implemented.

2.3
You have been approached for your advice on the proposed introduction of an incentive scheme for the direct operatives in the final production department of a factory producing one standard product. This department, the finishing shop, employs 30 direct operatives, all of whom are paid £3 per hour for a basic 40 hour week, with a guaranteed wage of £120 per week. When necessary, overtime is worked up to a maximum of 15 hours per week per operative and is paid at time rate plus one-half. It is the opinion of the personnel manager that no more direct operatives could be recruited for this department.

An analysis of recent production returns from the finishing shop indicate that the current average output is approximately 6 units of the standard product per productive man hour. The work study manager has conducted an appraisal of the working methods in the finishing shop and suggests that it would be reasonable to expect operatives to process 8 units of the product per man hour and that a piecework scheme be introduced in which the direct operatives are paid 55p for each unit processed. It is anticipated that, when necessary, operatives would continue to work overtime up to the previously specified limit, although as the operatives would be on piecework no premium would be paid.

Next year's budgeted production for the factory varies from a minimum of 7000 units per week to a maximum of 12 000 units per week, with the most frequent budgeted weekly output being 9600 units. The expected selling price of the product next year is £10 per unit and the budgeted variable production cost of the incomplete product passed into the finishing shop amounts to £8 per unit. Variable production overheads in the finishing shop, excluding the overtime premium of the direct operatives, are budgeted to be £0.48 per direct labour hour worked, and it is considered that variable overheads do vary directly with productive hours worked. Direct material costs are not incurred by the finishing shop. The fixed overheads incurred by the factory amount in total to £9000 per week.

Stocks of work in progress and finished goods are not carried.

You are required to:

(a) Calculate the effect on the company's budgeted weekly profits of the proposed incentive scheme in the finishing shop. Calculations should be to the nearest £. (15 marks)

(b) Explain the reasons for the changes in the weekly budgeted profits caused by the proposed incentive scheme. (7 marks)
(CACA Level 1 Costing, December 1984)

Answer
(a) Current average maximum production = 30 × 55 h × 6 units
= 9900 units
Proposed maximum production = 30 × 55 h × 8 units
= 13 200 units

Existing payment system

Output levels (units)	7 000	9 600	9 900
	£	£	£
Sales value (£10 per unit)	70 000	96 000	99 000
Pre-finishing VC	56 000	76 800	79 200
Direct labour:			
Guaranteed (30 × £120)	3 600	3 600	3 600
Overtime (W1)	–	1 800	2 025
Variable overhead (W2)	560	768	792
Fixed overhead	9 000	9 000	9 000
Total cost	69 160	91 968	94 617
Profit	840	4 032	4 383

For the existing incentive scheme, information should be presented for the minimum (7000 units), most frequent (9600 units) and maximum output levels. Note that maximum output is 9900 units for the existing incentive scheme. For the proposed incentive scheme the maximum output is 13 200 units but maximum sales demand is 12 000 units. You should therefore present information for 7000 9600 and 12 000 units. Information is also presented for the previous maximum output level of 9900 units, but it is not essential that you calculate profits for this level of output.

Proposed scheme

Output levels (units)	7 000	9 600	9 900	12 000
	£	£	£	£
Sales value	£70 000	£96 000	£99 000	£120 000
Pre-finishing VC	56 000	76 800	79 200	96 000
Direct labour at				
£0.55 per unit	3 850	5 280	5 445	6 600
Variable overhead (W3)	420	576	594	720
Fixed overhead	9 000	9 000	9 000	9 000
Total cost	69 270	91 656	94 239	112 320
Profit	730	4 344	4 761	7 680

Workings
(W1) 9600 units requires 1600 hrs (9600/6):
hence overtime = 400 h × £4.50
9900 units requires 1650 hrs (9900/6):
hence overtime = 450 h × £4.50
Basic hrs = 1200 hours (30 operatives at 40 hours per week)
(W2) 7000 units = 7000/6 × £0.48
9600 units = 9600/6 × £0.48
9900 units = 9900/6 × £0.48

(W3) 7000 units = 7000/8 × 0.48
9600 units = 9600/8 × £0.48
9900 units = 9900/8 × £0.48
12 000 units = 12 000/8 × £0.48

(b) At low output levels the average wage rate per unit is £0.50 (£3/6 hours) compared with £0.55 with the incentive scheme. However, once overtime is worked the wage rate per unit of output is £0.75 (£4.50/6) compared with £0.55 per unit under the incentive scheme. Overtime starts at 7200 units (1200 hours × 6 units). Hence savings will increase with the incentive scheme beyond 7200 units.

Variable overheads vary with productive hours. Therefore variable overhead per *unit* will be £0.08 (£0.48/6) under the old scheme and £0.06 per unit under the new scheme (£0.48/8).

The proposed incentive scheme will also enable the maximum output level to be achieved, thus enabling maximum sales demand to be achieved.

2.4

(a) Shown below is a summary of the previous week's payroll data for the moulding department in Peal PLC, a company manufacturing two different types of telephone receiver:

	Direct workers	*Indirect workers*
Hours worked:		
Ordinary time	3600 hours	800 hours
Overtime	630 hours	80 hours
Basic hourly rate of pay	£3.60	£2.10
Net wages paid	£12 864	£1420
Analysis of direct workers' time:		
Productive time:		
Type 1 receiver: 4800 units	2400 hours	
Type 2 receiver: 1500 units	1125 hours	
Non-productive down time	705 hours	

The moulding department employs 90 direct and 20 indirect operatives. All operatives are paid at hourly time rates; overtime, which is regularly worked to meet budgeted production targets, is paid at time rate plus one-third.

The company operates a batch costing system, using actual costs, which is fully integrated with the financial accounts.

You are required to construct the moulding department's wages control account for the previous week, *clearly* indicating the accounts into which the corresponding entries would be posted. (9 marks)

(b) The works manager of Peal PLC is considering introducing a piecework incentive scheme for the direct workers in the moulding department. Work study services have examined the manufacturing process in the moulding department, and consider that the operation to produce type 1 receivers should be performed under normal conditions by one operative in 24 minutes; for a type 2 receiver the corresponding time is 36 minutes. Unavoidable non-productive down time is expected to remain at approximately 20 per cent of productive time.

Having considered the above times, the works manager suggests that direct operatives should be paid a piecerate of £1.90 for each type 1 receiver produced and £2.85 for each type 2 receiver produced, and that non-productive down time should be paid at £2.50 per hour.

As the accountant of Peal PLC you have been asked to appraise the above scheme. It should be assumed that the previous week's payroll data shown in (a) represents an average week in the moulding department – although the weekly volume of production and consequent wages do fluctuate around this mean figure. No further information has been provided.

You are required to

(i) Examine the effect of the proposed scheme on the labour costs in the moulding department. Any assumptions you consider necessary should be clearly stated. (7 marks)
(ii) Briefly discuss any additional considerations which would need to be thoroughly examined before the feasibility of the proposed incentive scheme could be finally assessed. (6 marks)
(CACA Level 1 Costing, June 1982)

Answer
(a) *Calculation of gross wages*

	Direct £	Indirect £
Ordinary hours	15 228 (4230 × £3.60)	1848 (880 × £2.10)
Overtime premium	756 [630 × (1/3) × £3.60]	56 [80 × (1/3) × £2.10]
	15 984	1904

Total wages = £17 888 (£15 984 + £1904)

Allocation of gross wages	£
Direct workers production time: 3525 hours (2400 + 1125) at £3.60	12 690
Direct workers' non-production down time: 705 hours at £3.60	2 538
Direct workers' overtime premium	756
Indirect workers' gross wages	1 904
Wages charged to production overhead	5 198

Note that 4230 hours are worked by the direct operatives (3600 + 630). The question indicates that 3525 hours (2400 + 1125) were allocated to production and the balance of 705 hours was allocated to non-productive down time.

Gross wages are £17 888 and net wages are £12 864. The difference of £3604 represents deductions in respect of PAYE and National Insurance. This difference of £3604 is debited to the wages control account and credited to an expense creditors account for employees' deductions. You will find an explanation of the double entry procedure in Chapter 4.

Wages control account

	£		£
Cash (net wages paid as in question)	12 864	WIP A/C	12 690
	1 420	Production overhead A/C	5 198
Employees' deduction account (balance)	3 604		
	17 888		17 888

(b) (i) The effect of the proposed scheme is examined by comparing the previous week's earnings for the direct workers with the earnings that would have been earned if the proposed scheme had been in operation:

Proposed scheme:	£
Type 1 receiver (4800 units at £1.90)	9 120
Type 2 receiver (1500 units at £2.85)	4 275
Non-productive down time (see calculation below)	1 410
	14 805

Present scheme
Direct wages paid as in (a)   £15 984

Calculation of allowed hours for the previous week's production:

Type 1	4800 units × 24 minutes	1920 hours
Type 2	1500 units × 36 minutes	900 hours
		2820 hours

Non-productive down time
= 20% × 2820 hours × £2.50 = £1410.

Conclusion
It appears that the proposed incentive scheme will reduce the wages cost, but the factors outlined in (b)(ii) must be examined before a final decision is made. The above analysis assumes that the company will pay only for the hours worked by the direct operatives. If hours which are surplus to requirements are paid then the results of the proposed scheme should be adjusted as follows:

	hours
Total productive hours as in (i)	2820
Allowance for non-productive time (20%)	564
	3384
Ordinary time for direct operatives	3600
Shortfall	216

Assuming that the 216 hours are paid at £2.50 or £3.60, then the cost of the incentive scheme will be increased by the appropriate amount. However, the proposed scheme is still cheaper than the present scheme.

(ii) Additional factors to be examined are:

How will any surplus labour capacity (as in (b)(i)) be dealt with?

Will the opportunity for the direct workers to earn a higher wage be a source of grievance with the indirect workers and workers in other departments?

Will product quality be affected?

Will less supervision be required?

Will the scheme result in increased administration costs?

Will future output be significantly increased, and can it be sold? An estimate of future output with the incentive scheme and output without the incentive scheme is required. Cost and revenue comparisons should then be made for the different output levels.

Questions for Chapter 3

3.1

A company is preparing its production overhead budgets and determining the apportionment of these overheads to products.

Cost centre expenses and related information have been budgeted as follows:

	Total	Machine shop A	Machine shop B	Assembly	Canteen	Maintenance
Indirect wages (£)	78 560	8 586	9 190	15 674	29 650	15 460
Consumable materials (incl. maintenance) (£)	16 900	6 400	8 700	1 200	600	–
Rent and rates (£)	16 700					
Buildings insurance (£)	2 400					
Power (£)	8 600					
Heat and light (£)	3 400					
Depreciation of machinery (£)	40 200					
Area (ft^2)	45 000	10 000	12 000	15 000	6 000	2 000
Value of machinery (£)	402 000	201 000	179 000	22 000	–	–
Power usage: technical estimates (%)	100	55	40	3	–	2
Direct labour (hours)	35 000	8 000	6 200	20 800	–	–
Machine usage (hours)	25 200	7 200	18 000	–	–	–

You are required to:

(a) Determine budgeted overhead absorption rates for each of the production departments, using bases of apportionment and absorption which you consider most appropriate from the information provided. (13 marks)

(b) On the assumption that actual activity was:

	Machine shop A	Machine shop B	Assembly
Direct labour hours	8200	6 500	21 900
Machine usage hours	7300	18 700	–

and total production overhead expenditure was £176 533, prepare the production overhead control account for the year (you are to assume that the company has a separate cost accounting system). (6 marks)

(c) Explain the meaning of the word 'control' in the title of the account prepared in answer to (b). (3 marks)

(CACA Level 1 Costing, June 1986)

Answer

(a) *Overhead analysis*

Overhead	Basis of apportionment	Total £	Machine shop A £	Machine shop B £	Assembly £	Canteen £	Maintenance £
Indirect wages	Actual	78 560	8 586	9 190	15 674	29 650	15 460
Consumable materials	Actual	16 900	6 400	8 700	1 200	600	–
Rent and rates		16 700					
Building insurance	Area	2 400	5 000	6 000	7 500	3 000	1 000
Heat and light		3 400					
Power	Technical estimate	8 600	4 730	3 440	258	–	172
Depreciation	Value of machinery	40 200	20 100	17 900	2 200	–	–
		166 760	44 816	45 230	26 832	33 250	16 632
Maintenance	Machine usage hours		4 752	11 880			(16 632)
Canteen	DLHs		7 600	5 890	19 760	(33 250)	
		166 760	57 168	63 000	46 592		
Machine usage hours			7 200	18 000			
Direct labour hours					20 800		
Machine hour rate (£)			7.94	3.50			
Direct labour hour rate (£)					2.24		

Where the same basis of apportionment is used for different items of expense you can save time by merging them together and apportioning them in one calculation. For example, rent and rates, building insurance and heat and light are added together and apportioned on the basis of area.

Note that canteen and maintenance are service departments.

(b) It will be necessary to read Chapter 4 before you can answer this question.

Production overhead control account

	£		£
Cost ledger control account	176 533	WIP: overhead absorbed	
		Machine shop A (7300 × £7.94)	57 962
		Machine shop B (18 700 × £3.50)	65 450
		Assembly (21 900 × £2.24)	49 056
			172 468
		Under-absorbed overhead transferred to P & L account	4 065
	176 533		176 533

(c) For the answer to this question see Section 4.2.

3.2
AC Limited is a small company which undertakes a variety of jobs for its customers.

Budgeted profit and loss statement for year ending 31 December 1986

	£	£
Sales		750 000
Costs:		
Direct materials	100 000	
Direct wages	50 000	
Prime cost	150 000	
Fixed production overhead	300 000	
Production cost	450 000	
Selling, distribution and administration cost	160 000	610 000
Profit		£140 000

Budgeted data:
Labour hours for the year	25 000
Machine hours for the year	15 000
Number of jobs for the year	300

An enquiry has been received and the production department has produced estimates of the prime cost involved and of the hours required to complete job A57:

	£
Direct materials	250
Direct wages	200
Prime cost	£450
Labour hours required	80
Machine hours required	50

You are required to:

(a) Calculate by different methods *six* overhead absorption rates;
(6 marks)
(b) Comment briefly on the suitability of each method calculated in (a);
(8 marks)
(c) Calculate cost estimates for job A57 using in turn each of the six overhead absorption rates calculated in (a). (6 marks)
(CIMA Foundation Cost Accounting 1, November 1985)

Answer

(a) (i) Percentage of direct materials

$$= \frac{\text{production overhead}}{\text{direct materials}} \times 100$$

$$= \frac{£300\,000}{£100\,000} \times 100 = 300 \text{ per cent}$$

(ii) Percentage of direct wages

$$= \frac{\text{production overhead}}{\text{direct wages}} \times 100$$

$$= \frac{£300\,000}{£50\,000} \times 100 = 600 \text{ per cent}$$

(iii) Percentage of prime cost

$$= \frac{\text{production overhead}}{\text{prime cost}} \times 100$$

$$= \frac{£300\,000}{£150\,000} \times 100 = 200 \text{ per cent}$$

(iv) Unit

$$= \frac{\text{production overhead}}{\text{units}} = \frac{£300\,000}{300} = £1000 \text{ per unit}$$

(v) Labour hour rate

$$= \frac{\text{production overhead}}{\text{labour hours}} = \frac{£300\,000}{25\,000} = £12 \text{ per hour}$$

(vi) Machine hour rate

$$= \frac{\text{production overhead}}{\text{machine hours}} = \frac{£300\,000}{15\,000} = £20 \text{ per hour}$$

(b) The answer to this question is explained in Section 3.8.

(c)

	(i) Percentage of direct materials £	(ii) Percentage of direct wages £	(iii) Percentage of prime cost £	(iv) Unit £	(v) Labour hour rate £	(vi) Machine hour rate £
Direct materials	250	250	250	250	250	250
Direct wages	200	200	200	200	200	200
Prime cost	450	450	450	450	450	450
Production overhead	750[1]	1200[2]	900[3]	1000[4]	960[5]	1000[6]
Total cost	1200	1650	1350	1450	1410	1450

1 £250 × 300 per cent
2 £200 × 600 per cent
3 £450 × 200 per cent
4 1 unit of output at £1000
5 80 direct labour hours at £12 per hour
6 50 machine hours at £20 per hour

3.3

The following information relates to a manufacturing department of a company:

Manufacturing department

	Budgeted data	Actual data	Actual data relating to job 123
Direct material	£100 000	£140 000	£6000
Direct labour	£200 000	£250 000	£3000
Production overhead	£200 000	£230 000	
Direct labour hours	50 000	62 500	750
Machine hours	40 000	50 000	750

You are required to:

(a) Calculate the production overhead absorption rate predetermined for the period based on
   (i) Percentage of direct material cost, and
   (ii) Machine hours. (3 marks)
(b) Calculate the production overhead cost to be charged to job 123 based on the rates calculated in answer to (i). (3 marks)
(c) Assuming that a machine hour rate of absorption is used, calculate the under/over-absorption of production overheads for the period and state the appropriate treatment in the accounts. (3 marks)
(d) Comment briefly on the relative merits of the two methods of overhead absorption used in (i). (6 marks)

(AAT Pilot Paper)

Answer

(a) (i) Percentage direct material overhead rate

$$= \frac{\text{total department overheads}}{\text{total departmental material cost}} \times 100$$

$$= \frac{£200\,000}{£100\,000} \times 100 = 200 \text{ per cent}$$

(ii) Machine hour overhead rate

$$= \frac{\text{total departmental overheads}}{\text{total departmental machine hours}}$$

$$= \frac{£200\,000}{40\,000 \text{ h}} = £5 \text{ per hour}$$

(b)

	% direct material £	Machine hour rate £
Overhead charged to job 123	12 000 (200% × £6000)	3750 (750 h × £5)

		£
(c)	Overhead charged to production	250 000 (50 000 h × £5)
	Actual overhead incurred	230 000
	Over-recovery	20 000

The over-recovery should be regarded as a period cost adjustment and credited to the profit and loss account for the current period.

(d) For the answer to this question see Section 3.8. Your answer should stress that overhead recovery should normally relate to the time that jobs spend in various departments, and therefore the percentage direct material method cannot be recommended. For example, job 123 requires £6000 of materials and uses 750 departmental machine and direct labour hours. A job requiring £1000 of materials and using 1500 hours (twice the hours of job 123) would be charged £2000 for overheads (one-sixth of the amount charged to job 123).

A machine hour rate is related to the time that jobs spend in each department, and is appropriate when the machine hours of the department are the predominant activity and the majority of overhead expenditure is related to machinery. If these circumstances do not apply then the direct labour overhead hour rate is recommended.

3.4

Shown below is an extract from next year's budget for a company manufacturing three different products in three production departments:

	Product A	Product B	Product C
Production	4000 units	3000 units	6000 units
Direct material cost	£7 per unit	£4 per unit	£9 per unit
Direct labour requirements:	hours per unit	hours per unit	hours per unit
Cutting department:			
Skilled operatives	3	5	2
Unskilled operatives	6	1	3
Machining department	0.5	0.25	0.33
Pressing department	2	3	4
Machine hour requirements:			
Machining department	2	1.5	2.5

The skilled operatives employed in the cutting department are paid £4 per hour and the unskilled operatives are paid £2.50 per hour. All the operatives in the machining and pressing departments are paid £3 per hour.

	Production departments			Service departments	
	Cutting	Machining	Pressing	Engineering	Personnel
Budgeted total overheads	£154 482	£64 316	£58 452	£56 000	£34 000

Service department costs are incurred for the benefit of other departments as follows:

Engineering Services	20%	45%	25%	–	10%
Personnel Services	55%	10%	20%	15%	–

The company operates a full absorption costing system.

You are required to:

(a) Calculate, as equitably as possible, the total budgeted manufacturing cost of:
   (i) One completed unit of product A, and
   (ii) One incomplete unit of product B, which has been processed by the cutting and machining departments but which has not yet been passed into the pressing department. (15 marks)
(b) At the end of the first month of the year for which the above budget was prepared, the production overhead control account for the machining department showed a credit balance. Explain the possible reasons for that credit balance. (7 marks)

(CACA Level 1 Costing, June 1984)

Answer

(a) To calculate product cost we must calculate overhead absorption rates for the production departments. You can see from the question that the service departments serve each other, and it is therefore necessary to use the repeated distribution method or the simultaneous equation method to reallocate the service department costs. Both methods are illustrated below.

Repeated distribution method

	Cutting £	Machining £	Pressing £	Engineering £	Personnel £
Allocation per question	154 482	64 316	58 452	56 000	34 000
Engineering reallocation	11 200 (20%)	25 200 (45%)	14 000 (25%)	(56 000)	5 600 (10%)
Personnel reallocation	21 780 (55%)	3 960 (10%)	7 920 (20%)	5 940 (15%)	(39 600)
Engineering reallocation	1 188 (20%)	2 673 (45%)	1 485 (25%)	(5 940)	594 (10%)
Personnel reallocation	327 (55%)	59 (10%)	119 (20%)	89 (15%)	(594)
Engineering reallocation	20	44	25	(89)	–
	188 997	96 252	82 001	–	–

Simultaneous equation method

Let E be total overhead allocated to engineering department
Let P be total overhead allocated to personnel department

$$E = 56\,000 + 0.15P$$
$$P = 34\,000 + 0.10E$$

The costs are so small that any further apportionments are not justified. Consequently a return charge of 15 per cent is not made to the engineering department and the costs are apportioned in the ratio 20:45:25.

Rearranging the above equations gives

$$E - 0.15P = 56\,000 \quad (1)$$
$$-0.10E + P = 34\,000 \quad (2)$$

Multiply equation (2) by 0.15 and equation (1) by 1:

$$E - 0.15P = 56\,000$$
$$-0.015E + 0.15P = 5\,100$$

Adding the above equations gives

$$0.985E = 61\,100$$
$$E = £62\,030$$

Substituting for E in equation (1) gives

$$62\,030 - 0.15P = 56\,000$$
$$6030 = 0.15P$$
$$P = 40\,200$$

We now apportion the values of E and P to the production departments in the agreed percentages:

	Cutting £	Machining £	Pressing £
Allocation as in question	154 482	64 316	58 452
Allocation of engineering	12 408 (20%)	27 914 (45%)	15 508 (25%)
Allocation of personnel	22 110 (55%)	4 020 (10%)	8 040 (20%)
	189 000	96 250	82 000

Overhead absorption rates

A comparison of the machine and direct labour hours in the machine department indicates that machine hours are the dominant activity. Therefore a machine hour rate should be used. A direct labour hour rate is appropriate for the cutting and pressing departments. Note that unequal wage rates apply in the cutting department but equal wage rates apply in the pressing department. The direct wages percentage and the direct labour hour methods will therefore result in identical overhead charges to products passing through the pressing department and either method can be used. Because of the unequal wage rates in the cutting department, the direct wages percentage method is inappropriate.

The calculation of the overhead absorption rates are as follows:

		hours
Cutting	Product A (4000 × 9 hours)	36 000
	Product B (3000 × 6 hours)	18 000
	Product C (6000 × 5 hours)	30 000
		84 000

$$\text{Absorption rate} = \frac{£189\,000}{84\,000} = £2.25 \text{ per direct labour hour}$$

Machining	Product A (4000 × 2)	8 000
	Product B (3000 × 1.5)	4 500
	Product C (6000 × 2.5)	15 000
		27 500

$$\text{Absorption rate} = \frac{£96\,250}{27\,500} = £3.50 \text{ per machine hour}$$

Pressing	Product A (4000 × 2)	8 000
	Product B (3000 × 3)	9 000
	Product C (6000 × 4)	24 000
		41 000

$$\text{Absorption rate} = \frac{£82\,000}{41\,000} = £2 \text{ per direct labour hour}$$

Product cost calculations

		A (fully complete)	B (partly complete)
		£	£
Direct materials		7.00	4.00
Direct labour:	cutting (skilled)	12.00 (3 × £4)	20.00 (5 × £4)
	(unskilled)	15.00 (6 × £2.50)	2.50 (1 × £2.50)
	machining	1.50 (0.5 × £3)	0.75 (0.25 × £3)
	pressing	6.00 (2 × £3)	–
Prime cost		41.50	27.25
Overhead:	cutting	20.25 (9 × £2.25)	13.50 (6 × £2.25)
	machining	7.00 (2 × £3.50)	5.25 (1.5 × £3.50)
	pressing	4.00 (2 × £2)	–
		72.75	46.00

Note that product B has not yet been passed into the pressing department.

Answer to question: (a)(i)   (a)(ii)

(b) The accounting entries for overheads are presented in Chapter 4. You will find when you read this chapter that a credit balance in the overhead control account represents an over-recovery of overheads.

Possible reasons for this include:

(i) Actual overhead expenditure was less than budgeted expenditure.
(ii) Actual production activity was greater than budgeted production activity.

Questions for Chapter 4

4.1

You are required, using the information given below for the month of April 1980 in respect of D Manufacturing Company Limited, to:

(a) Write up the integrated accounts;
(b) Prepare a trading and profit and loss account for April 1980;
(c) Compile a trial balance as at 30 April 1980.

List of balances as at 1 April 1980

	£000
Land and buildings	500
Plant, machinery and office equipment	800
Provision for depreciation, plant, machinery and office equipment	200
Material stores	80
Work in progress	40
Finished goods stock	20
Debtors	260
Creditors	100
Bank overdrawn	50
Share capital	1100
Share premium	200
Profit and loss, appropriation: credit balance	35
Creditor for PAYE and National Insurance	15

Transactions for the month of April 1980

	£000
Cash received from debtors	190
Cash paid to creditors	70

	Gross wages £000	PAYE and NI £000	
Direct wages paid	40	10	30
Indirect wages paid	20	5	15
Administrative staff salaries paid	30	10	20
Selling staff salaries paid	20	5	15

Cash paid to creditor for PAYE and NI	30

Cash paid, expenses:
   Production   20
   Administration   10

Depreciation:
   Production plant and machinery   20
   Administrative office equipment   5

Employer's contribution NI:
   Production   5
   Administration   3
   Selling   2

Materials received and invoiced   50
Materials price variance, adverse:
   extracted as materials are received   5
Materials issued to production from stores   40
Materials issued to production maintenance   8
Transfers from work in progress to finished goods stock   110
Sales on credit   160
Production cost of goods sold   112

Accounting entries are presented for only those accounts which may cause you some difficulty in preparation: You should have no difficulty in preparing the omitted accounts — for example, debtors, creditors and cash accounts. You can check your closing balances for these accounts with the trial balance.

Production overhead is absorbed on the basis of 200 per cent on direct wages. Administration and selling costs are treated as period costs. (25 marks)
(CIMA Cost Accounting 1, May 1980)

Answer

(a)

Stores ledger control A/C	£000		£000
April 1 Balance B/F	80	April 30 Work in progress	40
30 Creditors (50 – 5)	45	Production overhead	8
		Balance C/F	77
	125		125

An explanation of the accounting entries for a material price variance is presented in Chapter 12.

Work in progress A/C			
April 1 Balance B/F	40	April 30 Finished goods	110
30 Wages and salaries	40	Balance C/F	90
Stores ledger	40		
Production overhead	80		
	200		200

Wages and salaries A/C			
April 30 Bank	80	April 30 Work in progress	40
PAYE and NI	30	Production overhead	20
		Administration overhead	30
		Selling overhead	20
	110		110

This entry of £80 000 consists of the total of the net wages paid (30 + 15 + 20 + 15) (£000). The £30 000 debit entry consists of the total amount owing for PAYE and national insurance (10 + 5 + 10 + 5) (£000).

PAYE and National Insurance A/C			
April 30 Bank	30	April 1 Balance B/F	15
Balance C/F	25	30 Wages and salaries	30
		Production overhead	5
		Administration overhead	3
		Selling overhead	2
	55		55

An explanation of the accounting entries for a material price variance is presented in Chapter 12.

Production overhead A/C

April 30	Wages and salaries	20	April 30	Work in progress	80
	Bank (expenses)	20		(200% × 40)	
	Provision for depreciation	20			
	PAYE and NI	5			
	Stores ledger	8			
	Profit and loss A/C				
	(over-absorption)	7			
		80			80

Administration overhead A/C

April 30	Wages and salaries	30	April 30	Profit and loss A/C	48
	Bank	10			
	Provision for depreciation	5			
	PAYE and NI	3			
		48			48

Selling overhead A/C

April 30	Wages and salaries	20	April 30	Profit and loss A/C	22
	PAYE and NI	2			
		22			22

Finished goods stock A/C

April 1	Balance B/F	20	April 30	Cost of sales	112
30	Work in progress	110		Balance C/F	18
		130			130

Material price variance A/C

April 30	Creditors account	5	April 30	Profit and loss A/C	5

Cost of sales A/C

April 30	Finished goods	112	April 30	Trading A/C	112

(b) *Trading and profit and loss A/C*

April 30	Cost of sales	112	April 30	Sales	160
	Gross profit C/F	48			
		160			160
	Administration overhead	48		Gross profit B/F	48
	Selling overhead	22		Production overhead	
	Material price variance	5		(over-absorbed)	7
				Net loss:	
				appropriation A/C	20
		75			75

(c) *Trial balance at 30 April 1980*

	DR £000	CR £000
Land and buildings	500	
Plant, machinery and office equipment	800	
Provision for depreciation		225
Material stores	77	
Work in progress	90	
Finished goods stock	18	
Debtors	230	

Creditors		80
Bank		70
Share capital		1100
Share premium		200
Profit and loss appropriation		15
PAYE and NI		25
	£1715	£1715

4.2

K Limited operates separate cost accounting and financial accounting systems. The following manufacturing and trading statement has been prepared from the financial accounts for the *quarter* ended 31 March:

	£	£
Raw materials:		
Opening stock	48 000	
Purchases	108 800	
	156 800	
Closing stock	52 000	
Raw materials consumed	104 800	
Direct wages		40 200
Production overhead		60 900
Production cost incurred		205 900
Work in progress:		
Opening stock	64 000	
Closing stock	58 000	
		6 000
Cost of goods produced carried down		211 900
Sales		440 000
Finished goods:		
Opening stock	120 000	
Cost of goods produced brought down	211 900	
	331 900	
Closing stock	121 900	
Cost of goods sold		210 000
Gross profit		230 000

From the cost accounts, the following information has been extracted:

Control account balances at 1 January	£
Raw material stores	49 500
Work in progress	60 100
Finished goods	115 400

Transactions for the quarter:	£
Raw materials issued	104 800
Cost of goods produced	222 500
Cost of goods sold	212 100
Loss of materials damaged by flood (insurance claim pending)	2 400

A notional rent of £4000 *per month* has been charged in the cost accounts. Production overhead was absorbed at the rate of 185 per cent of direct wages.

You are required to:
(a) Prepare the following control accounts in the cost ledger:
  Raw materials stores
  Work in progress
  Finished goods
  Production overhead (10 marks)
(b) Prepare a statement reconciling the gross profit as in the cost accounts and the financial accounts; (11 marks)
(c) Comment on the possible accounting treatment(s) of the under- or over-absorption of production overhead, assuming that the financial year of the company is 1 January to 31 December. (4 marks)

(CIMA Cost Accounting 1, May 1985)

Answer
(a) *Raw materials stores account*

	£		£
Balance B/D	49 500	Work in progress	104 800
Purchases	108 800	Loss due to flood to P & L A/C	2 400
		Balance C/D	51 100
	£158 300		£158 300
Balance B/D	51 100		

Work in progress control account

	£		£
Balance B/D	60 100	Finished goods	222 500
Raw materials	104 800	Balance C/D	56 970
Direct wages	40 200		
Production overhead	74 370		
	£279 470		£279 470
Balance B/D	56 970		

Note that the details for purchases, wages and production overhead are obtained from the financial accounts. In an integrated accounting system the corresponding credit entry would be in a financial account (for example, creditors or cash account). In an interlocking accounting system the corresponding credit entry will be in the general ledger control account. You should note that this account is also used to complete the double entry for notional rent. The question does not require a general ledger adjustment account, but this account has been prepared to help you gain a greater insight into an interlocking accounting system. The total of the closing balances for raw material, WIP and finished goods stock accounts agrees with the closing balance shown in the general ledger adjustment account.

Finished goods control account

	£		£
Balance B/D	115 400	Cost of sales	212 100
Work in progress	222 500	Balance C/D	125 800
	£337 900		£337 900
Balance B/D	125 800		

Production overhead

	£		£
General ledger control	60 900	Work in progress	74 370
Notional rent		(185% × £40 200)	
(3 × £4 000)	12 000		
Overhead over-absorbed	1 470		
	£74 370		£74 370

General ledger control account

	£		£
Sales	440 000	Balance B/D	
Balance C/D	233 870	(49 500 + 60 100 + 115 400)	225 000
		Purchases	108 800
		Direct wages	40 200
		Production overhead	60 900
		Notional rent	12 000
		P & L account	226 970
		(profit for period: see (b))	
	£673 870		£673 870

(b) *Calculation of profit in cost accounts*

			£
Sales			440 000
Cost of sales		212 100	
Loss of stores		2 400	
		214 500	
Less overhead over-absorbed		1 470	213 030
Profit			226 970

Reconciliation statement

			£
Profit as per cost accounts			226 970
Differences in stock values:			
Raw materials opening stock		1500	
Raw materials closing stock		900	
WIP closing stock		1030	3 430

Stock valuations in the financial accounts may differ from the valuation in the cost accounts. For example, raw materials may be valued on a LIFO basis in the cost accounts, whereas FIFO or weighted average may be used in the financial accounts. WIP and finished stock may be valued on a marginal (variable costing) basis in the cost accounts, but the valuation may be based on an absorption costing basis in the financial accounts. To reconcile the profits you should start with the profit from the cost accounts and consider what the impact would be on the profit calculation if the financial accounting stock valuations were used. If the opening stock valuation in the financial accounts exceeds the valuation in the cost accounts, then adopting the financial accounting stock valuation will reduce the profits. If the closing stock valuation in the financial accounts exceeds the valuation in the cost accounts, then adopting the financial accounting stock valuation will increase profits. Note that the notional rent is not included in the financial accounts and should therefore be deducted from the costing profit in the reconciliation statement.

WIP opening stock	3900		
Finished goods opening stock	4600		
Finished goods closing stock	3900	(12 400)	(8 970)
Add items not included in financial accounts			
Notional rent			12 000
Profit as per financial accounts			230 000

(c) The over-recovery of overhead could be apportioned between cost of goods sold for the current period and closing stocks. The justification for this is based on the assumption that the under/over-recovery is due to incorrect estimates of activity and overhead expenditure which leads to incorrect allocations being made to the cost of sales and closing stock accounts. The proposed adjustment is an attempt to rectify this incorrect allocation.

The alternative treatment is for the full amount of the under/over-recovery to be written off to the cost accounting profit and loss account in the current period as a period cost. This is the treatment recommended by SSAP 9.

4.3

Thornfield Ltd is a building contractor. During its financial year to 30 June 1984, it commenced three major contracts. Information relating to these contracts as at 30 June 1984 was as follows:

	Contract 1	*Contract 2*	*Contract 3*
Date contract commenced	1 July 1983	1 January 1984	1 April 1984
	£	£	£
Contract price	210 000	215 000	190 000
Expenditure to 30 June 1984:			
Materials and subcontract work	44 000	41 000	15 000
Direct wages	80 000	74 500	12 000
General expenses	3 000	1 800	700
Position at 30 June 1984:			
Materials on hand at cost	3 000	3 000	1 500
Accrued expenses	700	600	600
Value of work certified	150 000	110 000	20 000
Estimated cost of work completed but not certified	4 000	6 000	9 000
Plant and machinery allocated to contracts	16 000	12 000	8 000

The plant and machinery allocated to the contracts was installed on the dates the contracts commenced. The plant and machinery is expected to have a working life of four years in the case of contracts 1 and 3 and three years in the case of contract 2, and is to be depreciated on a straight line basis assuming nil residual values.

Since the last certificate of work was certified on contract number 1, faulty work has been discovered which is expected to cost £10 000 to rectify. No rectification work has been commenced prior to 30 June 1984.

In addition to expenditure directly attributable to contracts, recoverable central overheads are estimated to amount to 2 per cent of the cost of direct wages.

Thornfield Ltd has an accounting policy of taking two-thirds of the profit attributable to the value of work certified on a contract, once the contract is one-third completed. Anticipated losses on contracts are provided in full.

Progress claims equal to 80 per cent of the value of work certified have been invoiced to customers.

You are required to:

(a) Prepare contract accounts for each contract for the year to 30 June 1984, calculating any attributable profit or loss on each contract;
(12 marks)
(b) Calculate the amount to be included in the balance sheet of Thornfield Ltd as on 30 June 1984 in respect of these contracts.
(4 marks)
(ICAEW Accounting Techniques, November 1984)

Closing value of plant on site is calculated as follows:

Contract 1: £16000 − (£16 000/4)
Contract 2: £12000 − [(£12 000/3) (6/12)]
Contract 3: £ 8000 − [(£8000/4) (3/12)]

Answer

(a) *Contract accounts*

	Contract 1 £	Contract 2 £	Contract 3 £		Contract 1 £	Contract 2 £	Contract 3 £
Plant on site	16 000	12 000	8 000	Materials stock C/F	3 000	3 000	1 500
Materials	44 000	41 000	15 000	Cost of work not			
Wages	80 000	74 500	12 000	certified C/F	4 000	6 000	9 000
General expenses	3 000	1 800	700	Plant on site C/F	12 000	10 000	7 500
Central overheads	1 600	1 490	240	Cost of work certified			
Accrued expenses C/F	700	600	600	(balance)	136 300	112 390	18 540
Provision for faulty							
work C/F	10 000						
	155 300	131 390	36 540		155 300	131 390	36 540
Cost of work				Value of work certified	150 000	110 000	20 000
certified B/F	136 300	112 390	18 540	Loss taken		2 390	
Profit taken this period	9 133						
Profit not taken	4 567		1 460				
	150 000	112 390	20 000		150 000	112 390	20 000
Cost of work not				Accrued expenses B/F	700	600	600
certified B/F	4 000	6 000	9 000	Provision for faulty			
Material stock B/F	3 000	3 000	1 500	work B/F	10 000		
Plant on site B/F	12 000	10 000	7 500				

Profit calculations

Contract 1: (2/3) × £13 700 profit.
Contract 2: The loss to date (£112 390 − £110 000) is written off.
Contract 3: The contract is less than one-third complete. Therefore no profit is taken for the period.

(b) *Balance sheet (extracts)*

	£	£
Plant on site (£12 000 + £10 000 + £7500)		29 500
Raw material stock (£3000 + £3000 + £1500)		7 500
Cost of work completed to date		
(£140 300 + £118 390 + £27 540)	286 230	
Add profit taken (£9133 − £2390)	6 743	
	292 973	
Less progress payments received		
(£120 000 + £88 000 + £16 000)	224 000	68 973
Accrued expenses (£10 000 + £1900)		11 900

Note that completed work to date consists of the cost of uncertified work plus the cost of the certified work.

It is assumed that cash has been received in respect of the invoiced value of work certified.

Questions for Chapter 5

5.1

A product is manufactured by passing through three processes: *A*, *B* and *C*. In process *C* a by-product is also produced which is then transferred to process *D* where it is completed. For the first week in October, actual data included:

	Process A	Process B	Process C	Process D
Normal loss of input	5%	10%	5%	10%
Scrap value (per unit)	£1.50	£2.00	£4.00	£2.00
Estimated sales value of by-product (per unit)	−	−	£8.00	−
Output (units)	5760	5100	4370	−
Output of by-product (units)	−	−	510	450
	£	£	£	£
Direct materials (6000 units)	12 000	−	−	−
Direct materials added in process	5 000	9000	4000	220
Direct wages	4 000	6000	2000	200
Direct expenses	800	1680	2260	151

Budgeted production overhead for the week is £30 500
Budgeted direct wages for the week are £12 200

You are required to prepare:
(a) Accounts for processes *A*, *B*, *C* and *D*; (20 marks)
(b) Abnormal loss account and abnormal gain account. (5 marks)
(CIMA PI Cost Accounting 2, November 1986)

Answer
(a) The question does not indicate the method of overhead recovery. It is assumed that overheads are to be absorbed using the direct wages percentage method.

Process A account

	Units	Price £	Amount £		Units	Price £	Amount £
Direct materials	6000		12 000	Normal loss (scrap account)	300	1.5	450
Direct materials added			5 000				
Direct wages			4 000	Process B	5760	5.5	31 680
Direct expenses			800				
Production overhead (250% direct wages)			10 000				
			31 800				
Abnormal gain account	60	5.5	330				
	6060		32 130		6060		32 130

Cost per unit

$$= \frac{\text{cost of production (£31 800) less scrap value of normal loss (£450)}}{\text{expected output (5700 units)}}$$

$= £5.50$

Process B account

	Units	Price £	Amount £		Units	Price £	Amount £
Process A	5760	5.5	31 680	Normal loss (scrap account)	576	2.0	1 152
Direct materials added			9 000				
Direct wages			6 000	Process C	5100	12.0	61 200
Direct expenses			1 680	Abnormal loss	84	12.0	1 008
Production overhead (250% direct wages)			15 000				
	5760		63 360		5760		63 360

Cost per unit $= \dfrac{£63\,360 - £1152}{5760 - 576 \text{ units}}$

$= £12$

Process C account

	Units	Price £	Amount £		Units	Price £	Amount £
Process B	5100		61 200	Normal loss (scrap account)	255	4.0	1 020
Direct materials added			4 000				
Direct wages			2 000	Finished goods	4370	16.0	69 920
Direct expenses			2 260	Process D	510	8.0	4 080
Production overhead (250% direct wages)			5 000				
			74 460				
Abnormal gain	35	16.0	560				
	5135		75 020		5135		75 020

$$\text{Cost per unit} = \frac{£74\,460 - £1020 - £4080}{5100 - 255 - 510 \text{ units}}$$

$$= £16$$

Process D account (By Product)

By-product stock (process D) is recorded at the estimated net realizable value at split-off point (£4080) and the main product is credited (process C) with this amount. The separable processing costs are charged to the by-product stock account (process D). See section 6.4 in Part 2 for an explanation of accounting for by-products.

	Units	Price £	Amount £		Units	Price £	Amount £
Process C	510		4 080	Normal loss (scrap account)	51	2.0	102
Direct materials added			220				
Direct wages			200	Finished goods	450	11.0	4 950
Direct expenses			151	Abnormal loss	9	11.0	99
Production overhead (250% direct wages)			500				
	510		5 151		510		5 151

$$\text{Cost per unit} = \frac{£5151 - £102}{510 - 51 \text{ units}} = £11$$

(b) *Abnormal gain account*

	Units	Price £	Amount £		Units	Price £	Amount £
Normal loss A/C	60	1.5	90	Process A	60		330
Normal loss A/C	35	4.0	140	Process C	35		560
Profit and loss account			660				
	95		890		95		890

Abnormal loss account

	Units	Price £	Amount £		Units	Price £	Amount £
Process B	84		1 008	Normal loss A/C	84	2.0	168
Process D	9		99	Normal loss A/C	9	2.0	18
				Profit and loss account			921
	93		1 107		93		1 107

Normal loss account (income due)

	£		£
Process 1 normal loss	450	Abnormal gain A/C	90
Process 2 normal loss	1152	Abnormal gain A/C	140
Process 3 normal loss	1020		
Process 4 normal loss	102		
Abnormal loss A/C	168		
Abnormal loss A/C	18		

5.2
A manufacturing company makes a product by two processes and the data below relate to the second process for the month of April.

A work in progress balance of 1200 units brought forward from March was valued, at cost, as follows:

	£
Direct materials, complete	10 800
Direct wages, 60 per cent complete	6 840
Production overhead, 60 per cent complete	7 200

During April, 4000 units were transferred from the first process to the second process at a cost of £7.50 each, this input being treated as direct material within the second process.

Other costs incurred by the second process were:

	£
Additional direct materials	4 830
Direct wages	32 965
Production overhead	35 538

3200 completed units were transferred to finished goods store. A loss of 520 units, being normal, occurred during the process. The average method of pricing is used.

Work in progress at the end of April consisted of 500 completed units awaiting transfer to the finished goods store, and a balance of unfinished units which were complete as regards direct material and 50 per cent complete as regards direct wages and production overhead.

You are required to:

(a) Prepare for the month of April the account for the second process:
(14 marks)

(b) Present a statement for management setting out the:
   (i) Cost per unit of the finished product, by element of cost and total;
   (ii) Cost of production transferred to finished goods;
   (iii) Cost of production of completed units awaiting transfer to finished goods;
   (iv) Cost of uncompleted units in closing work in progress, by element of cost and in total. (6 marks)
   (CIMA Foundation Cost Accounting 1, May 1985)

Answer
Statement of input and output (units)

Input		Output	
Opening WIP	1200	Completed and transferred to finished stock	3200
Transferred in	4000	Normal loss	520
		WIP (completed units)	500
		Uncompleted WIP (balance)	980
	5200		5200

It is not clear from the question at what point in the process the loss occurs.

You could also have assumed that the loss was detected when the goods were completed and charged all of the loss to completed production. See Section 5.7 for an explanation of this approach. If the question does not specify when the loss occurs you should assume either that it occurs at the end of the process or that the WIP has just passed the inspection point. You should then prepare the unit cost calculations as shown in Sections 5.7 or 5.8. Do remember to state the assumptions you have made in your answer.

It is assumed that additional materials are added at the start of the process.

It is assumed that the WIP has just passed the inspection point and should be charged with a share of normal loss. By making no entry for normal losses in the cost per unit calculation, the normal loss is automatically apportioned between completed units and WIP.

Statement of cost per unit

	Opening WIP £	Current cost £	Total cost £	Completed units (W1)	Equiv. uncompleted WIP	Equiv. total units	Cost per unit £
Materials (W2)	10 800	34 830	45 630	3700	980	4680	9.75
Conversion cost	14 040	68 503	82 543	3700	490	4190	19.70
			128 173				29.45

	£
WIP: completed units (500 × £29.45)	14 725
uncompleted units: materials (980 × £9.75)	9 555
conv. cost (490 × £19.70)	9 653
	33 933
Completed units transferred to finished stock (3200 × £29.45)	94 240
	128 173

(W1) Completed units = 3200 + 500 (Completed WIP)
(W2) Materials include previous process cost (4000 units at £7.50 each is included in the current cost column).

Process account

	units	£		units	£
WIP B/F:	1200		Normal loss	520	
Materials		10 800	Transferred to		
Conv. cost		14 040	finished stock	3200	94 240
Transferred from			Completed WIP C/F	500	14 725
previous process	4000	30 000	Uncompleted WIP C/F	980	19 208
Materials		4 830			
Direct wages		32 965			
Overhead		35 538			
	5200	128 173		5200	128 173

5.3

Shown below is an extract from the accountant's working papers for the process cost accounts, for May 1982, of the final two operations in a factory producing one particular type of industrial chemical:

Process 4

	kg		kg
Opening stock	3 000	Transfers to process 5	8 000
Transfers from process 3	11 000	Loss	2 000
		Closing stock	4 000
	14 000		14 000

	Materials transferred from process 3	Process 4 materials	Process 4 conversion costs
Cost per equivalent whole unit of production	£2.80 per kg	£1.75 per kg	£2.50 per kg
Degree of completion:			
Opening stocks	100%	70%	60%
Losses	100%	60%	45%
Closing stocks	100%	80%	70%

Normally no losses are expected in process 4.

The company operates the first in, first out method of charging opening stock to production and, at the beginning of May 1982, the value of the opening stock in process 4 was £16 400.

Process 5

	kg		kg
Opening stock	nil	Transfers to finished	
Transfers from process 4	8000	goods store	7400
		Loss	600
		Closing stock	nil
	────		────
	8000		8000

Process 5 costs (in addition to the cost of transfers from process 4):
Materials   £10 175
Conversion costs   £18 000

Normally a loss of 10 per cent of input is expected in process 5; all losses may be sold as scrap at £2 per kg.

You are required to:

(a) Calculate the total cost of the 8000 kg of chemical transferred from process 4 to process 5 during May 1982; (5 marks)
(b) Calculate the total cost, incurred by process 4 during May 1982, for each of the following:
   (i) Materials transferred from process 3
   (ii) Process 4 materials
   (iii) Process 4 conversion costs; (10 marks)
(c) Prepare the process 5 Account for May 1982. (7 marks)
(CACA Level 1 Costing, June 1982)

Answer

(a) The company operates the FIFO method of charging opening stock to production. Therefore it is necessary to remove the opening stock equivalent production which is assumed to be contained within the completed production transferred to process 5. Our objective is to calculate the equivalent units which were started and completed during the period. The calculation is as follows:

	Completed units less opening WIP equivalent units	Unit cost (given)	Cost of equivalent units started and completed during period
Element of cost			
Transferred in costs	5000 (8000 − 3000 × 100%)	£2.80	£14 000
Materials	5900 (8000 − 3000 × 70%)	£1.75	£10 325
Conversion costs	6200 (8000 − 3000 × 60%)	£2.50	£15 500
			39 825
	Add opening work in progress (given)		£16 400
	Total cost of transfers to process 5		£56 225

(b)

Element of cost	Completed units less opening WIP equivalent units	Abnormal loss equiv. units	Closing WIP equiv. units	Total equiv. units
Transferred in costs	5000	2000 (100%)	4000 (100%)	11 000
Materials	5900	1200 (60%)	3200 (80%)	10 300
Conversion cost	6200	900 (45%)	2800 (70%)	9 900

The total costs incurred by process 4 are calculated as follows:

$$\text{Total equivalent units} \times \text{Cost per unit (given)}$$

(i) Transferred in costs   11 000   × £2.80 = £30 800
(ii) Process 4 materials   10 300   × £1.75 = £18 025
(iii) Conversion costs   9 900   × £2.50 = £24 750

(c) *Process 5 account*

Cost per unit =

$$\frac{\text{cost of production less scrap value of normal loss}}{\text{expected output}}$$

$$= \frac{£84\,400 - £1\,600}{7\,200 \text{ units}} = £11 \cdot 50$$

Abnormal gain = 200 units at £11·50 per unit.

	units	£		units	£
Opening stock			Transferred to finished		
Transfers from			goods store	7400	85 100
process 4 (from (a))	8000	56 225	Normal loss (10% × 8000)	800	1 600
Materials		10 175	Closing stock	−	−
Conversion costs		18 000			
		84 400			
Abnormal gains	200	2 300			
	8200	86 700		8200	86 700

Questions for Chapter 6

6.1
A process costing £200 000 produces three products, A, B and C. Output details are as follows:

Product A   6 000 litres
Product B   10 000 litres
Product C   20 000 tonnes

Each product may be sold at the completion of the process as follows:

	Sales value at end of first process
Product A	£10 per litre
Product B	£4 per litre
Product C	£10 per tonne

Alternatively, further processing of each individual product can be undertaken to produce an enhanced product thus:

	Subsequent processing costs	Sales value after final process
Enhanced product A	£14 per litre	£20 per litre
Enhanced product B	£2 per litre	£8 per litre
Enhanced product C	£6 per tonne	£16 per tonne

You are required to:

(a) Explain the following terms

    (i) Normal process loss
    (ii) Joint product
    (iii) By-product

and state the appropriate costing treatments for normal process loss and for by-products. (10 marks)

(b) Calculate the apportionment of joint process costs to products A, B and C. (8 marks)

(c) Explain whether the initial process should be undertaken and which, if any, of the enhanced products should be produced. (7 marks)

(AAT Pilot Paper)

Answer

(a) See Chapters 5 and 6 for the answer to this question.

(b) No specific apportionment method is asked for in the question. It is recommended that the joint costs should be apportioned (see Chapter 6) according to the sales value at the split-off point.

Product	Sales value £	Proportion to total (%)	Joint costs apportioned £
A	60 000	20	40 000
B	40 000	13.33	26 660
C	200 000	66.67	133 340
	300 000	100.00	200 000

(c) Assuming all of the output given in the question can be sold, the initial process is profitable – the sales revenue is £300 000 and the joint costs are £200 000.

To determine whether further processing is profitable, the additional relevant revenues should be compared with the additional relevant costs:

	A £	B £	C £
Additional relevant revenues	10 (20 − 10)	4 (8 − 4)	6 (16 − 10)
Additional relevant costs	14	2	6
Excess of relevant revenue over costs	(4)	2	–

Product B should be further processed; product A should not be further processed; and if product C is further processed then profits will remain unchanged.

6.2

A company manufactures two types of industrial sealant by passing materials through two consecutive processes. The results of operating the two processes during the previous month are as follows:

Process 1
Costs incurred:
   Materials 7000 kg at £0.50 per kg   £3500
   Labour and overheads   £4340
Output
   Transferred to process 2   6430 kg
   Defective production   570 kg

Process 2
Cost incurred:
   Labour and overheads   £12 129
Output
   Type E sealant   2000 kg
   Type F sealant   4000 kg
   By-product   430 kg

It is considered normal for 10 per cent of the total output from process 1 to be defective and all defective output is sold as scrap at £0.40 per kg. Losses are not expected in process 2.

There was no work in process at the beginning or end of the month and no opening stocks of sealants.

Sales of the month's output from process 2 were:

Type E sealant	1100 kg
Type F sealant	3200 kg
By-product	430 kg

The remainder of the output from process 2 was in stock at the end of the month.

The selling prices of the products are: type E sealant £7 per kg; type F sealant £2.50 per kg. No additional costs are incurred on either of the two main products after the second process. The by-product is sold for £1.80 per kg after being sterilized, at a cost of £0.30 per kg, in a subsequent process. The operating costs of process 2 are reduced by the net income receivable from sales of the by-product.

You are required to:
(a) Calculate, for the previous month, the cost of the output transferred from process 1 into process 2 and the net cost or saving arising from any abnormal losses or gains in process 1; (6 marks)
(b) Calculate the value of the closing stock of each sealant and the profit earned by each sealant during the previous month using the following methods of apportioning costs to joint products:
  (i) According to weight of output
  (ii) According to market value of output; (12 marks)
(c) Consider whether apportioning process costs to joint products is useful. Briefly illustrate with examples from your answer to (b).
(4 marks)
(CACA Level 1 Costing, June 1985)

Answer
(a) *Process 1*

	kg	£		kg	£
Materials	7000	3500	Normal loss (W2)	700	280
			Transferred to process (W1)	6430	7716
Labour and overhead		4340			
Abnormal gain (W3)	130	156			
	7130	7996		7130	7996

Note that the completed production transferred to process 2 and the abnormal gain is valued at £1·20 per unit.

Workings
1 Cost per unit

$$= \frac{\text{cost of production (£7840)} - \text{scrap value of normal loss (£280)}}{\text{expected output (6300 kg)}}$$

$$= £1.20 \text{ per kg}$$

2 Normal loss is 10 per cent of *total* output, which in this case is equivalent to total input. Therefore normal loss is 10 per cent of (6430 + 570).

3 Abnormal gain = actual output (6430) − expected output (6300)

Normal loss account				*Abnormal gain account*			
	£		£		£		£
Process 1 (700 × 40p)	280	Abnormal gain A/C (130 × 40p)	52	Normal loss (130 × 40p)	52	Process 1	156
		Cash (570 × 40p)	228	P & L A/C	104		
	280		280		156		156

(b) *Process 2*

	kg	£		kg	£
Previous process cost	6430	7 716	By-product net income	430	645
Labour and overhead		12 129	Output to be accounted for:		19 200
			E	2000	
			F	4000	
	6430	19 845		6430	19 845

The allocation of £19 200 to E and F depends on the apportionment method used.

(i) *Physical output method*

	E £	F £
1 Total output cost	$6400 \left(\frac{2000}{6000} \times £19\,200\right)$	$12\,800 \left(\frac{4000}{6000} \times £19\,200\right)$
2 Closing stock	$2880 \left(\frac{2000-1100}{2000} \times £6400\right)$	$2\,560 \left(\frac{4000-3200}{4000} \times £12\,800\right)$
3 Cost of sales	$3520 \left(\frac{1100}{2000} \times £6400\right)$	$10\,240 \left(\frac{3200}{4000} \times £12\,800\right)$
4 Sales revenue	7700 (1100 × £7)	8 000 (3200 × £2.50)
5 Profit (4 − 3)	4180	(2 240)

(ii) *Market value of output method*

	E £	F £
1 Market value of output	14 000 (2000 × £7)	10 000 (4000 × £2.50)
2 Cost of output	$11\,200 \left(\frac{14}{24} \times £19\,200\right)$	$8\,000 \left(\frac{10}{24} \times £19\,200\right)$
3 Closing stock	$5\,040 \left(\frac{900}{2000} \times £11\,200\right)$	$1\,600 \left(\frac{800}{4000} \times £8000\right)$
4 Cost of sales	$6\,160 \left(\frac{1100}{2000} \times £11\,200\right)$	$6\,400 \left(\frac{3200}{4000} \times £8000\right)$
5 Sales revenue	7 700	8 000
6 Profit (5 − 4)	1 540	1 600

(c) See Chapter 6 for the answer to this question. In particular the answer should stress that joint cost apportionments are necessary for stock valuation but such apportionments are inappropriate for decision-making. For decision-making, relevant costs should be used. It can be seen from the answer to (b) that one method of apportionment implies that F makes a loss whereas the other method indicates that F makes a profit. Product F should only be deleted if the costs saved from deleting it exceed the revenues lost.

6.3

A chemical company carries on production operations in two processes. Materials first pass through Process I, where a compound is produced. A loss in weight takes place at the start of processing. The following data, which can be assumed to be representative, relates to the month just ended:

Quantities (kilos)
Material input	200 000
Opening work-in-process (half processed)	40 000
Work completed	160 000
Closing work-in-process (two-thirds processed)	30 000

Costs (£)
Material input	75 000
Processing costs	96 000
Opening work-in-process – materials	20 000
– processing costs	12 000

Any quantity of the compound can be sold for £1.60 per kilo. Alternatively, it can be transferred to Process II for further processing and packing to be sold as Starcomp for £2.00 per kilo. Further materials are added in Process II such that for every kilo of compound used, two kilos of Starcomp result.

Of the 160 000 kilos per month of work completed in Process I, 40 000 kilos are sold as compound and 120 000 kilos are passed through Process II for sale as Starcomp. Process II has facilities to handle up to 160 000 kilos of compound per month if required. The monthly costs incurred in Process II (other than the cost of the compound) are:

	120 000 kilos of compound input	160 000 kilos of compound input
Materials	£120 000	£160 000
Processing costs	£120 000	£140 000

Required:

(a) Determine, using the average method, the cost per kilo of compound in Process I, and the value of both work completed and closing work-in-process for the month just ended. (11 marks)
(b) Demonstrate that it is worthwhile further processing 120 000 kilos of compound. (5 marks)

(c) Calculate the minimum acceptable selling price per kilo, if a potential buyer could be found for the additional output of Starcomp that could be produced with the remaining compound. (6 marks)

(CACA Level 1 Costing, June 1986)

Answer

(a) You can see from the question that the input is 240 000 kilos and the output is 190 000 kilos. It is assumed that the difference of 50 000 kilos is a normal loss in output which occurs at the start of processing. Therefore the loss should be charged to the completed production and WIP. By making no entry for normal losses in the cost per unit calculation the normal loss is automatically apportioned between completed units and WIP.

	Opening WIP £	Current cost £	Total cost £	Completed units	Closing WIP	Total equiv. units	Cost per unit £	WIP value £
Materials	20 000	75 000	95 000	160 000	30 000	190 000	0.50	15 000
Processing costs	12 000	96 000	108 000	160 000	20 000	180 000	0.60	12 000
			203 000				1.10	27 000

Completed units (160 000 units × £1.10) 176 000

203 000

(b) This question requires a comparison of incremental revenues and incremental costs. Note that the costs of Process I are irrelevant to the decision since they will remain the same whichever of the two alternatives is selected. You should also note that further processing 120 000 kilos of the compound results in 240 000 kilos of Starcomp.

Incremental sales revenue

	£	£
Starcomp (120 000 × 2 kilos × £2)	480 000	
Compound (120 000 × £1.60)	192 000	288 000
Incremental costs		
Materials	120 000	
Processing costs	120 000	240 000
Incremental profits		48 000

It is therefore worthwhile further processing the compound.

(c) The sales revenue should cover the additional costs of further processing the 40 000 kilos compound and the lost sales revenue from the 40 000 kilos compound if it is sold without further processing.

Additional processing costs:

	£
Materials (£160 000 − £120 000)	40 000
Processing costs (£140 000 − £120 000)	20 000
Lost compound sales revenue (40 000 × £1.60)	64 000
	124 000

$$\text{Minimum selling price per kilo of Starcomp} = \frac{£124\,000}{40\,000 \text{ kilos} \times 2}$$

$$= £1.55$$

Questions for Chapter 7

7.1
(a) A company manufactures and sells two products, A and B. The following information is available:

	A	B
Sales price (each)	£15	£20
Labour (unit)	£2 (1 hour)	£4 (2 hours)
Variable production overheads	£3	£6
Material	£4	£5
Production quantities: November	700	800
December	350	500
Quantities sold: November	600	700
December	400	400
Fixed overheads: November		£4600
December		£2700

You are required to prepare statements for November and December showing profit and closing stock valuations using the following methods:

(i) Marginal costing (7 marks)
(ii) Absorption costing (7 marks)

(b) Discuss absorption costing as a method of costing factory output.
(8 marks)
(AAT, December 1984)

Answer

(a) (i) *Marginal costing profit statements*

	November £		December £
Sales: A 9 000		A 6000	
B 14 000	23 000	B 8000	14 000
Variable cost of sales:			
A 5 400 (600 × £9)		A 3600 (400 × £9)	
B 10 500 (700 × £15)	15 900	B 6000 (400 × £15)	9 600

Contribution		7 100		4 400
Fixed costs		4 600		2 700
Profit		2 500		1 700
Stock valuations				
A 100 × £9		900	A 50 × £9	450
B 100 × £15		1 500	B 200 × £15	3 000
		2 400		3 450

(ii) *Absorption costing profit statements*

	November £		December £
Sales	23 000		14 000
Absorption cost of sales (W1)			
A 6 600 (600 × £11)		A 4400 (400 × £11)	
B 13 300 (700 × £19)	19 900	B 7600 (400 × £19)	12 000
Profit	3 100		2 000
Stock valuations			
A 100 × £11	1 100	A 50 × £11	550
B 100 × £19	1 900	B 200 × £19	3 800
	3 000		4 350

Remember to match costs against sales so that the costs refer to the sales quantities for each month. It appears that overheads are recovered on an actual basis. Consequently there will be no under/over-recoveries of fixed overheads.

Workings

(W1) It is recommended that fixed overheads are recovered on a direct labour hour basis. You will recall in Chapter 3 that it was argued that direct labour hours or machine hours were the most suitable methods for recovering overheads. The estimated direct labour hours are:

	hours
November: A: 700 units × 1 hour	700
B: 800 units × 2 hours	1600
	2300
December: A: 350 units × 1 hour	350
B: 500 units × 2 hours	1000
	1350

November fixed overhead absorption rate = £2 per hour (£4600/2300)

December fixed overhead absorption rate = £2 per hour (£2700/1350)

The product absorption costs are:

	A	B
Variable cost	9	15
Fixed cost	2	4
	11	19

(b) See Chapter 7 for the answer to this question.

7.2

X Limited commenced business on 1 March making one product only, the standard cost of which is as follows:

	£
Direct labour	5
Direct material	8
Variable production overhead	2
Fixed production overhead	5
Standard production cost	20

The fixed production overhead figure has been calculated on the basis of a budgeted normal output of 36 000 units per annum.

You are to assume that there were no expenditure or efficiency variances and that all the budgeted fixed expenses are incurred evenly over the year. March and April are to be taken as equal period months.

Selling, distribution and administration expenses are:

Fixed	£120 000 per annum
Variable	15 per cent of the sales value

The selling price per unit is £35 and the number of units produced and sold were:

	March units	April units
Production	2000	3200
Sales	1500	3000

You are required to:

(a) Prepare profit statements for each of the months of March and April using:
   (i) Marginal costing, and
   (ii) Absorption costing;   (15 marks)
(b) Present a reconciliation of the profit or loss figures given in your answer to (a) (i) and (a) (ii) accompanied by a brief explanation;
   (5 marks)
(c) Comment briefly on which costing principle, i.e. marginal or absorption, should be used for what purpose(s) and why, referring to any statutory or other mandatory constraints.   (5 marks)

(CIMA Stage 2 Cost Accounting, Pilot Paper)

Answer

(a) (i) *Marginal costing*

	March £		April £	
Sales: 1500 at £35	52 500			
3000 at £35			105 000	
less Variable cost of sales:				
Opening stock			7 500	
Variable manufacturing cost 2000 × £15	30 000		3200 × £15	48 000
			55 500	
less Closing stock 500 × £15	7 500		700 × £15	10 500
	22 500		45 000	
Variable selling, distribution and administration 15 per cent of sales	7 875		15 750	
		30 375		60 750
Contribution		22 125		44 250
less Fixed costs:				
Production (W1)	15 000		15 000	
Selling, distribution and administration	10 000	25 000	10 000	25 000
Profit (loss)		£(2 875)		£19 250

Note that non-manufacturing variable costs are not included in the marginal and absorption costing stock valuations.

(a) (ii) *Absorption costing*

	March £		April £	
Sales: 1500 at £35	52 500			
3000 at £35			105 000	
less Cost of sales:				
Opening stock	–		10 000	
Production cost 2000 × £20	40 000		3200 × £20	64 000
			74 000	
less Closing stock 500 × £20	10 000		700 × £20	14 000
	30 000		60 000	
Fixed production overhead under/(over) absorbed (W2)	5 000		(1 000)	
Production cost of sales		35 000		59 000
Gross profit		17 500		46 000
less Variable selling, distribution and administration. 15 per cent of sales	7 875		15 750	
Fixed selling, distribution and administration	10 000		10 000	
		17 875		25 750
(Loss) profit		(375)		20 250

Workings

(W1) Monthly fixed overheads = (36 000 units/12 months) × £5
= £15 000

(W2) In March the output is 1000 units less than the normal monthly activity of 3000 units, resulting in an under-recovery of £5000. In April output is 200 units in excess of normal activity, resulting in an over-recovery of £1000.

(b) *Reconciliation profit statement*

	March £	April £
Marginal costing profit (loss)	(2875)	19 250
Fixed overhead included in increase in stocks using absorption costing and not charged as an expense in current period	2500 (500 × £5)	1 000 (200 × £5)
Absorption costing profit (loss)	(375)	20 250

In March stocks have increased by 500 units. Absorption costing charges fixed overheads to products. Consequently £2500 (500 × £5) fixed overhead is included in the stock valuation and not charged as an expense in March. The fixed overheads incurred (£15 000) are charged as a period cost with the marginal costing system. In April stocks increase by 200 units and therefore the increase in the stock valuation includes £1000 fixed overheads. Thus £14 000 production fixed overheads are charged as an expense with the absorption costing system.

(c) Your answer should indicate that SSAP 9 requires that absorption costing should be used for external reporting. For internal reporting marginal costing (that is, variable costing) is normally favoured (see Section 7.4 for an explanation of why variable costing is preferable).

Questions for Chapter 8

8.1
Your company has just developed a new microcomputer to compete in the rapidly expanding home market. As management accountant, you are consulted as to the viability of marketing this computer.

In conjunction with the manager of research and development, the production manager, the buyer and the sales manager, you have been able to ascertain the following estimates:

Sales level units	Profit £
12 000	(30 000)
15 000	150 000
18 000	330 000

The selling price will be £150.

You are required to:

(a) Prepare a contribution–sales graph (sometimes known as a profit–volume graph), using the information given above, and read off the margin of safety; (15 marks)

(b) Calculate the estimated profit if the probabilities for each sales level are:

Sales level units	Probability
12 000	0.2
15 000	0.5
18 000	0.3
	1.0

(5 marks)

(CIMA P1 Cost Accounting 2, November 1985)

A question may require you to ascertain the fixed and variable cost when total costs are given at various activity levels. If variable costs are constant per unit then the variable cost per unit can be calculated by examining the changes in total cost and activity. For example, if total costs are £10 000 at an activity level of 5000 units and £11 000 at an activity level of 6000 units, the variable cost per unit is calculated as follows:

$$\frac{\text{increase in total costs}}{\text{increase in activity}} = \frac{£1000}{1000 \text{ units}} = £1 \text{ per unit}$$

Total variable costs will therefore be £5000 at an activity level of 5000 units and £6000 at an activity level of 6000 units. Fixed costs are calculated by deducting total variable cost from total cost. Fixed costs are therefore £5000. This method of analysing fixed and variable costs is called the high–low method.

Answer
(a) Workings

Units sold	12 000	15 000	18 000
	£	£	£
Total sales	1 800 000	2 250 000	2 700 000
Profit (loss)	(30 000)	150 000	330 000
Total cost	1 830 000	2 100 000	2 370 000

Profit (and therefore contribution) increases by £180 000 for each 3000 units increase in sales volume. Assuming that fixed costs remain unchanged, and selling price and variable cost are constant per unit, the contribution per unit is £60 (£180 000/3000 units). Contribution less fixed costs equals profit. At 15 000 units sales volume, contribution will be £900 000 and profit is £150 000. Therefore fixed costs are £750 000.

Sales value at break-even point

$$= \frac{\text{fixed costs (£750 000)}}{\text{contribution (£900 000)}} \times \text{sales (£2 250 000)}$$

$$= £1\,875\,000$$

The profit–volume graph can then be constructed as shown.

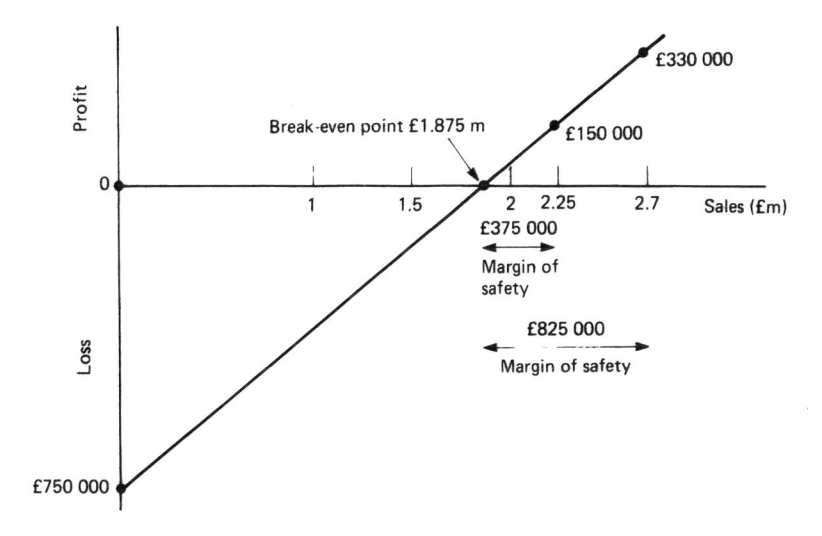

Profit–volume graph for Question 8.1(a)

(b)

1 Sales level	2 Probability	3 Weighted average (1 × 2)
12 000	0.2	2 400
15 000	0.5	7 500
18 000	0.3	5 400
Expected value		15 300

It is assumed that the question requires the expected value of the profits to be calculated. The expected value is the weighted average of the possible outcomes.

	£
Total contribution at a sales volume of 15 300 units	918 000
Less fixed costs	750 000
Estimated profit	168 000

8.2
A company producing and selling a single product expects the following trading results for the year just ending:

		£000	£000
Sales			900
Costs: Materials: direct		200	
Labour: direct		120	
indirect, fixed		38	
Other production overhead:	variable	50	
	fixed	80	
Administration overhead:	fixed	78	
Selling overhead:	variable	63	
	fixed	44	
Distribution overhead:	variable	36	
	fixed	20	729
Net profit			171

Budgets are now being prepared for the year ahead. The following information is provided:

(i) A selling price reduction from £9 to £8 per unit is expected to increase sales volume by 50 per cent.

(ii) Because of increased quantities purchased, a 5 per cent quantity discount will be obtained on the purchase of raw materials. Material usage per unit of output is expected to be 98 per cent of the current year.

(iii) Hourly direct wage rates will increase by 10 per cent. Labour efficiency should remain the same. 20 000 units will be produced in overtime hours at a premium of 25 per cent. Overtime premium is treated as a direct cost.

(iv) Variable selling overhead is expected to increase in total proportionately with total sales revenue.

(v) Variable production and distribution overhead should increase in total in proportion to the increase in sales volume.

(vi) Fixed overhead is forecast at 20 per cent above the level for the current year.

(vii) Monthly production will be scheduled so that finished goods stocks at the end of a month are sufficient to meet sales quantities forecast for the following one and a half months.

(viii) Materials will be purchased so that closing stocks of materials at the end of a month are sufficient to meet production requirements in the following month.

(ix) Monthly sales for the first six months are forecast as:

Month	1	2	3	4	5	6
000 units	10	12	15	11	12	12

You are to assume that:

(i) Prices and efficiency have been at a constant level throughout the year just ending.

(ii) Stocks of materials and finished goods at the end of the current year are consistent with the above assumptions for the year ahead, e.g. closing stocks of raw materials will be sufficient for production requirements in month 1 of the new year.

You are required to:

(a) Prepare a budgeted profit statement for the year ahead in marginal costing format; (10 marks)
(b) Calculate and compare the break-even points for the two years; (8 marks)
(c) Prepare a monthly production budget for the first quarter of the new year. (4 marks)

(CACA Level 1 Costing, June 1986)

Answer

(a)

	£000	£000
Sales ([(900/£9) × 1.5] × £8)		1200.00
Direct materials (£200 × 1.5 × 0.95 × 0.98)	279.3	
Direct labour (W1)	204.6	
Variable production overhead (50 × 1.5)	75.0	
Variable selling overhead (63 × 1200/900): see (W2)	84.0	
Variable distribution overhead (36 × 1.5)	54.0	696.90
Contribution		503.10
Fixed costs: production (118 × 1.2)	141.6	
administration (78 × 1.2)	93.6	
selling (44 × 1.2)	52.8	
distribution (20 × 1.2)	24.0	312.00
Net profit		191.10

Workings £

(W1) Labour cost without overtime
 = £120 000 × 1.10 × 1.5   198 000
Labour cost per unit is £1.32 (£198 000/150 000)
Extra cost of 20 000 units produced in overtime
(20 000 × £1.32 × 0.25)   6 600
   ―――――
   204 600

(W2) Selling overheads are variable with sales revenue and not production.

(b) Current year BE point

$$= \frac{\text{fixed costs (£260 000)}}{\text{contribution (431 000)}} \times \text{sales (£900 000)}$$

$$= £542\,923 \text{ (or 60 325 units)}$$

For the budget year it is likely that the overtime will be incurred after the break-even point. The contribution per unit at the lower levels of activity will be £3.398 [(£503 100 + £6600 overtime)/150 000]. Therefore

Budget BE point

$$= \frac{\text{fixed costs (£312 000)}}{\text{unit contribution (£3.398)}}$$

$$= 91\,819 \text{ units (or £734 552 sales value)}$$

The break-even point has increased because the fixed costs have increased and the selling price has been reduced.

It is important that in your answer to (b) you show you can calculate break-even points and explain why the break-even point has increased. You should not be too concerned if you fail to take into account the overtime adjustment. The examiner is likely to award you the majority of the marks if the rest of the answer is correct.

(c) *Production budget (units)*

	Month 1	Month 2	Month 3
Closing stock	19 500 (12 000 + 15 000/2)	20 500 (15 000 + 11 000/2)	17 000 (11 000 + 12 000/2)
add Sales	10 000	12 000	15 000
	29 500	32 500	32 000
less Opening stock	16 000 (10 000 + 12 000/2)	19 500	20 500
Production	13 500	13 000	11 500

8.3

Mr Belle has recently developed a new improved video cassette, and shown below is a summary of a report by a firm of management consultants on the sales potential and production costs of the new cassette.

Sales potential

The sales volume is difficult to predict and will vary with the price, but it is reasonable to assume that at a selling price of £10.00 per cassette, sales would be between 7500 and 10 000 units per month. Alternatively, if the selling price was reduced to £9.00 per cassette, sales would be between 12 000 and 18 000 units per month.

Production costs

If production is maintained at or below 10 000 units per month, then variable manufacturing costs would be approximately £8.25 per cassette and fixed costs £12 125 per month. However, if production is planned to exceed 10 000 units per month, then variable costs would be reduced to £7.75 per cassette, but the fixed costs would increase to £16 125 per month.

Mr Belle has been charged £2000 for the report by the management consultants and, in addition, he has incurred £3000 development costs on the new cassette.

If Mr Belle decides to produce and sell the new cassette it will be necessary for him to use factory premises which he owns, but are leased to a colleague for a rental of £400 per month. Also he will resign from his current post in an electronics firm where he is earning a salary of £1000 per month.

You are required to:
(a) Identify in the question an example of
   (i) An opportunity cost
   (ii) A sunk cost. (3 marks)
(b) Making whatever calculations you consider appropriate, analyse the report from the consultants and advise Mr Belle of the potential profitability of the alternatives shown in the report. Any assumptions considered necessary or matters which may require further investigation or comment should be clearly stated. (19 marks)
(CACA Level 1 Costing, December 1983)

Answer
(a) (i) The opportunity costs of producing cassettes are the salary forgone of £1000 per month and the rental forgone of £400 per month.
   (ii) The consultants' fees and development costs represent sunk costs.
(b) The following information can be obtained from the report:

	£10 selling price	£9 selling price
Sales quantity	7500–10 000 units	12 000–18 000 units
Fixed costs (W1)	£13 525	£17 525
Profit at maximum sales (W2)	£3 975	£4 975
Profit (loss) at minimum sales (W3)	(£400)	(£2 525)
Break-even point (W4)	7 729 units	14 020 units
Margin of safety:		
Below maximum	2 271 units	3 980 units
Above minimum	229 units	2 020 units

Workings
(W1) Fixed production cost + £1400 opportunity cost
(W2) (10 000 units × £1.75 contribution) − £13 525 fixed costs
    = £3975 profit
   (18 000 units × £1.25 contribution) − £17 525 fixed costs
    = £4975 profit
(W3) (7 500 units × £1.75 contribution) − £13 525 fixed costs
    = £400 loss
   (12 000 units × £1.25 contribution) − £17 525 fixed costs
    = £2525 loss
(W4) Fixed costs/contribution per unit

There is no specific answer to this question. With questions like this you should present information which you think will be useful to management. Where a range of volumes is given you could present details of profits/losses for minimum, maximum and the mid-point of the range. You should also calculate break-even points.

Conclusions
  (i) The £10 selling price is less risky than the £9 selling price. With the £10 selling price the maximum loss is lower and the break-even point is only 3 per cent above minimum sales (compared with 17 per cent for a £9 selling price).
  (ii) The £9 selling price will yield the higher profits if maximum sales quantity is achieved.
  (iii) In order to earn £3975 profits at a £9 selling price Mr Belle must sell 17 200 units (required contribution of 17 525 fixed costs plus £3975 divided by a contribution per unit of £1.25).

Additional information required
  (i) Details of capital employed for each selling price.
  (ii) Details of additional finance required to finance the working capital and the relevant interest cost so as to determine the cost of financing the working capital.
  (iii) Estimated probability of units sold at different selling prices.
  (iv) How long will the project remain viable?
  (v) Details of range of possible costs. Are the cost figures given in the question certain?

8.4

A company produces and sells two products with the following costs:

	Product X	Product Y
Variable costs (per £ of sales)	£0.45	£0.6
Fixed costs	£1 212 000 per period	

Total sales revenue is currently generated by the two products in the following proportions:

Product X	70%
Product Y	30%

Required:
(a) Calculate the break-even sales revenue per period, based on the sales mix assumed above. (6 marks)
(b) Prepare a profit volume chart of the above situation for sales revenue up to £4 000 000. Show on the same chart the effect of a change in the sales mix to Product X 50%, Product Y 50%. Clearly indicate on the chart the break-even point for each situation. (11 marks)
(c) Of the fixed costs £455 000 are attributable to Product X. Calculate the sales revenue required on Product X in order to recover the attributable fixed costs and provide a net contribution of £700 000 towards general fixed costs and profit. (5 marks)

(CACA Level 1 Costing, June 1987)

Answer
(a) Break-even point

$$= \frac{\text{fixed costs } (\pounds 1\,212\,000)}{\text{average contribution per } \pounds \text{ of sales } (\pounds 0.505)}$$

$$= \pounds 2\,400\,000$$

Average contribution per £ of sales
$$= [0.7 \times (\pounds 1 - \pounds 0.45)] + [0.3 \times (\pounds 1 - \pounds 0.6)]$$

(b) The graph is based on the following calculations:
Zero activity: Loss = £1 212 000 (fixed costs)
£4m existing sales: (£4m × £0.505) − £1 212 000 = £808 000 profit
£4m revised sales: (£4m × £0.475) − £1 212 000 = £688 000 profit
Existing break-even point: £2 400 000
Revised break-even point: £2 551 579 (£1 212 000/£0.475)
Revised contribution per £ of sales
$$= (0.5 \times \pounds 0.55) + (0.5 \times \pounds 0.40) = \pounds 0.475$$

Each £1 sales generates an average contribution of £0.505 with a sales mix of 50% of X and 50% of Y. If the sales mix changes then the average contribution, break-even point and profits at different activity levels will change.

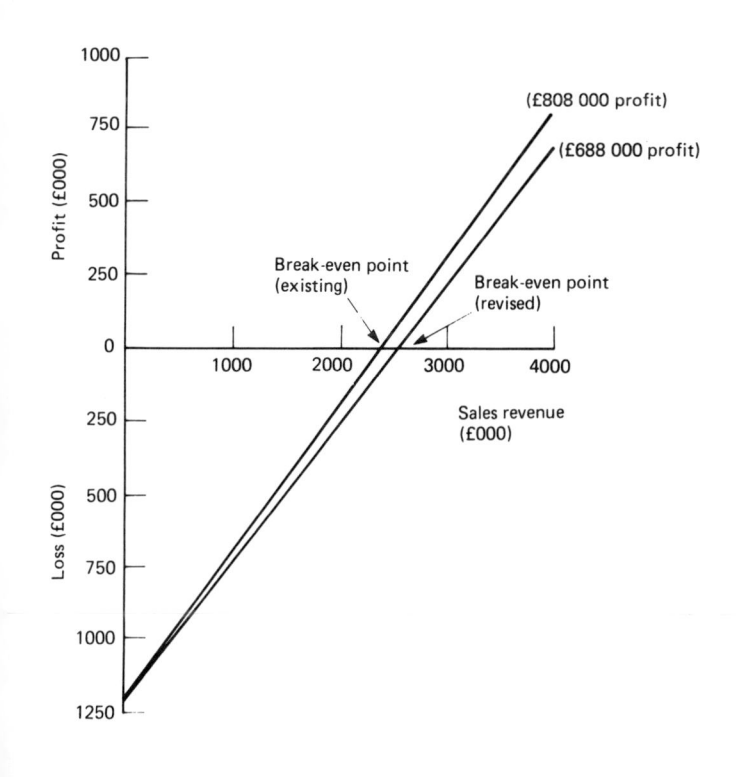

(c) $\dfrac{\text{required contribution}}{\text{contribution per } \pounds \text{ of sales}} = \dfrac{\pounds 455\,000 + \pounds 700\,000}{\pounds 0.55} = \pounds 2\,100\,000$

Profit–volume graph for Question 8.4(b)

Questions for Chapter 9

9.1
JB Limited is a small specialist manufacturer of electronic components and much of its output is used by the makers of aircraft for both civil and military purposes. One of the few aircraft manufacturers has offered a contract to JB Limited for the supply, over the next twelve months, of 400 identical components.

The data relating to the production of each component are as follows:
(i) *Material requirements:*
3 kg material M1 – see note 1 below
2 kg material P2 – see note 2 below
1 Part No. 678 – see note 3 below

Note 1: Material M1 is in continuous use by the company. 1000 kg are currently held in stock at a book value of £4.70 per kg but it is known that future purchases will cost £5.50 per kg.

Note 2: 1200 kg of material P2 are held in stock. The original cost of this material was £4.30 per kg but as the material has not been required for the last two years it has been written down to £1.50 per kg scrap value. The only foreseeable alternative use is as a substitute for material P4 (in current use) but this would involve further processing costs of £1.60 per kg. The current cost of material P4 is £3.60 per kilogramme.

Note 3: It is estimated that the Part No. 678 could be bought for £50 each.

(ii) *Labour requirements:*
Each component would require five hours of skilled labour and five hours of semi-skilled. An employee possessing the necessary skills is available and is currently paid £5 per hour. A replacement would, however, have to be obtained at a rate of £4 per hour for the work which would otherwise be done by the skilled employee. The current rate for semi-skilled work is £3 per hour and an additional employee could be appointed for this work.

(iii) *Overhead:*
JB Limited absorbs overhead by a machine hour rate, currently £20 per hour of which £7 is for variable overhead and £13 for fixed overhead. If this contract is undertaken it is estimated that fixed costs will increase for the duration of the contract by £3200. Spare machine capacity is available and each component would require four machine hours.

A price of £145 per component has been suggested by the large company which makes aircraft.

You are required to:
(a) State whether or not the contract should be accepted and support your conclusion with appropriate figures for presentation to management. (16 marks)
(b) Comment briefly on *three* factors which management ought to consider and which may influence their decision. (9 marks)

(CIMA Cost Accounting Stage 2, May 1987)

Answer
(a) The relevant costs for the production of 400 components are as follows:

	£	£
Materials:		
M1: 1200 kg at £5.50 replacement cost	6 600	
P2: 800 kg at £2 per kg (see note)	1 600	
Part No. 678: 400 at £50 replacement cost	20 000	28 200
Labour:		
Skilled: 2000 hours at £4 per hour	8 000	
Semi-skilled: 2000 hours at £3 per hour	6000	14 000
Overheads:		
Variable: 1600 machine hours at £7 per hour		11 200
Fixed: Incremental fixed costs		3 200
Total relevant cost		56 600
Contract price (400 components at £145 per component)		58 000
Contribution to general fixed costs		1 400

The incremental revenues exceed the incremental costs. Therefore the contract should be accepted subject to the comments in (b) below.

Note: If materials P2 are not used on the contract they will be used as a substitute for material P4. Using P2 as a substitute for P4 results in a saving of £2 (£3.60 – £1.60) per kg. Therefore the relevant cost of P2 consists of the opportunity cost of £2 per kg.

(b) Three factors which should be considered are:
   (i) Can a price higher than £145 per component be negotiated? The contract only provides a contribution of £1400 to general fixed costs. If the company generates insufficient contribution from its activities to cover general fixed costs then it will incur losses and will not be able to survive in the long term. It is assumed that acceptance of the contract will not lead to the rejection of other profitable work.
   (ii) Will acceptance of the contract lead to repeat orders which are likely to provide a better contribution to general fixed costs?
   (iii) Acceptance of the contract will provide additional employment for 12 months and this might have a significant effect on the morale of the workforce.

It is preferable to use P2 as a substitute for P4 (thus saving £2 per kg) rather than disposing of the materials at a scrap value of £1·50 per kg.

The fixed overheads of £13 per hour are common and unavoidable to all alternatives and will not change if the components are produced.

9.2
A company is preparing its production budget for the year ahead. Two of its processes are concerned with the manufacture of three components

which are used in several of the company's products. Capacity (machine hours) in each of these two processes is limited to 2000 hours.

Production costs are as follows:

	Component X £/unit	Component Y £/unit	Component Z £/unit
Direct materials	15.00	18.50	4.50
Direct labour	12.00	12.50	8.00
Variable overhead	6.00	6.25	4.00
Fixed overhead: process M	6.00	6.00	4.50
process N	10.50	10.50	3.50
	49.50	53.75	24.50

Requirements for components X, Y and Z for the following year are:

Component X	300 units
Component Y	300 units
Component Z	450 units

Fixed overhead is absorbed on the basis of machine hours at the following rates:

Process M	£3.00 per hour
Process N	£3.50 per hour

Components X and Z could be obtained from an outside supplier at the following prices:

Component X	£44.00 per unit
Component Z	£23.00 per unit

You are required to:
(a) Demonstrate that insufficient capacity is available to produce the requirements for components X, Y and Z in the year ahead, and calculate the extent of the shortfall; (6 marks)
(b) Determine the requirements for bought-in components in order to satisfy the demand for components at minimum cost; (8 marks)
(c) Consider briefly any other factors which may be relevant to decisions regarding these components in the longer term. (8 marks)

(CACA Level 1 Costing, June 1986)

Answer
(a)

			X	Y	Z	Total
(i)	Machine hrs required	M	2	2	1.5	
(ii)	see (W1)	N	3	3	1	
(iii)	Output (units)		300	300	450	
(iv)	Process M hours (i × iii)		600	600	675	1875
(v)	Process N hours (ii × iii)		900	900	450	2250

(W1) Fixed overhead per unit/hourly fixed overhead rate.

There is a shortfall of 250 hours in process N, and a surplus of 125 hours in process M.

It is important that you determine the capacity limitations for each process and not for the total combination of both processes.

(b)

	X	Z
	£	£
Variable cost	33	16.50
Buying-in price	44	23.00
Extra buying-in cost	11	6.50
Hours required per unit in N	3	1
Extra buying in cost per hour	£3.67	£6.50

The company should therefore minimize production costs by obtaining the 250 process N hours from purchasing 84 units (250/3) of component X.

(c) The following factors should be considered:
  (i) Possible alternative uses of the process facilities
  (ii) Ways of increasing existing capacity such as overtime and shift work
  (iii) Security and quality of outside supply
  (iv) Stability of outside price
  (v) An investigation of why the purchase price from outside is less than the *total* cost of manufacture. The total cost could be regarded as a long-run cost and it might be in the interest of the company to obtain all the output from the outside supplier and not to reinvest in producing the components internally.

An alternative approach would be to determine the number of components of Y and Z which should be purchased and compare the total buying-in costs. For example, the shortfall can be met by purchasing 84 units of X or 250 units of Z (250/1 hour). It is therefore cheaper to purchase component X.

Questions for Chapter 10

10.1
The following data are supplied relating to two investment projects, only one of which may be selected:

	Project A	Project B
	£	£
Initial capital expenditure	50 000	50 000
Profit (loss): year 1	25 000	10 000
year 2	20 000	10 000
year 3	15 000	14 000
year 4	10 000	26 000
Estimated resale value end of year 4	10 000	10 000

Profit is calculated after deducting straight-line depreciation.
The cost of capital is 10 per cent.
Present value £1 received at the end of: year 1   0.909
                                          year 2   0.826
                                          year 3   0.751
                                          year 4   0.683
                                          year 5   0.620

You are required to:
(a) Calculate for each project
 (i) Average annual rate of return on average capital invested
 (ii) Payback period
 (iii) Net present value; (12 marks)
(b) Briefly discuss the relative merits of the three methods of evaluation mentioned in (a); (10 marks)
(c) Explain which project you would recommend for acceptance.
(3 marks)
(AAT Pilot Paper)

Answer
(a) (i) Average capital invested

$$= \frac{£50\,000 + £10\,000}{2} = £30\,000$$

The diagram shows why the project's scrap value is added to the initial cost to calculate the average capital employed. You can see that at the mid-point of the project's life, the capital invested is equal to £30 000.

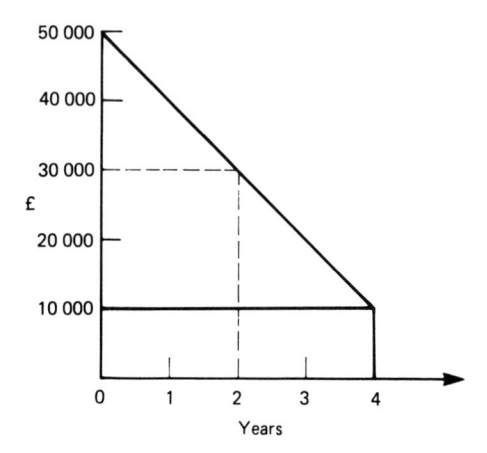

Note that the mid-point of the project's life is 2 years. From the graph you can read off the net investment cost at the end of year 2. It is £30 000, and this represents the average cost of the investment.

Average capital employed for Question 10.1

Average annual profit (project A)

$$= \frac{£25\,000 + £20\,000 + £15\,000 + £10\,000}{4} = £17\,500$$

Average annual profit (project B)

$$= \frac{£10\,000 + £10\,000 + £14\,000 + £26\,000}{4} = £15\,000$$

Average annual return:
Project A   58.33 per cent [(£17 500/£30 000) × 100]
Project B   50 per cent [(£15 000/£30 000) × 100]

(ii) Payback period:
Project A   1.5 years [1 + (£15 000/£30 000)]
Project B   2.4 years [2 + (£10 000/£24 000)]

(iii)

Year	Project A cash inflows (W1) £	Project B cash inflows (W1) £	Discount factor	Project A PV £	Project B PV £
1	35 000	20 000	0.909	31 815	18 180
2	30 000	20 000	0.826	24 780	16 520
3	25 000	24 000	0.751	18 775	18 024
4	20 000	36 000	0.683	13 660	24 588
4	10 000	10 000	0.683	6 830	6 830
				95 860	84 142
			Investment cost	(50 000)	(50 000)
			NPV	45 860	34 142

(W1) Cash flows = profit + depreciation
Note that the estimated resale value is included as a year 4 cash inflow.

(b) See Chapter 10 for the answer to this question.
(c) Project A is recommended because it has the highest *NPV* and also the shortest payback period.

10.2

(a) The management of the Primetaste Restaurant has been experiencing losses in the most recent months and is considering converting its operations to fast-food takeaways.

The fitting out of the premises will cost £40 000, and the equipment will have a life of ten years with a residual value of £1000. However, an £8000 overhaul will be necessary at the end of the fifth year.

Currently the restaurant costs £30 000 per annum to operate and did break even in this past year. The new service will save £10 000 of these costs.

Projected sales are 1000 units per week, for a full 52 weeks per year, except in year 5 when the overhaul will enforce a 4 week shutdown. Each unit will provide a contribution of 20 pence.

You are required to give

(i) The annual cash inflows expected from the new project;
(ii) The net present value of the operation if the management is expecting a 20 per cent rate of return.   (14 marks)

(b) (i) Define the 'payback period'; and
(ii) Calculate it using the above example. What advantages are claimed for this method?   (14 marks)

Note: PV of 20 per cent:

Year		Year	
1	0.833	6	0.335
2	0.694	7	0.279
3	0.579	8	0.233
4	0.482	9	0.194
5	0.402	10	0.162

(AAT, June 1985)

Answer
(a) The relevant cash inflows are £10 000 per annum cost savings, £1000 residual value of the equipment and the *additional* contribution. It is assumed that the £200 per week cash inflow represents an additional contribution above that earned from the existing business. If the £200 per week represents the contribution that would be received before and after conversion there would be no additional contribution from the conversion. Consequently the £200 per week would not be included in the analysis apart from the four weeks lost contribution in year 5.

If the annual cash flows are identical you can add the discount factors together and multiply the total by the annual cash flow. This approach has been adopted for years 1–4 and years 6–9. Separate calculations are necessary for years 5 and 10.

Year	Cash inflow (W1) £	Cash outflows £	Net cash flow £	Discount factor[1]
1	20 400		20 400	0.833 ⎫
2	20 400		20 400	0.694 ⎬ = 2.588
3	20 400		20 400	0.579
4	20 400		20 400	0.482 ⎭
5	19 600	8000	11 600	0.402
6	20 400		20 400	0.335 ⎫
7	20 400		20 400	0.279 ⎬ = 1.041
8	20 400		20 400	0.233
9	20 400		20 400	0.194 ⎭
10	21 400		21 400	0.162

		£
PV of cash flows: years 1–4	(£20 400 × 2.588) =	52 795
year 5	(£11 600 × 0.402) =	4 663
years 6–9	(£20 400 × 1.041) =	21 236
year 10	(£21 400 × 0.162) =	3 467
		82 161
Investment cost		40 000
NPV		42 161

(W1) Years 1–9 (excluding year 5) = £10 000 savings + (£200 × 52 weeks)
Year 5 includes 48 weeks × £200 contribution.
Year 10 includes the residual value of the equipment.

(b) (i) See Section 10.6 for a definition of payback period.
  (ii) The payback period is just under 2 years. The precise calculation is 1.96 years [1 + (£19 600/£20 400)].

Questions for Chapter 11

11.1

The management of Beck PLC have been informed that the union representing the direct production workers at one of their factories, where a standard product is produced, intends to call a strike. The accountant has been asked to advise the management of the effect the strike will have on cash flow.

The following data have been made available:

	Week 1	Week 2	Week 3
Budgeted sales	400 units	500 units	400 units
Budgeted production	600 units	400 units	nil

The strike will commence at the beginning of week 3 and it should be assumed that it will continue for at least four weeks. Sales at 400 units per week will continue to be made during the period of the strike until stocks of finished goods are exhausted. Production will stop at the end of week 2. The current stock level of finished goods is 600 units. Stocks of work in progress are not carried.

The selling price of the product is £60 and the budgeted manufacturing cost is made up as follows:

	£
Direct materials	15
Direct wages	7
Variable overheads	8
Fixed overheads	18
Total	£48

Direct wages are regarded as a variable cost. The company operates a full absorption costing system and the fixed overhead absorption rate is based upon a budgeted fixed overhead of £9000 per week. Included in the total fixed overheads is £700 per week for depreciation of equipment. During the period of the strike direct wages and variable overheads would not be incurred and the cash expended on fixed overheads would be reduced by £1500 per week.

The current stocks of raw materials are worth £7500; it is intended that these stocks should increase to £11 000 by the end of week 1 and then remain at this level during the period of the strike. All direct materials are paid for one week after they have been received. Direct wages are paid one week in arrears. It should be assumed that all relevant overheads are paid for immediately the expense is incurred. All sales are on credit; 70 per cent of the sales value is received in cash from the debtors at the end of the first week after the sales have been made, and the balance at the end of the second week.

The current amount outstanding to material suppliers is £8000 and direct wage accruals amount to £3200. Both of these will be paid in week 1. The current balance owing from debtors is £31 200, of which £24 000 will be received during week 1 and the remainder during week 2. The current balance of cash at bank and in hand is £1000.

You are required to:

(a) (i) Prepare a cash budget for weeks 1 to 6 showing the balance of cash at the end of each week together with a suitable analysis of the receipts and payments during each week. (13 marks)

(ii) Comment upon any matters arising from the cash budget which you consider should be brought to management's attention. (4 marks)

(b) Explain why the reported profit figure for a period does not normally represent the amount of cash generated in that period. (5 marks)

(CACA Level 1 Costing, June 1983)

Answer

(a) (i) *Cash budget for weeks 1–6*

	Week 1 £	Week 2 £	Week 3 £	Week 4 £	Week 5 £	Week 6 £
Receipts from debtors (W1)	24 000	24 000	28 200	25 800	19 800	5 400
Payments:						
To material suppliers (W3)	8 000	12 500	6 000	nil	nil	nil
To direct workers (W4)	3 200	4 200	2 800	nil	nil	nil
For variable overheads (W5)	4 800	3 200	nil	nil	nil	nil
For fixed overheads (W6)	8 300	8 300	6 800	6 800	6 800	6 800
Total payments	24 300	28 200	15 600	6 800	6 800	6 800
Net movement	(300)	(4 200)	12 600	19 000	13 000	(1 400)
Opening balance (week 1 given)	1 000	700	(3 500)	9 100	28 100	41 100
Closing balance	700	(3 500)	9 100	28 100	41 100	39 700

Workings

(W1) *Debtors*

	Week 1	Week 2	Week 3	Week 4	Week 5	Week 6
Units sold (W2)	400	500	400	300	–	–
Sales (£)	24 000	30 000	24 000	18 000	–	–
Cash received (£): 70%			16 800	21 000	16 800	12 600	–
30%				7 200	9 000	7 200	5 400
given	24 000	7 200				
Total receipts (£)	24 000	24 000	28 200	25 800	19 800	5 400

(W2) Sales in week 4
 = opening stock (600 units)
 add production in weeks 1 and 2 (1000 units)
 less sales in weeks 1–3 (1300 units) = 300 units

(W3) *Creditors*

	Week 1 £	2 £	3 £	4 £	5 £	6 £
Materials consumed at £15	9 000	6 000	–	–	–	–
Increase in stocks	3 500	–				
Materials purchased	12 500	6 000				
Payment to suppliers	8 000 (given)	12 500	6 000	nil	nil	nil

(W4) *Wages*

	Week 1 £	2 £	3 £	4	5	6
Wages consumed at £7	4 200	2 800		nil	nil	nil
Wages paid	3 200 (given)	4 200	2 800	–	–	–

Material and wages consumed are ascertained by multiplying the weekly production by the materials and wages cost per unit of output.

(W5) Variable overhead payment = budgeted production
 × budgeted cost per unit

(W6) Fixed overhead payments for weeks 1–2
 = fixed overhead per week (£9000)
 less weekly depreciation (£700)
 Fixed overhead payments for weeks 3–6
 = £8300 normal payment
 less £1500 per week

(ii) *Comments*
 (1) Finance will be required to meet the cash deficit in week 2, but a lowering of the budgeted material stocks at the end of week 1 would reduce the amount of cash to be borrowed at the end of week 2.
 (2) The surplus cash after the end of week 2 should be invested on a short-term basis.
 (3) After week 6 there will be no cash receipts but cash outflows will be £6800 per week. The closing balance of £39 700 at the end of week 6 will be sufficient to finance outflows for a further 5–6 weeks (£39 700/£6800 per week).

(b) The answer should include a discussion of the matching concept, emphasizing that revenues and expenses may not be attributed to the period when the associated cash inflows and outflows occur. Also some items of expense do not affect cash outflow (e.g. depreciation).

11.2

(a) A company manufactures three products: chairs, tables and benches. From the following information you are to produce:

   (i) A production budget showing quantities to be manufactured and factory unit costs of each product; (5 marks)
   (ii) A purchasing budget detailing quantities to be purchased and the total cost of materials; (5 marks)
   (iii) A direct wages budget showing hours to be worked in total and gross wages to be paid. (5 marks)

	Chairs	Tables	Benches
Sales in the next trading period (units)	4000	1000	500
Material requirements:			
Timber (per unit)	0.5 m^2	1.2 m^2	2.5 m^2

Price of timber: £8 m^2

| Upholstery | 0.2 m^2 | – | – |

Price of upholstery: £4 m^2

Fixing and finishing material costs: 5 per cent of total material cost.

Labour requirements:

| Carpenters (hours per unit) | 0.75 | 0.8 | 1.3 |
| Fixers and finishers (hours per unit) | 0.25 | 0.3 | 1.0 |

Carpenters' rate per hour: £6
Fixers and finishers' rate per hour: £4.80

Fixed factory overheads are estimated at £6253 for the trading period, and these are recovered on the basis of labour hours.

	Chairs	Tables	Benches
Finished stocks at:			
beginning of period	200	300	40
end of period	400	100	50
Material stocks at beginning of period: timber	600 m^2	Upholstery	400 m^2
Material stocks at end of period: timber	650 m^2	Upholstery	260 m^2

(b) The trading period to which this budget relates is of four weeks' duration. The labour force is expected to perform as follows:

	Carpenters	Fixers
Normal hours per week, per person	40	40
Absenteeism and lateness	10%	15%

Calculate how many carpenters and fixers should be employed.
(4 marks)

(c) From the information in (a), which is considered the 100 per cent level of activity, show a production budget flexed to output levels of 80, 90 and 110 per cent of the target production budget. (All calculations to nearest £1.) (9 marks)

(AAT, June 1983)

Answer

(a) (i) Production budget

	Sales	Stock adjustment	Production
Chairs	4000	+200	4200
Tables	1000	−200	800
Benches	500	+ 10	510

Factory cost per unit

		Chairs		Tables		Benches
Materials: timber		4.00		9.60		20.00
upholstery		0.80		–		–
fixing and finishing		0.24		0.48		1.00
		5.04		10.08		21.00
Wages: carpenters	4.50		4.80		7.80	
fixers	1.20	5.70	1.44	6.24	4.80	12.60
Factory overheads		1.00		1.10		2.30
Factory cost (per unit)		11.74		17.42		35.90

Budgeted direct labour hours are: Hours
Chairs   (4200 × 1 hour)   4200
Tables   (800 × 1.1 hrs)   880
Benches   (510 × 2.3 hrs)   1173
   6253

Fixed overhead rate = £1 per direct labour hour (£6253/6253 hours)

(ii) Purchasing budget

Timber production requirements (m²)

Chairs	2100	(4200 × 0.5)
Tables	960	(800 × 1.2)
Benches	1275	(510 × 2.5)
Stock increase	50	
	4385 at £8	£35 080

Upholstery production requirements (m²)

Chairs	840	(4200 × 0.2)
Stock decrease	140	
	700 at £4	2 800
		37 880

Fixing and finishing

5 per cent of material cost (5% × £37 880)   1 894

   39 774

(iii) Direct wages budget

		Hours	Rate	Total £
Carpenters:				
Chairs	0.75 × 4200 =	3150		
Tables	0.8 × 800 =	640		
Benches	1.3 × 510 =	663		
		4453	£6	26 718

Fixers and finishers:
Chairs   0.25 × 4200 = 1050
Tables   0.3 × 800 = 240
Benches   1.0 × 510 = 510

                                    1800   £4.80   8 640

                                                              £35 358

(b)

	Carpenters	Fixers
Hours per week, normal	40	40
less Lost time	4	6
Effective hours per week	36	34
(1) Effective hours × 4 weeks	144	136
(2) Hours required per wages budget	4453	1800
(3) (2)/(1)	30.9	13.2
Employ	31	14

(c) *Flexible production budget*

	100%	80%	90%	110%
Units produced				
Chairs	4200	3 360	3 780	4 620
Tables	800	640	720	880
Benches	510	408	459	561
Variable costs				
Materials:	£	£	£	
Chairs		16 934	19 051	23 285
Tables		6 451	7 258	8 870
Benches		8 568	9 639	11 781
Wages		28 286	31 822	38 894
Fixed costs		6 253	6 253	6 253
		£66 492	£74 023	£89 083

Materials (80% activity)

                              £
Chairs   3360 × £5.04 = 16 934
Tables   640 × £10·08 = 6 451
Benches   408 × £21   = 8 568

Wages (80% activity)

                  £
3360 × £5·70 = 19 152
 640 × £6·24 = 3 994
 408 × £12·60 = 5 140
                  28 286

11.3

A manufacturing company has the following budgeted costs for one month which are based on a normal capacity level of 40 000 hours. A departmental overhead absorption rate of £4.40 per hour has been calculated, as follows:

Overhead item	*Fixed* £000	*Variable* (£/hour)
Management and supervision	30	–
Shift premium	–	0.10
National Insurance and pension costs	6	0.22
Inspection	20	0.25
Consumable supplies	6	0.18
Power for machinery	–	0.20

Lighting and heating	4	–
Rates	9	–
Repairs and maintenance	8	0.15
Materials handling	10	0.30
Depreciation of machinery	15	–
Production administration	12	–
	120	

Overhead rate per hour: variable	1.40
fixed	3.00
total	£4.40

During the month of April, the company actually worked 36 000 hours producing 36 000 standard hours of production and incurred the following overhead costs:

	£000
Management and supervision	30.0
Shift premium	4.0
National Insurance and pension costs	15.0
Inspection	28.0
Consumable supplies	12.7
Power for machinery	7.8
Lighting and heating	4.2
Rates	9.0
Repairs and maintenance	15.1
Materials handling	21.4
Depreciation of machinery	15.0
Production administration	11.5
Idle time	1.6
	175.3

You are required to:

(a) Prepare a statement showing for April the flexible budget for the month, the actual costs and the variance for each overhead item.
(14 marks)
(b) Comment on each variance of £1000 or more by suggesting possible reasons for the variances reported;
(c) State, for control purposes, with reasons to support your conclusions:
  (i) Whether (b) is adequate, and
  (ii) Whether the statement prepared in respect of the request in (a) could be improved and, if so, how;
(d) Calculate:
  (i) The overhead absorbed
  (ii) The total amount under/over-spent
  (iii) The overhead volume variance. (11 marks for (b), (c) and (d))
(CIMA Stage 2 Cost Accounting Pilot Paper)

Answer

(a) *Budget statement*

Overhead	Budget Fixed £	Budget variable £	Budget Total £	Actual £	Variance Adv. £	Variance Fav. £
Management	30 000	–	30 000	30 000	–	–
Shift premium	–	3 600	3 600	4 000	400	
National Insurance	6 000	7 920	13 920	15 000	1080	
Inspection	20 000	9 000	29 000	28 000		1000
Supplies	6 000	6 480	12 480	12 700	220	
Power	–	7 200	7 200	7 800	600	
Light and heat	4 000	–	4 000	4 200	200	
Rates	9 000	–	9 000	9 000		
Repairs	8 000	5 400	13 400	15 100	1700	
Materials handling	10 000	10 800	20 800	21 400	600	
Depreciation	15 000	–	15 000	15 000		
Administration	12 000	–	12 000	11 500		500
Idle time	–	–	–	1 600	1600	
	120 000	50 400	170 400	175 300	6400	1500

£4900A

(b) *National Insurance* It appears that National Insurance rates have increased. If this assumption is correct then the variance will be beyond the control of management. Note that actual activity is less than budgeted activity. It is therefore unlikely that total wages will have increased because of an increase in the number of labour hours worked. It is possible that wage rates might have increased, thus increasing the National Insurance payments.

Note that National Insurance payments are a fixed percentage of wages.

Inspection It is possible that the standard of inspection has been lowered, thus resulting in a saving in costs. If this has not been a policy decision taken by management then the variance should be investigated. Another possibility is that a member of staff has resigned. Consequently the actual labour cost will be less than the budget.

Repairs and maintenance This variance may be due to unexpected repairs which were not envisaged when the budget was set. It is likely that variances for repairs and maintenance will fluctuate considerably from month to month. It is therefore appropriate to compare budgeted and actual expenditure for several months rather than focus on a single month.

Variable overheads may be a function of more than one variable. In this question they are assumed to fluctuate in relation to hours of activity. In practice variable overhead costs may be a function of direct labour hours of input, machine hours, units produced or quantities of materials used. Consequently budgeted expenses based on only one variable will not represent truly accurate estimates.

Idle time No allowance for normal idle time is included in the budget. Consequently the idle time must be of an abnormal nature. Possible uncontrollable causes include power failure or machine breakdowns. Controllable causes include bottlenecks arising from poor production scheduling or a lack of materials.

(c) (i) Commenting on variances in excess of a specific figure may not be satisfactory for control purposes. Variances should only be investigated if the investigation is likely to yield benefits in terms of identifying inefficiencies and remedying them. It may be preferable to use statistical tests to establish the probability that the variance is out of control.

(ii) The statement could be improved by analysing the expense items into their controllable and non-controllable elements. Where possible variances should be analysed according to whether they are due to price and quantity changes. The statement should also include non-financial measures such as a comparison of actual hours worked with standard hours produced.

(d) (i) Overhead absorbed = £158 400 (£4.40 × 36 000 hours)
(ii) Over-spending = £4900 (see part (a) of answer)
(iii) Actual production was 4000 standard hours less than budgeted production and this decline in output has resulted in a failure to recover £12 000 fixed overheads. This under recovery of £12 000 is also known as the volume variance.

Questions for Chapter 12

12.1

(a) A manufacturer produces a single product Brand X, which has the following standard data:

	Per unit of Brand X (£)
Direct material 2 units at £10 per unit	20
Direct wages 5 hours at £10 per hour	50
Selling price	100

500 units of Brand X are budgeted to be produced and sold for each of the 13 reporting periods in the year. Administrative fixed costs of £2000 per period are also budgeted.

In the fourth reporting period the actual data were as follows:

Units of Brand X produced	500 units
Sales of Brand X	450 units
Total revenue from sales	£49 500
Units of material purchased	1200 units
Total cost of purchases	£10 800
Direct wages: hours	2000 hours
total cost	£18 000
Administrative fixed costs	£3000

There are no opening or closing stocks of materials, and no opening stocks of finished goods.

Stocks are valued at standard cost.

Although 2000 labour hours were paid for, this includes 100 hours of idle time caused by machine breakdown.

You are required to
(i) Calculate the actual profit for period 4; (5 marks)
(ii) Calculate the relevant variances for materials and labour; (5 marks)
(iii) Prepare a statement which reconciles the actual profit with the profit budgeted for in period 4. (6 marks)

(b) Material price variances may be calculated and recorded

1 *Either* at the time of receiving the goods into store (method A)
2 *Or* at the time of issue to production (method B).

You are required to:

(i) Explain which method you prefer; (6 marks)
(ii) Show the journal entries to record the information given below, using method A only:

Goods received: 100 units of material X
standard cost £1 per unit,
actual cost £1.50 per unit.
Goods subsequently issued to production: 60 units. (3 marks)
(AAT, June 1986)

Answer
(a) (i) *Actual profit: period 4*

	£	£
Sales (450 × £110)		49 500
Materials	10 800	
Wages	18 000	
	28 800	
Less closing stock (50 × £70)	3 500	25 300
Gross profit		24 200
Admin. fixed costs		3 000
Profit		21 200

(ii) Material price
= (standard price − actual price) × actual quantity

$$= \left(£10 - \frac{£10\,800}{1200}\right) \times 1200 \qquad = £1200F$$

Material usage
= (standard quantity − actual quantity) × standard price

$$= (500 \times 2 = 1000 - 1200) \times £10 \qquad = £2000A$$

Wage rate
= (standard rate − actual rate) × actual hours

$$= \left(£10 - \frac{£18\,000}{2000}\right) \times 2000 \qquad = £2000F$$

Labour efficiency
= (standard hours − actual hours) × standard rate
= (500 × 5 = 2500 − 1900) × £10   = £6000F

Idle time variance
= 1000 hours × £10   = £1000A

(iii) To reconcile actual and budgeted profits it is necessary to compute the sales margin variances.

Sales margin price
= (actual margin − standard margin) × actual quantity

$$= \left[\left(\frac{49\,500}{£450} - £70\right) - (£100 - £70)\right] \times 450 = £4500F$$

Sales margin quantity
= (actual quantity − budgeted quantity) × standard margin
= (450 − 500) × £30   = £1500A

Reconciliation of actual profit and budgeted profit

		£
Budgeted profit (W1)		13 000
Add favourable variances:	£	
Material price	1200	
Wage rate	2000	
Labour efficiency	6000	
Sales margin price	4500	13 700
		26 700
Less adverse variances:		
Material usage	2000	
Idle time	1000	
Sales margin quantity	1500	
Admin. fixed expenses (£2000–£3000)	1000	5 500
Actual profit		21 200

(W1) Budgeted profit: 500 units at £30 budgeted profit
    margin   £15 000
    Less admin. expenses   2 000
          13 000

(b) (i) See Section 12.6 for the answer to this question.

	£	£
(ii) DR stores ledger control A/C (100 × £1)	100	
DR material price variance A/C	50	
CR creditors A/C		150
Being purchase of materials		
DR WIP A/C (60 × £1)	60	
CR stores ledger control A/C		60

It is assumed that there is no material usage variance, so that the 60 units issued represents the standard and actual quantity.

12.2
A company manufactures a number of products, data for one of which are shown below:

Standard cost
Direct materials	8 units at £2 per unit
Direct labour	4 hours at £5 per hour
Production overhead	4 hours at £6 per hour
Administration and selling overhead	50 per cent of production cost
Profit	$16\frac{2}{3}$ per cent of selling price

Budget for April
Sales	5000 units
Production	5200 units

Actual results during April
Sales	5150 units valued at £566 500
Direct materials used	£77 040
Direct labour costs	£110 770
Production overhead incurred	£122 800

Variances calculated in April
Direct materials:	price	£8560F
	usage	£800A
Direct labour:	rate	£6270A
	efficiency	£1500F

You are required to calculate the:

(a)	Actual output	(8 marks)
(b)	Actual price per unit of direct material	(4 marks)
(c)	Actual rate per hour of direct labour	(4 marks)
(d)	Overhead expenditure variance	(2 marks)
(e)	Overhead volume variance	(4 marks)
(f)	Selling price variance	(4 marks)
(g)	Sales volume profit variance.	(4 marks)

(CIMA Cost Accounting 2, May 1986)

Answer
(a) Standard material cost
 = actual cost (£77 040) + price variance (£8560)
 − usage variance (£800) = £84 800

Therefore £84 800 = actual output × standard material cost per unit of output (£16)

Actual output = 5300 units (£84 800/£16)

Actual output can also be calculated by adopting the same approach with labour costs.

(b) Actual material cost (£77 040) = actual quantity × actual price

The usage variance is £800 adverse. Therefore actual quantity used is 400 units (£800 usage variance/£2 standard material price) in excess of standard quantity. Standard quantity is 42 400 units (5300 units actual output × 8 units). Thus actual quantity of materials used is 42 800 units. Therefore

Actual material price = £1.80 (£77 040/42 800 units)

(c) Actual direct labour cost (£110 770) = actual hours × actual wage rate

The efficiency variance is £1500 favourable. Therefore actual hours are 300 hours less than the standard hours (£1500 efficiency variance/£5 standard wage rate). Standard hours produced are 21 200 (5300 units actual output × 4 hours). Therefore 20 900 actual hours are worked. Therefore

Actual wage rate = £5.30 (£110 770/20 900 hours)

(d) It is assumed that the question refers to *production* overhead expenditure variance and that all of the production overheads are fixed.

Note that no data are given to separate production overheads into fixed and variable elements.

Expenditure variance
= budgeted fixed overhead − actual fixed overhead
= (5200 units × £24) − (£122 800) = £2000F

(e) Volume variance
= (actual production − budgeted production) × fixed overhead rate
= (5300 units − 5200 units) × £24 = £2400F

(f) Selling price variance
= (actual selling price − budgeted selling price) × actual sales volume

$$= \left(\frac{£566\,500}{5150\ \text{units}} - £108\right) \times 5150 = £10\,300F$$

(g) Sales volume profit variance
= (actual sales volume − budgeted sales volume) × standard margin
= (5150 − 5000) × £18 = £2700F

The calculation for the standard profit margin and selling price is:

Standard product cost:	£
Direct materials	16
Direct labour	20
Production overhead	24
Production cost	60
Administration and selling overhead	30
Total cost	90
Profit (16⅔/83⅓ × £90)	18
Selling price	108

12.3
Fischer Ltd manufactures a range of chess sets, and operates a standard costing system. Information relating to the 'Spassky' design for the month of March 1985 is as follows:

(1) Standard costs per 100 sets

	£
Raw materials:	
Plaster of Paris, 20 kg at £8 per kg	160
Paint, 0.5 litre at £30 per litre	15
Direct wages, 2.5 hours at £10 per hour	25
Fixed production overheads, 400 per cent of direct wages	100
	300

(2) Standard selling price per set. £3.80
(3) Raw materials, work in progress and finished goods stock records are maintained at standard cost.
(4) Stock levels at the beginning and end of March 1985 were as follows:

	1 March 1985	31 March 1985
Plaster of Paris	2800 kg	2780 kg
Paint	140 litres	170 litres
Finished sets	900 sets	1100 sets

There was no work in progress at either date.

(5) Budgeted production and sales during the month were 30 000 sets. Actual sales, all made at standard selling price, and actual production, were 28 400 and 28 600 sets respectively.
(6) Raw materials purchased during the month were 5400 kg of plaster of Paris at a cost of £43 200 and 173 litres of paint at a cost of £5800.
(7) Direct wages were 730 hours at an average rate of £11 per hour.
(8) Fixed production overheads amounted to £34 120.

You are required to prepare for the month of March 1985:

(a) The cost ledger accounts for raw materials, work in progress and finished goods; (10 marks)
(b) (i) Budget trading statement
 (ii) Standard cost trading statement
 (iii) Financial trading statement
 (iv) A reconciliation between these statements identifying all relevant variances. (14 marks)

(ICAEW Accounting Techniques, May 1985)

Answer

Workings
Parts (a) and (b) require a detailed variance analysis. The variance calculations are as follows:

Throughout the answer actual production and sales are expressed in 100 sets.

Material price
= (standard price − actual price) × actual quantity purchased

Plaster of Paris

$$= \left[£8 - \frac{£43\,200}{5400}\right] \times 5400 \qquad = \begin{array}{c}£\\0\end{array}$$

Paint

$$= \left[£30 - \frac{£5800}{173}\right] \times 173 \qquad = 610A$$

Material usage
 = (standard quantity − actual quantity) × standard price
 Plaster of Paris
 = (286 × 20 = 5720 − 5420) × £8   = 2400F

Note that actual material usage is calculated as follows:

Opening stock + purchases − closing stock

Paint = (286 × ½ = 143 − 143) × £30   = 0

Wage rate
 = (standard rate − actual rate) × actual hours
 = (£10 − £11) × 730   = 730A

Labour efficiency
 = (standard hours − actual hours) × standard rate
 = (286 × 2.5 = 715 − 730) × £10   = 150A

Fixed overhead expenditure
 = (budgeted fixed overheads − actual fixed overheads)
 = (300 × £100 = £30 000 − £34 120)   = 4120A

Volume efficiency
 = (standard hours − actual hours) × fixed overhead rate
 = (715 − 730) × £40   = 600A

The fixed overhead rate is expressed as a rate per standard hour (that is, 1 hour × £10 × 400%).

Volume capacity
 = (actual hours − budgeted hours) × fixed overhead rate
 = (730 − 300 × 2.5 = 750) × £40   = 800A

Sales margin price
 = (actual selling price − budgeted selling price) × actual sales volume
 = (£380 − £380) × 284   = 0

Sales margin volume
 = (actual sales quantity − budgeted sales quantity) × standard margin
 = (284 − 300) × £80   = 1280A

(a) *Stores ledger control account (plaster of Paris)*

	kg	£		kg	£
Balance B/F	2800	22 400	WIP (SQ × SP)	5720	45 760
Creditors	5400	43 200	Balance C/F	2780	22 240
Material usage variance	300	2 400	(closing stock)		
	8500	68 000		8500	68 000

The entries in the creditors, wages and fixed overhead accounts are as follows:

Creditors

	£
Stores ledger (plaster)	43200
Stores ledger (paint)	5190
Material price variance A/C	610

Wages control

	£		£
Wages accrued A/C	8030	WIP	7150
		Wage rate variance A/C	730
		Labour efficiency variance A/C	150
	8030		8030

Fixed overhead control

	£		£
Expense creditors	34 120	Overhead expenditure variance	4120
		Volume efficiency	600
		Volume capacity	800
		WIP A/C	28600
	34 120		34120

Note that budgeted production and sales are expressed in 100 sets.

Stores ledger control account (paint)

	litres	£		litres	£
Balance C/F	140	4200	WIP A/C (SQ × SP)	143	4290
Creditors	173	5190	Balance C/F (closing stock)	170	5100
	313	9390		313	9390

WIP account

	£		£
Stores ledger control A/C:		Finished goods stock A/C	85 800
Plaster	45 760		
Paint	4 290		
Wages control A/C (SQ × SP)	7 150		
Fixed overhead A/C	28 600		
	85 800		85 800

Finished goods stock account

	£		£
Opening balance (9 × £300)	2 700	Cost of sales (284 × £300)	85 200
WIP A/C	85 800	Closing stock C/F	3 300
	88 500		88 500

(b) It is assumed that (ii) refers to a statement showing standard profit on actual sales and (iii) refers to a statement showing actual profit.

(i) *Budget trading statement*

	£	£
Sales revenue (300 × £380)		114 000
Cost of sales:		
Materials: plaster (300 × £160)	48 000	
paint (300 × £15)	4 500	
Direct wages (300 × £25)	7 500	
Fixed production overheads (300 × £100)	30 000	90 000
Budgeted profit		24 000

(ii) *Standard cost trading statement*

	£
Actual sales (284 × £380)	107 920
Standard cost of sales (284 × £300)	85 200
Standard profit on actual sales	22 720

(iii) *Financial trading statement*

	£	£
Actual sales		107 920
Opening stock (£22 400 + £4200 + £2700)	29 300	
Materials (£43 200 + £5800)	49 000	
Labour	8 030	
Fixed overhead	34 120	
	120 450	
Less closing stock (£22 240 + £5100 + £3300)	30 640	89 810
Actual profit		18 110

Note that opening and closing stocks are valued at standard cost. The variances are written off as period costs.

(iv) *Reconciliation*

	£
Budgeted profit (i)	24 000
Less sales margin volume variance	1 280
Standard profit on actual sales (ii)	22 720

Cost variances	Fav. £	Adv. £	
Paint price		610	
Plaster usage	2400		
Wage rate		730	
Labour efficiency		150	
Fixed overhead expenditure		4120	
Volume efficiency		600	
Volume capacity		800	
	2400	7010	4 610A
Actual profit (iii)			18 110

Index

Abnormal gain, 48–50
Abnormal loss, 48–50
Absorption costing, 65–71
Accounting entries for a job costing system, 34–41
Accounting rate of return, 96–7
Average cost, see Weighted average cost

Basic cost standards, 112
Bin card, 12
Bonus schemes, 18
Break-even analysis, see Cost-volume-profit analysis
Break-even point:
   calculation of, 75
   graphical approach, 78–80
   see also Cost-volume-profit analysis
Budget(s):
   administration of, 98–9
   cash, 103–5
   communication and, 98
   co-ordination of, 100–1
   defined, 98
   fixed, 108
   flexible, 108–10
   master, 101
   production, 102–3
   sales, 100
   stages in the budget process, 99–101
Budget committee, 99
Budget manual, 99
Budget period, 98–9
By-products, 64

Capacity variance, see Variance analysis
Capital budgeting:
   accounting rate of return and, 96–7
   cost of capital, 90
   internal rate of return method for, 94–5
   net present value method for, 92–4
   payback method for, 95
Cash budgets, 103–5

Classification of costs, 7–9
Compounding, 90–1
Contract costing, 41–5
Contribution graph, 79
Contribution margin, 75, 87
Control accounts, 34
Controllable and non-controllable costs, 9, 107–8
Conversion cost, 53
Cost estimation:
   high-low method, 172
Cost of capital, 90
Cost objectives, 6
Cost of work certified, 43
Cost-volume-profit analysis:
   accountants' approach, 73–4
   assumptions of, 74–5
   break-even chart, 77–80
   contribution graph, 79
   economists' approach, 72–3
   margin of safety and, 78
   profit-volume graph, 79–80
Costing profit and loss account, 41
Currently attainable standards, 112

Decision-making:
   discounting a segment, 82
   joint products and, 63–4
   limiting factors and, 87–9
   make or buy illustration, 85–7
   opportunity costs, 87
   relevant costs and, see Relevant costs
   selling price decisions, 83–4
   see also Capital budgeting
Direct cost, 6–7
Direct labour hour rate, 28

Efficiency variance, see Variance analysis
Equivalent production, 50

First in, first out (FIFO):
   process costing, 55–6
   stores pricing, 13–15

Fixed costs:
  definition, 8
  semi-fixed, 9
Flexible budgets, 108–10

Goods received note, 12

High-low method, 172

Ideal cost standards, 111
Idle time, 16
Incentive schemes, 17
Incremental cost, 6
Integrated accounts, 34–9
Interlocking accounts, 39–41
Internal rate of return, 94–5

Job-costing:
  accounting entries for, 34–41
  defined, 46
  labour cost accounting, 15–18
  materials cost accounting, 11–15
  overhead allocation and, 19–33
Joint products, 59–64

Key factors, *see* Limiting factors

Labour cost accounting, 15–18
Labour variances, *see* Variance analysis
Last in, first out (LIFO), 14–15
Limiting factors, 87–9

Machine hour rate, 28–9
Manufacturing cost:
  elements of, 6–7
Margin of safety, 78
Marginal costing, *see* Variable costing
Master budget, 101
Material requisitions, *see* Stores requisitions
Materials control, 11–15
Materials variances, *see* Variance analysis

Net present value, *see* Present value
Non-controllable cost, 9, 108
Normal losses, 46–7, 52–5

Opportunity cost, 7–8, 87
Overheads:
  absorption rates:
    calculation of, 20–9
    direct labour hours method, 28
    direct materials percentage, 29
    direct wages percentage, 28
    machine hour rate, 28
  prime cost percentage, 29
  units of output, 29
  accounting for, 35
  analysis sheet, 22
  apportionment of, 22–3
  blanket rates, 19–20
  defined, 19
  departmental *vs* blanket, 19–20
  disposition of under/over recovery, 25
  over/under recovery, 25
  pre-determined rates, 24–5
  service department reallocation, 29–33
Overtime premium, 16

Payback method, 95
Performance evaluation and reporting, 107–10
Period cost, 6
Perpetual inventory methods, 13
Piecework payments, 18
Present value:
  defined, 91
  net present value, 92–4
Previous process cost, 56
Prime cost, 6
Process costing:
  abnormal gains, 48–50
  abnormal losses, 48–50
  defined, 46
  equivalent production, 50
  first in, first out method, 55–7
  normal losses, 46–7, 52–5
  previous process cost, 56
  weighted average method, 57–8
Product cost, 6
Production budget, 102–3
Progress payments, 42
Purchase order, 11
Purchase requisition, 11

Rate of return, *see* Required rate of return
Reciprocal allocation of service costs, 29–32
Reconciliation of budget and actual profit, 120
Relevant costs, 7, 81
Relevant range, 73–4
Repeated distribution method, 30–1
Replacement cost, 14–15
Required rate of return, *see* Cost of capital
Responsibility accounting, 9, 107–8
Responsibility centre, 9
Retention money, 42

Returns to scale, 73

Sales budget, 100
Sales margin variances, 119
Semi-fixed costs, 9
Semi-variable costs, 9
Service department overheads, 29–32
Shift premium, 16
Simultaneous equation method:
   service department reallocation of, 31–2
Spending variance, 116
Standard cost, *see* Standard costing
Standard costing:
   accounting entries for, 121–4
   defined, 111
   illustration of, 112–20
   setting standards, 111
   types of standards, 111–12
   variances, *see* Variance analysis
Standard hour, 111
Step costs, 9
Stores ledger account, 12
Stores requisitions, 12
Sunk cost, 7

Value of work certified, 42
Variable costing, 65–71
Variable costs, 8
Variance analysis:
   accounting entries for, 121–4
   direct labour variances, 114–15
   direct materials variances, 113–14
   expenditure (spending) variance, 116, 118
   overhead (fixed) variances, 115–17
   overhead (variable) variances, 117–18
   reconciliation of budget and actual profit, 120
   sales margin, 119
   sales price, 119
   volume capacity variance, 117
   volume efficiency variance, 117
   volume variance, 116

Weighted average cost:
   process costing and, 57–8
   stores pricing and, 14
Work in progress account, 35–40